MATHEMATICS 4

FOR YOUNG CATHOLICS

WRITTEN BY
SETON STAFF

SETON PRESS
FRONT ROYAL, VA

Executive Editor: Dr. Mary Kay Clark
Editors: Seton Staff

Seton Home Study School
1350 Progress Drive
Front Royal, VA 22630
Phone: (540) 636-9990
Fax: (540) 636-1602

For more information, visit us on the Web at www.setonhome.org
Contact us by e-mail at info@setonhome.org

ISBN: 978-1-60704-017-0

Cover: *Madonna and Child by Sassoferrato*

DEDICATED TO THE SACRED HEART OF JESUS

Contents

Review of Basic Arithmetic Facts

Facts Review

Complete each number sentence.

1. $8 + 8 =$ _____   2. $3 + 6 =$ _____   3. $7 + 8 =$ _____   4. $9 + 2 =$ _____

5. $5 + 7 =$ _____   6. $7 + 6 =$ _____   7. $1 + 3 =$ _____   8. $4 + 6 =$ _____

9. $9 + 0 =$ _____   10. $3 + 8 =$ _____   11. $8 + 2 =$ _____   12. $3 + 4 =$ _____

13. $12 - 6 =$ _____   14. $13 - 9 =$ _____   15. $8 - 5 =$ _____   16. $14 - 5 =$ _____

17. $12 - 4 =$ _____   18. $8 - 0 =$ _____   19. $4 - 1 =$ _____   20. $6 - 2 =$ _____

21. $10 - 3 =$ _____   22. $11 - 4 =$ _____   23. $16 - 8 =$ _____   24. $11 - 2 =$ _____

25. $5 \times 8 =$ _____   26. $6 \times 0 =$ _____   27. $5 \times 4 =$ _____   28. $6 \times 8 =$ _____

29. $9 \times 3 =$ _____   30. $8 \times 9 =$ _____   31. $4 \times 6 =$ _____   32. $8 \times 8 =$ _____

33. $4 \times 4 =$ _____   34. $6 \times 3 =$ _____   35. $3 \times 8 =$ _____   36. $3 \times 3 =$ _____

37. $40 \div 8 =$ _____   38. $16 \div 8 =$ _____   39. $18 \div 9 =$ _____   40. $35 \div 7 =$ _____

41. $0 \div 2 =$ _____   42. $20 \div 5 =$ _____   43. $14 \div 7 =$ _____   44. $6 \div 3 =$ _____

45. $8 \div 1 =$ _____   46. $4 \div 4 =$ _____   47. $10 \div 5 =$ _____   48. $1 \div 1 =$ _____

Place Value

All numerals in our system can be written with only ten **digits**. The digits are the whole numbers from 0 to 9:   0, 1, 2, 3, 4, 5, 6, 7, 8, 9

It is the **place** that the digit occupies that gives the number its **value**.

For example: 987 and 789 have the same digits but they are not the same number.

Last year, we looked at numbers up to six places. This year, we will work with numbers up to nine places. The biggest number with nine places is 999,999,999. We say it as:

nine hundred ninety-nine million, nine hundred ninety-nine thousand, nine hundred ninety-nine.

$$100,000,000 = 10^8$$
$$10,000,000 = 10^7$$
$$1,000,000 = 10^6$$
$$100,000 = 10^5$$
$$10,000 = 10^4$$
$$1,000 = 10^3$$
$$100 = 10^2$$
$$10 = 10^1$$
$$1 = 10^0$$

hundred millions	ten millions	millions	hundred thousands	ten thousands	thousands	hundreds	tens	ones
9	9	9,	9	9	9,	9	9	9

100,000,000s	10,000,000s	1,000,000s	100,000s	10,000s	1,000s	100s	10s	1s
9	9	9,	9	9	9,	9	9	9

What is the value of the underlined digit?

1. 2<u>5</u>6 _____

2. <u>5</u>93 _____

3. 37<u>5</u> _____

4. <u>3</u>,695 _____

5. 8,24<u>7</u> _____

6. 9,<u>2</u>37 _____

7. 2<u>9</u>,326 _____

8. <u>4</u>5,163 _____

9. 36,9<u>4</u>5 _____

10. 654,<u>9</u>83 _____

11. <u>3</u>19,567 _____

12. 231,<u>1</u>964 _____

13. 9,7<u>2</u>3,284 _____

14. <u>6</u>,221,397 _____

15. 6,<u>8</u>49,347 _____

16. <u>4</u>7,592,256 _____

17. 7<u>2</u>,391,652 _____

18. 70,003,<u>2</u>56 _____

19. 54<u>6</u>,733,821 _____

20. <u>5</u>64,213,793 _____

21. 1<u>2</u>3,453,967 _____

22. <u>7</u>22,333,974 _____

Find each sum or difference.

23.
$$\begin{array}{r} 2 \\ +\ 4 \\ \hline \end{array}$$

24.
$$\begin{array}{r} 8 \\ +\ 4 \\ \hline \end{array}$$

25.
$$\begin{array}{r} 9 \\ +\ 3 \\ \hline \end{array}$$

26.
$$\begin{array}{r} 7 \\ -\ 1 \\ \hline \end{array}$$

27.
$$\begin{array}{r} 6 \\ -\ 0 \\ \hline \end{array}$$

28.
$$\begin{array}{r} 5 \\ -\ 2 \\ \hline \end{array}$$

Multiply.

29.
$$\begin{array}{r} 4 \\ \times\ 3 \\ \hline \end{array}$$

30.
$$\begin{array}{r} 5 \\ \times\ 5 \\ \hline \end{array}$$

31.
$$\begin{array}{r} 9 \\ \times\ 9 \\ \hline \end{array}$$

32.
$$\begin{array}{r} 4 \\ \times\ 9 \\ \hline \end{array}$$

33.
$$\begin{array}{r} 8 \\ \times\ 6 \\ \hline \end{array}$$

34.
$$\begin{array}{r} 6 \\ \times\ 6 \\ \hline \end{array}$$

Divide.

35. $4\overline{)12}$

36. $4\overline{)16}$

37. $4\overline{)24}$

38. $7\overline{)21}$

Thousands, Hundreds, Tens, and Ones

When we are dealing with larger numbers, we can separate the numbers into periods of three. Each period has 3 digits. When the numbers are larger than 9999, use a comma to separate the periods. Four-digit numbers may be written with or without a comma.

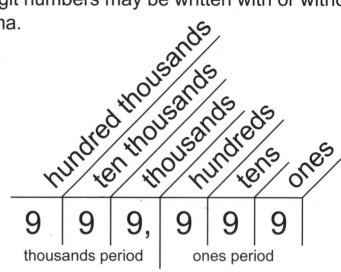

thousands period   ones period

In the number 345,678, we first look at the thousands period and we see that it is 345 or three hundred forty-five thousand. Then we move to the ones period and see 678 and we say six hundred seventy-eight. Altogether we say:

Words: three hundred forty-five thousand, six hundred seventy-eight

Standard form: 345,678

Example: Write the word name for **269,872.**

We look first at the thousands period (269) and we say:

two hundred sixty-nine **thousand**.

Then we look at the ones period (872) and we say:

eight hundred seventy-two.

Then we put it all together and say:

two hundred sixty-nine thousand, eight hundred seventy-two.

Exercise

Write the word name for each number.

1. 265,000 _____

2. 732,000 _____

4

3. 679,000 _____

4. 500,709 _____

5. 408,305 _____

6. 521,478 _____

7. 647,493 _____

8. 904,276 _____

9. 243,093 _____

10. 115,347 _____

11. 331,721 _____

12. 569,932 _____

13. 684,478 _____

14. 939,939 _____

15. 976,326 _____

16. 896,469 _____

17. 800,865 _____

18. 735,107 _____

19. 962,321 _____

Millions

According to the U.S. Bureau of the Census, the population of the United States on July 1, 1999, was 272,690,813. In the number 272,690,813, we first look at the millions period and we see that it is 272, so we say two hundred seventy-two million. Then we move on to the thousands period and we see 690 and we say six hundred ninety thousand. Finally, we move to the ones period and see 813 and we say eight hundred thirteen. Altogether we say:

Words: two hundred seventy-two million
six hundred ninety thousand
eight hundred thirteen.

Standard form: 272,690,813

Example: Write the word name for 379,486,245.

We look first at the millions period (379) and we say:

three hundred seventy-nine **million**.

Then we look at the thousands period (486) and we say:

four hundred eighty-six **thousand**.

Then we look at the ones period (245) and we say:

two hundred forty-five.

Then we put it all together and say:

three hundred seventy-nine million,
four hundred eighty-six thousand, two hundred forty-five.

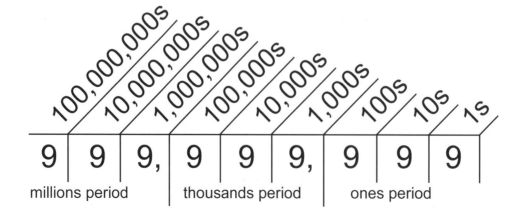

Write the word name for each number.

1. 482,076,153 _____

   _____

2. 165,531,010 _____

   _____

3. 16,920,692 _____

   _____

4. 38,354,534 _____

   _____

5. 296,876,217 _____

   _____

6. 145,904,310 _____

   _____

7. 412,628,105 _____

   _____

Example: Fill in the number for each period.

617,465,123:

<u>617</u> **million** <u>465</u> **thousand** <u>123</u>

Example: Write the words for each period.

617,465,123:

<u>six hundred seventeen</u> **million**

<u>four hundred sixty-five</u> **thousand**

<u>one hundred twenty-three</u>

Fill in the number for each period.

1. 324,759,432

   _____ million _____ thousand _____

2. 397,692,438

   _____ million _____ thousand _____

3. 712,689,473

   _____ million _____ thousand _____

4. 491,222,347

   _____ million _____ thousand _____

5. 748,972,369

   _____ million _____ thousand _____

8

Write the words for each period.

6. 479,897,321

_____ million

_____ thousand

_____

7. 391,682,745

_____ million

_____ thousand

_____

8. 273,342,791

_____ million

_____ thousand

_____

9. 796,221,475

_____ million

_____ thousand

_____

Expanded Notation

To write a number in what we call expanded form, we simply break it down into the value of each of its digits and make an addition sentence. Let's use the population number that we used on page 6. The number was 272,690,813. We will start at the left and work our way through each digit until we get to the ones place.

The first digit is 2. What place is it in? The one hundred millions place, so we write 200,000,000. What is the next digit? 7. What place is it in? The ten millions place, so we write 70,000,000.

We continue to the millions place and write 2,000,000.

To review, so far we have covered the millions period and have written:

hundred millions	ten millions	millions	hundred thousands	ten thousands	thousands	hundreds	tens	ones
2	7	2,	6	9	0,	8	1	3

200,000,000 + 70,000,000 + 2,000,000.

We continue to the thousands period and write 600,000 for the hundred thousands place and 90,000 for the ten thousands place and then we see that in the thousands place, we have a 0.

If the digit for a place is 0, then we don't write anything and we move on to the next place. So far, we have gotten through the millions period and the thousands period and have written

200,000,000 + 70,000,000 + 2,000,000 + 600,000 + 90,000.

We now move to the last period and add 800 + 10 + 3.

Altogether we have:

200,000,000 + 70,000,000 + 2,000,000 + 600,000 + 90,000 + 800 + 10 + 3

272,690,813

Example: Write 34,872,321 in expanded notation.

30,000,000 + 4,000,000 + 800,000 + 70,000 + 2,000 + 300 + 20 + 1

Example: Write 23,492,570 in expanded notation.

20,000,000 + 3,000,000 + 400,000 + 90,000 + 2,000 + 500 + 70

Exercise

Write each number in expanded notation.

1. 27,810,392

_____

2. 4,864,326

_____

3. 35,972,601

_____

4. 170,372,444

_____

5. 210,036,341

_____

6. 704,350,491

_____

7. 691,047,021

_____

What is the value of the underlined digit?

1. 6<u>5</u>4,983 _____

2. 319,5<u>6</u>7 _____

3. 231,96<u>4</u> _____

4. 9,<u>7</u>23,284 _____

5. 6,22<u>1</u>,397 _____

6. 6,84<u>9</u>,347 _____

7. <u>5</u>2,545,256 _____

Write the word name for each number.

8. 502,670,351 _____

_____

9. 295,345,198 _____

_____

10. 37,029,296 _____

_____

Fill in the number for each period.

11. 423,957,234

_____ million _____ thousand _____

12. 793,296,834

_____ million _____ thousand _____

13. 217,986,374

_____ million _____ thousand _____

Write the words for each period.

14. 974,798,123

_____ million

_____ thousand

_____

15. 193,286,547

_____ million

_____ thousand

_____

Write each number in expanded notation.

16. 35,018,293

_____

17. 8,649,723

_____

18. 53,279,106

_____

19. 410,273,786

_____

The land area of the United States is 3,537,438 square miles. If we wanted to make it a little simpler, we would say that it is between 3 and 4 million square miles. In order to round this number to the nearest million, we look at the value of the digit to the right of the millions place. If it is 5 or greater, then we round up. If it is less than 5, we round down. What is the land area of the United States rounded to the closest million?

3,537,438

rounding digit   determining digit

We need to concern ourselves with only two digits. One is the digit we are rounding to, and the other is the digit in the next place that will determine whether we leave the rounding digit as is, or add one to it.

3,537,438

rounding digit

Step one is to identify the digit we are rounding to. In this case, it is the millions digit, which is 3. Either this digit will remain a 3 or we will add 1 and make it 4. All the digits after this will become 0.

3,500,000 all the digits to the right become 0

determining digit

Step two is to look at the determining digit in the next place. If the determining digit is 5 or more, we add 1 to the rounding digit. If the determining digit is less than 5, then the rounding digit will remain the same. In this case, the determining digit is a 5, so we must add 1 to the rounding digit and then change the determining digit to 0.

4,000,000

add 1 to the rounding digit and change the determining digit to 0

The land area of the United States rounded to the nearest million is:

4,000,000 square miles

Example: Round 9,684,352 to the nearest thousand.

We first identity the rounding digit, which is in the thousands place.

9,684,352

rounding digit

Then look at the determining digit in the next place and change the rest to 0.

9,684,300

determining digit

The determining digit is a 3, which is less than 5 so we change it to 0 and leave the rounding digit the same.

9,684,000

9,684,352 rounded to the nearest thousand is 9,684,000

Example: Round 9,684,352 to the nearest hundred thousand.

We first identity the rounding digit, which is in the hundred thousands place.

9,684,352

Then look at the determining digit in the next place and change the rest to 0.

9,680,000

The determining digit is an 8, which is 5 or more,
so we change it to 0 and add 1 to the rounding number.

9,700,000

9,684,352 rounded to the nearest hundred thousand is 9,700,000

Example: Round 9,684,352 to the nearest hundred.

We first identity the rounding digit, which is in the hundreds place and then look at the determining digit in the next place and change the rest to 0.

9,684,350

The determining digit is a 5, which is 5 or more, so we change it to 0 and add 1 to the rounding number.

9,684,400

9,684,352 rounded to the nearest hundred is 9,684,400

Round each number to the indicated place.

1. 934,328,674 to the nearest **hundred thousand** _____

2. 785,723,945 to the nearest **million** _____

3. 327,492,743 to the nearest **hundred** _____

4. 384,657,396 to the nearest **thousand** _____

5. 757,895,563 to the nearest **ten thousand** _____

6. 492,730,913 to the nearest **hundred million** _____

7. 124,482,130 to the nearest **ten million** _____

8. 109,578,234 to the nearest **ten** _____

9. 77,744,505 to the nearest **million** _____

10. 5,791,519 to the nearest **million** _____

We have studied **place value** in our **system of numeration**. We learned that our system has 10 basic symbols which we call digits. We further learned that the place of the digit determines its value. We explored this with expanded notation. Our **system of numeration** is called the **Hindu-Arabic System of Numeration**. It is also known as the **decimal system** because it is a **base-ten** system. The prefix *deci* is from Latin and means "ten." We have ten digits and each place is based on ten, as we saw on page 2.

The **decimal system** reached Europe in the 11th century. Before that, the **Roman System of Numeration** was used.

The seven basic symbols of the Roman system are:

I V X L C D M

These are the equivalents in our decimal system:

$$I = 1 \qquad V = 5 \qquad X = 10 \qquad L = 50$$

$$C = 100 \qquad D = 500 \qquad M = 1000$$

To write other numerals in the Roman system, we use addition and subtraction. First, let's look at the addition pattern.

VI = 5 + 1 = 6	XI = 10 + 1 = 11
LX = 50 + 10 = 60	CX = 100 + 10 = 110
DC = 500 + 100 = 600	MC = 1000 + 100 = 1100

Do you begin to see the pattern? Let's look at some more examples:

VII = 5 + 2 = 7	XII = 10 + 2 = 12
LXX = 50 + 20 = 70	CXX = 100 + 20 = 120
DCC = 500 + 200 = 700	MCC = 1000 + 200 = 1200
VIII = 5 + 3 = 8	XIII = 10 + 3 = 13
LXXX = 50 + 30 = 80	CXXX = 100 + 30 = 130
DCCC = 500 + 300 = 800	MCCC = 1000 + 300 = 1300

We are going to spend a little more time with Roman numerals in order to look for patterns. Sometimes, in order to figure something out, we come up with rules or steps to explain how something works or to solve a problem. Sometimes, we try to see patterns and then we figure out the rules. We are going to look at some more patterns and then try to figure out the rules.

Remember the seven basic symbols of the Roman system are:

I V X L C D M

These are the equivalents in our decimal system:

I = 1   V = 5   X = 10   L = 50

C = 100   D = 500   M = 1000

To write other numerals in the Roman system, we use addition and subtraction. We have looked at addition; now let's look at the subtraction pattern.

IV = 5 − 1 = 4   IX = 10 − 1 = 9

XL = 50 − 10 = 40   XC = 100 − 10 = 90

CD = 500 − 100 = 400   CM = 1000 − 100 = 900

Look at these examples and try to see the pattern:

MMCDXLIV = 2000 + 400 + 40 + 4 = 2444   XLI = 40 + 1 = 41

MCDXLIII = 1000 + 400 + 40 + 3 = 1443   DV = 500 + 5 = 505

MMCDXXX = 2000 + 400 + 30 = 2430   DXL = 500 + 40 = 540

Exercise

Write each of the following in standard form.

1. CXLIV _____

2. LXIX _____

3. MCMLXVI _____

4. LXVIII _____

5. DCIX _____

6. MMI _____

7. XXXIV _____

8. CV _____

9. MDCXV _____

10. MIV _____

11. MCMII _____

12. MCMLVI _____

Round each number to the indicated place.

13. 374,694,321 to the nearest hundred million _____

14. 51,632,427 to the nearest million _____

15. 6,329,742 to the nearest hundred _____

16. 963,847 to the nearest thousand _____

Write the word name for each number.

17. 437,694,510 _____

_____

18. 379,287,345 _____

_____

19. 101,305,086 _____

_____

20. 738,942 _____

Properties of Addition

Commutative Property of Addition (Order)
Changing the order of the addends does not change the sum.

Study these examples.

$2 + 4 = 6$ $4 + 2 = 6$ $1 + 3 = 4$ $3 + 1 = 4$

$3 + 2 = 5$ $2 + 3 = 5$ $6 + 3 = 9$ $3 + 6 = 9$

We can add in any order.

Associative Property of Addition (Grouping)
Changing the grouping of the addends does not change the sum.

We can add only two numbers at a time.
The Associative Property lets us group any two addends at a time.

Study these examples.

$(1 + 2) + 3 = 6$ $1 + (2 + 3) = 6$ $2 + (4 + 6) = 12$ $(2 + 4) + 6 = 12$

$3 + (6 + 2) = 11$ $(3 + 6) + 2 = 11$ $(1 + 4) + 5 = 10$ $1 + (4 + 5) = 10$

We can group any two addends.

Identity Property of Addition (Zero)
Adding zero to a number does not change the number.

The Identity Property of Addition tells us that adding zero to a number does not change the number. It maintains its **identity**.

$8 + 0 = 8$ $0 + 9 = 9$ $12 + 0 = 12$

$0 + 3 = 3$ $5 + 0 = 5$ $0 + 7 = 7$

Find the sums.

1. 6 + 8 = _____   8 + 6 = _____   2. 3 + 4 = _____   4 + 3 = _____

3.   4   2   4.   8   2   5.   3   8
     + 2   + 4   + 2   + 8   + 8   + 3

6. 9 + 7 = _____   7 + 9 = _____   7. 8 + 6 = _____   6 + 8 = _____

8.   5   9   9.   5   6   10.   4   5
     + 9   + 5   + 6   + 5   + 5   + 4

Find the sums. Add the numbers in parentheses first.

11. (9 + 4) + 2 = _____   9 + (4 + 2) = _____

12. 6 + (3 + 4) = _____   (6 + 3) + 4 = _____

13. 2 + (3 + 9) = _____   (2 + 3) + 9 = _____

14.   2 ☐   2   15.   2 ☐   2   16.   8 ☐   8
        6   6 ☐   4   4 ☐   1   1 ☐
     + 3   + 3   + 3   + 3   + 6   + 6

17.   5 ☐   5   18.   1 ☐   1   19.   2 ☐   2
        4   4 ☐   5   5 ☐   2   2 ☐
     + 5   + 5   + 3   + 3   + 3   + 3

Six players on the St. John's basketball team scored points in the last game.

How many total points did they score?

Player	# points
James	9
John	7
Tony	5
Mike	6
Mark	8
Dennis	2

The problem is to find the total number of points scored by the 6 players.

We can add only 2 numbers at a time, so we have to be patient and just work it through, step by step. Let's add the 6 numbers and find the total number of points.

First, we write the numbers in a column.
Then there are several ways to proceed. Study the examples.

$$
\begin{array}{l}
9 \\
7 \\
5 \\
6 \\
8 \\
+2
\end{array}
\quad
\begin{array}{l}
16 \\
11 \\
10
\end{array}
\quad 27 \quad 37
$$

$$
\begin{array}{l}
9 \\
7 \\
5 \\
6 \\
8 \\
+2
\end{array}
\quad
\begin{array}{l}
16 \\
21 \\
27 \\
35 \\
37
\end{array}
$$

$$
\begin{array}{l}
9 \\
7 \\
5 \\
6 \\
8 \\
+2
\end{array}
\quad
\begin{array}{l}
15 \\
15 \\
7
\end{array}
\quad 30 \quad 37
$$

Study the examples.

$$
\begin{array}{l}
3 \\
7 \\
5 \\
5 \\
8 \\
+2 \\
\hline 30
\end{array}
\quad
\begin{array}{l}
10 \\
10 \\
10
\end{array}
\quad 20 \quad 30
$$

$$
\begin{array}{l}
8 \\
4 \\
6 \\
3 \\
7 \\
+5 \\
\hline 33
\end{array}
\quad
\begin{array}{l}
12 \\
18 \\
21 \\
28 \\
33
\end{array}
$$

$$
\begin{array}{l}
8 \\
9 \\
5 \\
7 \\
6 \\
+5 \\
\hline 40
\end{array}
\quad
\begin{array}{l}
15 \\
15 \\
10
\end{array}
\quad 30 \quad 40
$$

Find the sum of each column.

1.	2.	3.	4.	5.
6	8	9	5	6
7	2	5	2	5
4	6	4	7	7
+ 3	+ 1	+ 3	+ 3	+ 8

6.	7.	8.	9.	10.
3	9	5	6	4
5	6	3	8	5
8	4	2	3	6
2	7	5	2	8
7	4	7	1	3
+ 6	+ 6	+ 3	+ 0	+ 2

11.	12.	13.	14.	15.
5	3	8	7	3
7	4	3	6	7
9	6	5	5	2
2	5	6	3	5
+ 8	+ 2	+ 4	+ 2	+ 6

16.	17.	18.	19.	20.
3	3	9	6	5
8	6	5	5	3
+ 2	+ 7	+ 4	+ 8	+ 8

21.	22.	23.	24.	25.
7	1	2	2	7
4	3	4	1	7
9	8	6	3	8
2	5	3	5	8
1	6	5	6	5
+ 3	+ 9	+ 7	+ 2	+ 5

Examine the sentences.

The sum of five and seven is twelve.   5 + 7 = 12

We look for key words like "sum" which tells us this is an addition sentence. We see the word "is" and that tells us that this is an **equation** and has an equal sign. Then we fill in the numbers.

The sum of five and seven is twelve.   5 + 7 = 12

Write a number sentence for each word sentence.

Example: The sum of three and six is nine.

We note the key words and then fill in the numbers.

3 + 6 = 9

Try These

Write a number sentence for each word sentence.

1.   The sum of eight and four is twelve.   _____

2.   The sum of nine and seven is sixteen.   _____

3.   Eight is the sum of three and five.   _____

4.   The sum of two and one is three.   _____

5.   Eleven is the sum of five and six.   _____

6.   The sum of six and seven is thirteen.   _____

Sentences and Missing Numbers

Examine the sentences.

What is the sum of five and seven? $5 + 7 = n$

In this case, the sentence asks a question. We can still write a number sentence by using a letter like "n" to stand for the unknown number.

<u>What is</u> the <u>sum</u> of five and seven? $n = \underline{\hspace{1cm}} + \underline{\hspace{1cm}}$

We translate "What is" into $n =$. We see the key word "sum" which tells us this is an addition sentence. Then we fill in the numbers.

What is the sum of <u>five</u> and <u>seven</u>? $n = 5 + 7$

Write a number sentence for each word sentence.

Example: The sum of six and four is what?

We translate "is what": $\overset{\text{is what}}{= n}$

Then "sum" and the numbers: $6 + 4 = n$

The sum of six and four is what? $6 + 4 = n$

Try These

Write a number sentence for each word sentence.

1. What is the sum of six and nine?   _____

2. The sum of two and three is what?   _____

3. What is the sum of four and six?   _____

4. The sum of eight and four is what?   _____

5. What is the sum of seven and seven?   _____

Write a number sentence for each word sentence.

1. What is the sum of nine and three? _____

2. Fifteen is the sum of seven and eight. _____

3. The sum of five and nine is fourteen. _____

4. The sum of five and seven is what? _____

5. What is the sum of five and three? _____

6. The sum of four and five is nine. _____

7. What is the sum of eight and eight? _____

8. The sum of six and four is ten. _____

Find the sums.

9.
$$\begin{array}{r} 3 \\ 4 \\ + 5 \\ \hline \end{array}$$
10.
$$\begin{array}{r} 7 \\ 6 \\ + 8 \\ \hline \end{array}$$
11.
$$\begin{array}{r} 9 \\ 3 \\ + 1 \\ \hline \end{array}$$
12.
$$\begin{array}{r} 5 \\ 2 \\ 7 \\ + 3 \\ \hline \end{array}$$
13.
$$\begin{array}{r} 6 \\ 5 \\ 7 \\ + 8 \\ \hline \end{array}$$

14. $(4 + 6) + 5 =$ _____ $4 + (6 + 5) =$ _____

Write in standard form.

15. CXLIII _____   16. LXVI _____

Find each sum or difference.

17.
$$\begin{array}{r} 7 \\ + 6 \\ \hline \end{array}$$
18.
$$\begin{array}{r} 9 \\ + 9 \\ \hline \end{array}$$
19.
$$\begin{array}{r} 8 \\ + 7 \\ \hline \end{array}$$
20.
$$\begin{array}{r} 8 \\ - 1 \\ \hline \end{array}$$
21.
$$\begin{array}{r} 8 \\ - 3 \\ \hline \end{array}$$
22.
$$\begin{array}{r} 5 \\ - 0 \\ \hline \end{array}$$

Write the word name.

23. 345,722,691 _____

_____

Write in expanded notation.

24. 78,092,001

_____

25. 8,568,321

_____

Multiply.

26.	27.	28.	29.	30.	31.
5	8	3	2	7	6
× 7	× 9	× 4	× 2	× 1	× 0

Divide.

32. 5)15   33. 5)25   34. 6)36   35. 3)27

36. Tom has three apples and Jane has five apples.
How many apples do they have altogether?   _____

37. Sam scored 4 points in the game and Mike scored
6 points. How many points did they score together?   _____

38. Susan had three goals and Rebecca had two goals.
How many goals did they have altogether?   _____

Facts Review

Complete each number sentence.

1. 2 + 6 = _____   2. 9 + 4 = _____   3. 6 + 5 = _____   4. 7 + 3 = _____

5. 6 + 9 = _____   6. 4 + 5 = _____   7. 8 + 4 = _____   8. 4 + 7 = _____

9. 6 + 3 = _____   10. 9 + 6 = _____   11. 4 + 3 = _____   12. 5 + 2 = _____

13. 12 − 9 = _____   14. 14 − 6 = _____   15. 10 − 9 = _____   16. 11 − 5 = _____

17. 10 − 8 = _____   18. 15 − 7 = _____   19. 9 − 3 = _____   20. 12 − 7 = _____

21. 13 − 8 = _____   22. 7 − 5 = _____   23. 6 − 0 = _____   24. 17 − 9 = _____

25. 1 × 7 = _____   26. 5 × 7 = _____   27. 3 × 0 = _____   28. 5 × 1 = _____

29. 3 × 2 = _____   30. 0 × 2 = _____   31. 1 × 4 = _____   32. 6 × 2 = _____

33. 7 × 5 = _____   34. 9 × 1 = _____   35. 2 × 5 = _____   36. 1 × 6 = _____

37. 0 ÷ 5 = _____   38. 12 ÷ 6 = _____   39. 15 ÷ 5 = _____   40. 2 ÷ 1 = _____

41. 30 ÷ 5 = _____   42. 6 ÷ 2 = _____   43. 14 ÷ 2 = _____   44. 20 ÷ 4 = _____

45. 0 ÷ 7 = _____   46. 35 ÷ 5 = _____   47. 5 ÷ 5 = _____   48. 10 ÷ 2 = _____

Examine the sentence and write the number sentence.

What number, when added to five, is twelve? $5 + n = 12$

What number will make the number sentence true?
Because we know that $5 + 7 = 12$, we see that the solution is: $n = 7$

Examine these sentences and write a number sentence.
If you know your facts, you can solve the problems very easily.

What number, when you add four to it, is twelve?

$$n + 4 = 12$$

The fact is:
$$\begin{array}{r} 8 \\ +\ 4 \\ \hline 12 \end{array}$$
The solution is simple. $n = 8$

In order to get a sum of sixteen,
what number should you add to nine? $9 + n = 16$

The fact is:
$$\begin{array}{r} 9 \\ +\ 7 \\ \hline 16 \end{array}$$
The solution is simple. $n = 7$

Another simple way to find the solution is to
use a related subtraction sentence.

Examine the sentence and write the number sentence.

What number, when added to eight, is fifteen? $8 + n = 15$

Look at the number sentence and think of a related subtraction sentence.

The related subtraction sentence is: $15 - 8 = n$
so we see that the solution is: $n = 7$

Examine these sentences and write a number sentence.
Then think of a related subtraction sentence and solve the problem.

What number, when you add six to it, is thirteen? $n + 6 = 13$

The related subtraction sentence is: $13 - 6 = n$
so we see that the solution is: $n = 7$

What number do you add to seven to get ten? $7 + n = 10$

The related subtraction sentence is: $10 - 7 = n$
We see that the solution is: $n = 3$

Write a number sentence for each word sentence, then find the solution, using your knowledge of the arithmetic facts, fact families, and related sentences. The first one is done for you.

1. What number, when added to three, will give a sum of nine?

    $3 + n = 9$ $9 - 3 = n$ $n = 6$

2. What number, when added to five, will give a sum of fourteen?

    _____   _____

3. What number, when you add four to it, is seven?

    _____   _____

4. In order to get a sum of eighteen, what number should you add to nine?

    _____   _____

5. What number do you add to six to get fifteen?

    _____   _____

6. What number, when added to eight, will give a sum of eleven?

    _____   _____

7. What number, when you add nine to it, is sixteen?

    _____   _____

8. In order to get a sum of fifteen, what number should you add to eight?

_____   _____

9. What number do you add to six to get fourteen?

_____   _____

10. What number, when added to seven, will give a sum of fifteen?

_____   _____

11. What number, when you add three to it, is seven?

_____   _____

Find the solution to each number sentence, using your knowledge of the arithmetic facts, fact families, and related sentences.

12. $6 + 6 = n$

$n =$ _____

13. $1 + n = 7$

$n =$ _____

14. $n + 5 = 10$

$n =$ _____

15. $5 + 8 = n$

$n =$ _____

16. $3 + n = 5$

$n =$ _____

17. $n + 6 = 13$

$n =$ _____

18. $8 + 4 = n$

$n =$ _____

19. $2 + n = 11$

$n =$ _____

20. $n + 8 = 17$

$n =$ _____

21. What number must you add to three, in order to obtain a sum of three? _____

22. If the Junior Legion of Mary group has fourteen members and five of them are girls, then how many are boys? _____

31

Subtraction is the inverse operation of addition. It is the opposite of addition.

As with addition, zero is also the Identity element for subtraction.

Identity Property of Addition and Subtraction (Zero)
Adding zero to a number or subtracting zero from a number does not change the number.

There are different types of subtraction problems. The most basic is the "take away" type of problem. Here is an example:

There were twelve eggs in the carton. We *took four* eggs and cooked them and ate them. *How many* eggs *were left* in the carton?

In this problem we *take some away* and find how many *remain*. *n* is *how many are left*.

$$12 - 4 = n \qquad 12 - 4 = 8 \qquad n = 8$$

There were 8 eggs *left* in the carton.

Another type of subtraction problem is the "comparing" type problem. This is an example:

John ate seven tacos and Joan ate three tacos. *How many more* tacos did John eat *than* Joan?

In this problem, we compare two things and find the difference. *n* is the difference between the two things.

$$7 - 3 = n \qquad 7 - 3 = 4 \qquad n = 4$$

John ate 4 *more* tacos *than* Joan.

Also, we have the "how many more are needed" or "completion" type problem. This is an example:

Mark has fourteen math problems to do on the quiz. He has done six. How many more problems does he need to do to *complete* the math?

In this problem, we look at the *total needed* and subtract the *amount already completed* to find the *amount needed* to get the total. *n* is the amount needed to complete the total.

$$14 - 6 = n \qquad 14 - 6 = 8 \qquad n = 8$$

Mark needs to do 8 *more* problems *to complete* the quiz.

Solve each problem. Try to write a number sentence first.

1. Elijah played cards with his mother. At the end of the game, he scored fourteen and his mother scored six. By how many points did he win? _____

2. Rosie baked a "baker's dozen" (13) cookies. She gave four to her brother. How many were left? _____

3. There were eleven ducks on the pond. Six flew away. How many remained on the pond? _____

4. There are ten Hail Marys in each decade of the Rosary. We have prayed five in the first decade. How many are left to say in the decade? _____

5. Twelve Boy Scouts went on the overnight camping trip. Seven Scouts helped to pitch the tent while the rest gathered firewood. How many looked for firewood? _____

6. Jesus chose twelve Apostles. Three were present at the Agony in the Garden. How many were not? _____

7. Ten chickens were sunning in the barnyard. Two of them laid eggs. How many did not? _____

8. Eleven children were playing at the playground. Five were swinging on the swings. How many were not? _____

9. Twelve Knights of Columbus helped out at the Corpus Christi procession. Four carried the canopy while the rest served at the ice cream social afterwards. How many served at the ice cream social afterwards? _____

$$\underline{} - \underline{} = \underline{}$$
minuend   subtrahend   difference

☐	minuend
– ☐	subtrahend
☐	difference

PRINCIPLE	EXAMPLE
IF: $a + b = c$	$3 + 4 = 7$
THEN: $c - a = b$	$7 - 3 = 4$
AND: $c - b = a$	$7 - 4 = 3$

Other Subtraction Sentences

Study the boxes above carefully. Make sure you understand the concepts.

We have *studied addition number sentences that were missing the sum:*

$6 + 6 = n$ $7 + 8 = n$ $5 + 3 = n$

We have studied addition sentences that were missing an addend:

$6 + n = 12$ $7 + n = 15$ $n + 3 = 8$

We have studied subtraction sentences that were missing the difference:

$12 - 6 = n$ $15 - 8 = n$ $8 - 3 = n$

Now we will study subtraction sentences that are missing the minuend or the subtrahend:

$n - 5 = 3$ $12 - n = 5$ $15 - n = 8$

We will start by looking at each of the three subtraction sentences above and making either a related addition sentence or another subtraction sentence, so that the n is all by itself on one side of the equal sign.

$n = 5 + 3$ $12 - 5 = n$ $15 - 8 = n$

Write a related number sentence for each of the following so that the *n* is all by itself on one side of the equal sign.

Examples:	$n - 7 = 3$	$14 - n = 6$	$n - 8 = 5$
Solutions:	$n = 3 + 7$	$14 - 6 = n$	$n = 5 + 8$

Study the above examples very carefully.

Read each problem and write a subtraction sentence. Then write a related sentence so that the n is all by itself on one side of the equal sign. Then solve.

Example: What number when you subtract three will leave seven?

$$n - 3 = 7 \qquad n = 7 + 3 \qquad n = 10$$

Example: If the difference is nine and the minuend is sixteen, what is the subtrahend?

$$16 - n = 9 \qquad n = 16 - 9 \qquad n = 7$$

Study the above examples very carefully.

Write a related number sentence for each of the following so that the n is all by itself on one side of the equal sign. Then solve.

1. $n - 2 = 3$

2. $12 - n = 8$

_____ _____   _____ _____

3. $11 - n = 6$

4. $n - 2 = 9$

_____ _____   _____ _____

5. $n - 4 = 8$

6. $8 - n = 8$

_____ _____   _____ _____

Read each problem and write a subtraction sentence. Then write a related sentence so that the n is all by itself on one side of the equal sign. Then solve.

Ex.   If the minuend is 9 and the difference is 3, what is the subtrahend?

$$\underline{\quad 9 - n = 3 \quad} \qquad \underline{\quad 9 - 3 = n \quad} \qquad \underline{\quad n = 6 \quad}$$

7. A family of 14 went on a hike. Seven people wore sneakers and the rest wore hiking boots. How many wore hiking boots?

_____ _____ _____

8. Sixteen tulips came up in the spring in the front garden. Nine of the tulips were yellow and the rest were red. How many were red?

_____ _____ _____

Write a related number sentence for each of the following so that the n is all by itself on one side of the equal sign. Then solve.

1. $n - 7 = 3$

   _____ _____

2. $11 - n = 8$

   _____ _____

3. $7 - n = 6$

   _____ _____

4. $n - 4 = 7$

   _____ _____

5. $n - 5 = 5$

   _____ _____

6. $13 - n = 5$

   _____ _____

7. $10 - n = 4$

   _____ _____

8. $n - 0 = 2$

   _____ _____

9. $n - 9 = 4$

   _____ _____

10. $14 - n = 6$

   _____ _____

Read each problem and write a subtraction sentence. Then write a related sentence so that the n is all by itself on one side of the equal sign. Then solve.

11. The difference is nine and the minuend is 16. What is the subtrahend?

   _____ _____

12. Fourteen people were at the meeting. After the meeting, five people stayed to clean up and the rest left. How many left?

   _____ _____

13. There were 18 goats grazing by the pond. Nine of the goats wandered up the hill while the rest remained at the pond. How many of the goats remained at the pond?

   _____ _____

Solve each problem. Try to write a number sentence first.

14. The choir sang thirteen songs at the concert.
Five of them were in Latin. How many were not in Latin? _____

15. The Whittaker family has twelve children.
Seven are outside doing chores while the rest
are studying inside. How many are indoors? _____

Write a number sentence for each word sentence, then find the solution.

16. What number, when added to 0, will give a sum of 4?

_____ _____

17. What number, when you add 8 to it, is 13?

_____ _____

18. Write **42,756,210** in expanded notation.

_____

Find the sums.

19.
$$\begin{array}{r} 9 \\ 4 \\ +\ 7 \\ \hline \end{array}$$

20. (1 + 7) + 6 = _____   1 + (7 + 6) = _____

21. Round **1,324,551** to the nearest hundred _____

22. Write the word name for **348,772,412**.

_____

More Number Sentences and Problem Solving

Find the missing number

1. $8 + 6 = n$

n = _____

2. $0 + n = 4$

n = _____

3. $n + 8 = 13$

n = _____

4. $16 - 9 = n$

n = _____

5. $7 - n = 6$

n = _____

6. $n - 9 = 9$

n = _____

7. $9 + 5 = n$

n = _____

8. $11 - n = 6$

n = _____

9. $n + 5 = 6$

n = _____

10. $10 - 9 = n$

n = _____

11. $5 + n = 9$

n = _____

12. $n - 7 = 5$

n = _____

13. $9 - 9 = n$

n = _____

14. $n + 0 = 0$

n = _____

15. $15 - n = 8$

n = _____

16. $2 + 4 = n$

n = _____

17. $14 - n = 5$

n = _____

18. $n - 7 = 2$

n = _____

19. $8 - 3 = n$

n = _____

20. $6 - n = 1$

n = _____

21. $n - 2 = 8$

n = _____

22. $6 + 9 = n$

n = _____

23. $7 - n = 4$

n = _____

24. $n + 8 = 9$

n = _____

Solve each problem. Try to write a number sentence first.

25. Eleven students were able to go to the concert.
Four were boys. How many were girls? _____

26. There are ten pins in bowling. Mary knocked down six
pins in her first attempt. How many pins were left standing? _____

27. Giovanni took thirteen shots in the basketball game.
He made eight baskets. How many did he miss? _____

28. There are fourteen Stations of the Cross. Father has
finished the third Station. How many Stations remain? _____

29. Phillip scored twelve points in the game.
He scored eight points in the second half.
How many points did he score in the first half? _____

30. If you start with eleven, and you end up with
four, how many did you lose? _____

31. Nine blue votive candles on the left side of the church
were lit by children after Mass. Eight more were lit that
afternoon. How many candles were lit altogether? _____

32. One early morning, Mom spotted ten deer grazing
in the clearing. Two had antlers. How many did not? _____

33. Felicity is eighteen years old. Elijah is nine years old.
How much older than Elijah is Felicity? _____

34. There are eight children in the Schmitt family.
There are six children in the Jones family. How
many children are there in the two families? _____

35. If you study for 5 hours today and you study
for 3 hours tomorrow, how many hours will you
have studied in those two days?

_____

36. What is the sum of 7 and 8?

_____

Addition Beyond the Facts

When adding whole numbers, we always start with the ones place and move to the left, while regrouping as necessary. Here is an example:

$$\begin{array}{r} \overset{1\ 1}{435} \\ +276 \\ \hline 711 \end{array}$$

First, add the ones and regroup if necessary.

Then move to the tens and regroup as necessary.

Finally, move to the hundreds and finish up and we're done.

Example: The Empire State building in New York has 102 stories and the Sears Tower in Chicago has 108 stories. How many stories do the two buildings have altogether?

Solution:

$$\begin{array}{r} \overset{1}{102} \\ +108 \\ \hline 210 \end{array}$$

Write the problem, then add the ones and regroup if necessary. Then move to the tens and regroup as necessary. Finally, move to the hundreds and regroup if necessary. We have our solution.

The two buildings have 210 stories altogether.

Try These

Add.

1.
$$\begin{array}{r} 714 \\ +239 \\ \hline \end{array}$$

2.
$$\begin{array}{r} 528 \\ +357 \\ \hline \end{array}$$

3.
$$\begin{array}{r} 681 \\ +149 \\ \hline \end{array}$$

4.
$$\begin{array}{r} 432 \\ +398 \\ \hline \end{array}$$

5.
$$\begin{array}{r} 325 \\ +467 \\ \hline \end{array}$$

6.
$$\begin{array}{r} 236 \\ +673 \\ \hline \end{array}$$

7.
$$\begin{array}{r} 632 \\ +185 \\ \hline \end{array}$$

8.
$$\begin{array}{r} 994 \\ +384 \\ \hline \end{array}$$

9.
$$\begin{array}{r} 843 \\ +195 \\ \hline \end{array}$$

10.
$$\begin{array}{r} 572 \\ +238 \\ \hline \end{array}$$

11.
$$\begin{array}{r} 343 \\ +599 \\ \hline \end{array}$$

12.
$$\begin{array}{r} 466 \\ +285 \\ \hline \end{array}$$

13. The team had 138 yards rushing and 142 yards passing. How many total passing and rushing yards did they have? _____

Four-Digit Addition

No matter how large the numbers we add, we always start with the ones place and move to the left, while regrouping as necessary. We just keep following the procedure and moving to the left until we get to the end. Here is an example:

¹ ¹
2353
+ 4289
———
6642

First, add the ones and regroup if necessary.

Then move to the tens and regroup as necessary. Move to the hundreds next and continue to regroup as necessary.

Finally, move to the thousands, add, and we're done!

Example: The Arkansas River is 2364 kilometers long.
The Ohio River is 1579 kilometers long.
How many kilometers long are the two rivers altogether?

Solution:
¹ ¹
2364
+ 1579
———
3943

Write the problem, then add the ones and regroup if necessary. Then move to the tens and the hundreds, regrouping each as necessary. After that, we finish up with the thousands and we have our solution.

The two rivers are 3943 kilometers altogether.

Try These

Add.

1. 5390
  + 6475

2. 2615
  + 9218

3. 3742
  + 8616

4. 3099
  + 1908

5. 7465
  + 6592

6. 4175
  + 5450

7. 6549
  + 8290

8. 7875
  + 1855

9. The Missouri River is 2341 miles long.
The Mississippi River is 2320 miles long.
How many miles long are the two rivers altogether?   _____

Adding Larger Numbers

The rules and principles of addition stay the same even if the numbers are really big. We always start on the right side and move left until done, regrouping along the way, as necessary. Just for fun and exercise, try to add the problem below.

$$235,345,766,793,487,259,618,843,559,012$$
$$+428,932,987,543,892,164,534,829,467,231$$

The answer is 664,278,754,337,379,424,153,673,026,243.

Example: There were 364,521 pinto beans in a very large container. In another large container, there were 215,987 kidney beans. If all the beans were mixed into an even larger container, how many beans would there be altogether?

Solution:
$$\begin{array}{r} \overset{1}{3}\overset{1}{6}\overset{1}{4},521 \\ +215,987 \\ \hline 580,508 \end{array}$$

Write the problem, then add the ones and regroup if necessary. Then keep moving to the left, continuing to regroup as necessary. Just keep going until you have the solution.

There were 580,508 beans altogether.

Try These

Add.

1. 27,895
    + 97,132

2. 321,476
    +335,569

3. 58,977
    + 22,891

4. 542,321
    +128,754

5. 527,397
    +354,214

6. 45,391
    + 23,549

7. 472,765
    +397,000

8. 91,362
    + 48,231

9. The state of Alaska covers 570,380 square miles. It has the largest land area of the 50 states. Texas is the second largest state. It has a land area of 268,820 square miles. What is the area of the two largest states when you add them together? _____

As is the case with adding larger numbers, the rules and principles stay the same when adding multiple addends. If you are adding three or more addends, you must be very careful to make sure all the places (ones, tens, hundreds, etc.) are correctly lined up with one another. Then we begin as usual at the right with the ones column, adding two digits at a time and then adding that sum to the next digit. Here is an example.

```
  2 1
  234
  579
  182
+ 361
 1356
```

First, add the ones. Add the first two digits and then add that sum to the next digit and add that sum to the last digit and regroup as necessary. Then move to the tens and follow the same procedure. Move to the hundreds next, adding the first two digits and continuing with adding that sum to the next digit and that one to the next. Don't forget the regroupings as necessary. Since there are more addends, it would be wise to check your answer.

Example: The three largest islands in the United States are Hawaii, Kodiak Island, and Puerto Rico. The largest, Hawaii, has an area of 4028 square miles. Kodiak Island in Alaska has an area of 3588 square miles and Puerto Rico has an area of 3435 square miles. What is the area of all three islands altogether?

Solution:
```
  1 1 2
   4028
   3588
 + 3435
 11,051
```

Think about the problem, then line up the addends. Add the ones and regroup if necessary. Move to the tens, add and regroup. Continue to move to the left until finished and check the solution.

The total area of the three islands is 11,051 square miles.

Try These

Add.

1.
```
  109
  275
+976
```

2.
```
  499
  485
  353
+452
```

3.
```
  539
  293
+612
```

4.
```
  247
  191
  322
+423
```

5.
```
  5806
  4155
  9760
+ 4243
```

6.
```
  3219
  8604
+ 6154
```

7.
```
  4129
  2083
  9611
+ 6072
```

8.
```
  1352
  8440
+ 2566
```

Exercise

Add.

1. 229
    +543

2. 480
    +253

3. 675
    +162

4. 837
    +162

5. 828
    +781

6. 973
    +964

7. 168
    +743

8. 643
    +259

9. 4837
    + 4616

10. 5885
    + 2280

11. 8291
    + 3472

12. 1279
    + 2355

13. 4780
    + 2956

14. 6438
    + 1725

15. 5067
    + 2545

16. 3165
    + 2917

17. 376,142
    +394,672

18. 16,214
    + 56,850

19. 391,897
    +355,654

20. 22,456
    + 67,381

21. 143,785
    +675,352

22. 49,025
    + 38,484

23. 798,456
    +105,555

24. 39,454
    + 12,926

25. 421
    145
    +162

26. 231
    178
    103
    +407

27. 214
    513
    +223

28. 641
    412
    372
    +444

44

29.
$$\begin{array}{r} 459 \\ 524 \\ +425 \\ \hline \end{array}$$

30.
$$\begin{array}{r} 723 \\ 240 \\ 568 \\ +000 \\ \hline \end{array}$$

31.
$$\begin{array}{r} 312 \\ 211 \\ +631 \\ \hline \end{array}$$

32.
$$\begin{array}{r} 491 \\ 475 \\ 327 \\ +135 \\ \hline \end{array}$$

33.
$$\begin{array}{r} 7289 \\ 3723 \\ 1454 \\ +1323 \\ \hline \end{array}$$

34.
$$\begin{array}{r} 2317 \\ 6035 \\ +4218 \\ \hline \end{array}$$

35.
$$\begin{array}{r} 4287 \\ 3652 \\ 4564 \\ +1748 \\ \hline \end{array}$$

36.
$$\begin{array}{r} 4257 \\ 2545 \\ +3162 \\ \hline \end{array}$$

37.
$$\begin{array}{r} 2225 \\ 5424 \\ 8542 \\ +5631 \\ \hline \end{array}$$

38.
$$\begin{array}{r} 4316 \\ 7312 \\ +6321 \\ \hline \end{array}$$

39.
$$\begin{array}{r} 1127 \\ 6135 \\ 5743 \\ +1424 \\ \hline \end{array}$$

40.
$$\begin{array}{r} 2816 \\ 6355 \\ +2143 \\ \hline \end{array}$$

Solve each problem.

41. Twenty-two girls were preparing to receive the Sacrament of Confirmation. Seventeen boys were also going to be confirmed. How many confirmandi were there altogether? _____

42. The land area of Rhode Island is 1545 square miles and the land area of Delaware is 2490 square miles. What is the total land area of the two states? _____

43. The Arkansas River is 1469 miles long and the Ohio River is 981 miles long. The Tennessee River is 652 miles long and the Cumberland River is 675 miles long. How many miles long are all the rivers together? _____

44. The Arkansas River passes through the states of Colorado, Kansas, Oklahoma, and Arkansas. The land area of Colorado is 104,185 square miles. The land area of Kansas is 82,227 square miles. The land area of Oklahoma is 69,898 square miles and the land area of Arkansas is 53,179 square miles. What is the total land area of the four states that the river travels through? _____

When subtracting whole numbers, we always start with the ones place and move to the left, while regrouping as necessary. Here is an example:

$$\begin{array}{r} \overset{8\ 15}{49\cancel{5}} \\ -276 \\ \hline 9 \end{array}$$

First, we check and see if there are enough ones to subtract. In this case, more ones are needed so we regroup one ten from the tens place and add it to ones place. We rewrite the new number in the tens place and the new number in the ones place. Now we can subtract.

$$\begin{array}{r} \overset{8\ 15}{49\cancel{5}} \\ -276 \\ \hline 219 \end{array}$$

Then we move left to the next place and continue in the same way until we are finished.

Study these examples.

$$\begin{array}{r} \overset{5\ 15}{76\cancel{5}} \\ -347 \\ \hline 418 \end{array} \qquad \begin{array}{r} \overset{3\ 14}{4\cancel{4}9} \\ -273 \\ \hline 176 \end{array} \qquad \begin{array}{r} \overset{8\ 12}{49\cancel{2}} \\ -247 \\ \hline 245 \end{array} \qquad \begin{array}{r} \overset{12}{\overset{3\ \cancel{2}\ 11}{4\cancel{3}\cancel{1}}} \\ -289 \\ \hline 142 \end{array}$$

Subtract.

1. $\begin{array}{r} 646 \\ -519 \\ \hline \end{array}$ 2. $\begin{array}{r} 441 \\ -193 \\ \hline \end{array}$ 3. $\begin{array}{r} 938 \\ -256 \\ \hline \end{array}$ 4. $\begin{array}{r} 898 \\ -350 \\ \hline \end{array}$

5. $\begin{array}{r} 256 \\ -148 \\ \hline \end{array}$ 6. $\begin{array}{r} 763 \\ -237 \\ \hline \end{array}$ 7. $\begin{array}{r} 827 \\ -173 \\ \hline \end{array}$ 8. $\begin{array}{r} 435 \\ -258 \\ \hline \end{array}$

9. $\begin{array}{r} 665 \\ -276 \\ \hline \end{array}$ 10. $\begin{array}{r} 810 \\ -229 \\ \hline \end{array}$ 11. $\begin{array}{r} 830 \\ -433 \\ \hline \end{array}$ 12. $\begin{array}{r} 851 \\ -619 \\ \hline \end{array}$

13. $911 - 743 =$ _____   14. $872 - 543 =$ _____

Sometimes, when subtracting, we may have to regroup a place that we had already regrouped. We just regroup it again.
Regroup one place value at a time.
Here is an example:

$$\begin{array}{r} \overset{1\ 11}{57\cancel{2}\cancel{1}} \\ -\ 3946 \\ \hline 5 \end{array}$$

First, we check and see if there are enough ones to subtract. In this case, more ones are needed so we regroup 1 ten from the tens place and add it to the ones place. We rewrite the new number in the tens place and the new number in the ones place. Now we can subtract.

$$\begin{array}{r} \overset{\ \ \ 11}{\overset{6\ \diagdown\ 11}{5\cancel{7}\cancel{2}\cancel{1}}} \\ -\ 3946 \\ \hline 75 \end{array}$$

Then we move left to the next place and see if we have enough tens to subtract. We don't, so we have to regroup 1 hundred as 10 tens and add them to the tens place. We rewrite the new number in the hundreds place and the new number in the tens place. Now we can subtract the tens place.

$$\begin{array}{r} \overset{16\ 11}{\overset{4\ \diagdown\ \diagdown\ 11}{5\cancel{7}\cancel{2}\cancel{1}}} \\ -\ 3946 \\ \hline 1775 \end{array}$$

Then we move left to the hundreds place and repeat the procedure. Then we move to the thousands and finish up the subtraction.
Study the example carefully.

Study these examples.

$$\begin{array}{r} \overset{15\ 11}{\overset{4\ \diagdown\ \diagdown\ 11}{5\cancel{6}\cancel{2}\cancel{1}}} \\ -\ 2999 \\ \hline 2622 \end{array} \qquad \begin{array}{r} \overset{12\ 14}{\overset{3\ \diagdown\ \diagdown\ 14}{4\cancel{3}\cancel{5}\cancel{4}}} \\ -\ 1465 \\ \hline 2889 \end{array} \qquad \begin{array}{r} \overset{10\ 11}{\overset{6\ \diagdown\ \diagdown\ 16}{7\cancel{1}\cancel{2}\cancel{6}}} \\ -\ 4987 \\ \hline 2139 \end{array} \qquad \begin{array}{r} \overset{12\ 13}{\overset{8\ \diagdown\ \diagdown\ 18}{9\cancel{3}\cancel{4}\cancel{8}}} \\ -\ 3359 \\ \hline 5989 \end{array}$$

Try These

Subtract.

$$\begin{array}{r} 1. \quad 7149 \\ -\ 3861 \\ \hline \end{array} \qquad \begin{array}{r} 2. \quad 5460 \\ -\ 1509 \\ \hline \end{array} \qquad \begin{array}{r} 3. \quad 8432 \\ -\ 5954 \\ \hline \end{array} \qquad \begin{array}{r} 4. \quad 4990 \\ -\ 2495 \\ \hline \end{array}$$

$$\begin{array}{r} 5. \quad 3721 \\ -\ 1888 \\ \hline \end{array} \qquad \begin{array}{r} 6. \quad 9126 \\ -\ 3087 \\ \hline \end{array} \qquad \begin{array}{r} 7. \quad 8532 \\ -\ 2999 \\ \hline \end{array} \qquad \begin{array}{r} 8. \quad 6541 \\ -\ 1892 \\ \hline \end{array}$$

Zeros in Subtraction

When we have zeros in the minuend, we may need to regroup more than once before we subtract. Regroup just one place value at a time.

Here is an example:

Subtract. $3000 - 1946 =$

Rewrite the problem vertically and then proceed.

$$\begin{array}{r} {\scriptstyle 2\ 10} \\ 3000 \\ -\ 1946 \\ \hline \end{array}$$

First, we check and see if there are enough ones to subtract. No, there are not. Can we regroup 1 ten from the tens place? There are no tens so we look in the hundreds place. Is there 1 hundred we could regroup?

$$\begin{array}{r} {\scriptstyle \quad 9} \\ {\scriptstyle 2\ 10\ 10} \\ 3000 \\ -\ 1946 \\ \hline \end{array}$$

No, so we must move on to the thousands place. Are there any thousands? Yes, so we regroup 1 thousand as 10 hundreds and add it to the hundreds place. Then we regroup 1 of those 10 hundreds into 10 tens and add it to the tens place. Then we regroup 1 ten of those tens

$$\begin{array}{r} {\scriptstyle \quad 9\ 9} \\ {\scriptstyle 2\ 10\ 10\ 10} \\ 3000 \\ -\ 1946 \\ \hline 4 \end{array}$$

and add it to the ones place. Now we have enough ones so that we can finally subtract the ones. We rewrite the new number in the tens place and the new number in the ones place. Now we can subtract.

We continue to move left to the next place and subtract the tens.

$$\begin{array}{r} {\scriptstyle \quad 9\ 9} \\ {\scriptstyle 2\ 10\ 10\ 10} \\ 3000 \\ -\ 1946 \\ \hline 1054 \end{array}$$

Then we move left to the hundreds place and repeat the procedure.

Then we move to the thousands and finish up the subtraction.

Study the example carefully.

Study these examples.

$$\begin{array}{r} {\scriptstyle \quad 9\ 9} \\ {\scriptstyle 4\ 10\ 10\ 10} \\ 5000 \\ -\ 2812 \\ \hline 2188 \end{array} \qquad \begin{array}{r} {\scriptstyle \quad 9} \\ {\scriptstyle 6\ 10\ 10} \\ 7006 \\ -\ 4142 \\ \hline 2864 \end{array} \qquad \begin{array}{r} {\scriptstyle 2\ 10\ 3\ 10} \\ 3040 \\ -\ 1325 \\ \hline 1715 \end{array} \qquad \begin{array}{r} {\scriptstyle \quad 11\ 9} \\ {\scriptstyle 5\ 1\ 10\ 10} \\ 6200 \\ -\ 3333 \\ \hline 2867 \end{array}$$

Try These

Subtract.

$$\begin{array}{r} 1.\quad 9002 \\ -\ 7865 \\ \hline \end{array} \qquad \begin{array}{r} 2.\quad 4000 \\ -\ 1695 \\ \hline \end{array} \qquad \begin{array}{r} 3.\quad 3030 \\ -\ 1967 \\ \hline \end{array} \qquad \begin{array}{r} 4.\quad 5005 \\ -\ 1178 \\ \hline \end{array}$$

5. $200 - 119 =$ _____

6. $403 - 238 =$ _____

Subtracting Larger Numbers

When subtracting larger numbers, we may have to do several regroupings. We just stay calm and take things one place at a time.
Here is an example.

$$\begin{array}{r} \overset{\scriptstyle 12}{\underset{}{\overset{6\ \cancel{3}\ 11}{587,7\cancel{3}1}}} \\ -265,954 \\ \hline 77 \end{array}$$

First, we check and see if there are enough ones to subtract. In this case, more ones are needed so we regroup one ten from the tens place and add it to ones place. We rewrite the new number in the tens place and the new number in the ones place. Now we can subtract. Then repeat the procedure with the tens place. Then again with the hundreds.

$$\begin{array}{r} \overset{\scriptstyle 16\ 12}{\underset{}{\overset{6\ \cancel{8}\ \cancel{3}\ 11}{587,7\cancel{3}1}}} \\ -265,954 \\ \hline 777 \end{array}$$

$$\begin{array}{r} \overset{\scriptstyle 16\ 12}{\underset{}{\overset{6\ \cancel{8}\ \cancel{3}\ 11}{587,7\cancel{3}1}}} \\ -265,954 \\ \hline 321,777 \end{array}$$

Continue moving left to the next place and subtracting and regrouping in the same way until you are finished.
Study the example carefully.

Study these examples.

$$\begin{array}{r} \overset{\scriptstyle 9\ \ 9}{\overset{8\ \cancel{10}\ \cancel{10}\ 10}{490,007}} \\ -478,810 \\ \hline 11,197 \end{array}$$

$$\begin{array}{r} \overset{\scriptstyle 13}{\overset{3\ \cancel{3}\ 13}{44,376}} \\ -\ 16,542 \\ \hline 27,834 \end{array}$$

$$\begin{array}{r} \overset{\scriptstyle 14}{\overset{2\ \cancel{4}\ 12\ 6\ 13}{35,273}} \\ -\ 18,435 \\ \hline 16,838 \end{array}$$

$$\begin{array}{r} \overset{\scriptstyle 11}{\overset{6\ 11\ \ \ 6\ \cancel{1}\ 17}{714,727}} \\ -330,689 \\ \hline 384,038 \end{array}$$

Try These

Subtract.

1. $\begin{array}{r}421,653\\-298,123\\\hline\end{array}$	2. $\begin{array}{r}69,766\\-24,873\\\hline\end{array}$	3. $\begin{array}{r}397,211\\-104,989\\\hline\end{array}$	4. $\begin{array}{r}59,796\\-44,518\\\hline\end{array}$
5. $\begin{array}{r}715,007\\-219,351\\\hline\end{array}$	6. $\begin{array}{r}26,371\\-15,999\\\hline\end{array}$	7. $\begin{array}{r}864,231\\-397,421\\\hline\end{array}$	8. $\begin{array}{r}23,772\\-12,599\\\hline\end{array}$

Exercise

Subtract.

1. 258
    −139

2. 441
    −208

3. 996
    −589

4. 813
    −431

5. 624
    −252

6. 877
    −296

7. 671
    −352

8. 921
    −237

9. 8273
    − 4829

10. 6456
    − 3343

11. 9522
    − 3569

12. 4226
    − 1332

13. 5491
    − 1776

14. 7265
    − 2588

15. 4415
    − 1544

16. 8462
    − 4784

17. 985,321
    −498,456

18. 69,278
    − 34,569

19. 841,759
    −221,878

20. 57,821
    − 22,594

21. 726,786
    −341,297

22. 73,816
    − 41,623

23. 549,009
    −239,143

24. 81,987
    − 27,789

25. 952
    −278

26. 4791
    − 2843

27. 32,654
    − 24,456

28. 654,279
    −468,321

50

29.	727 −568	30.	8475 − 2243	31.	54,982 − 26,968	32.	359,121 −144,600

Add.

33.	5679 3699 2796 + 4165	34.	2871 1544 + 4415	35.	2459 2626 1986 + 3814	36.	1949 2843 + 3692

37.	1959 4237 2813 + 1985	38.	5796 2980 + 7886	39.	5681 2998 3752 + 2985	40.	9828 5423 + 3251

Solve each problem.

41. The land area of Rhode Island is 1545 square miles and the land area of Delaware is 2490 square miles. How much smaller is Rhode Island than Delaware? _____

42. At the second apparition of Our Lady of Fatima, in June, 70 people were present. By the last apparition in October, The Miracle of the Sun, the crowd had swelled to 70,000. How many more people attended the last apparition than the second one in June? _____

43. The Missouri River is 2341 miles long. The Mississippi River is 2320 miles long. How many miles long are the two rivers altogether? _____

44. The state of Alaska covers 570,380 square miles. It has the largest land area of the 50 states. Texas is the second largest state. It has a land area of 268,820 square miles. How much bigger is Alaska than Texas? _____

Problem Solving

Solve each problem.

1. There are 365 days in one year. If you spend 120 days in Florida to avoid the winter cold and the rest up north, how many days will you spend up north? _____

2. There are 52 cards in a deck of playing cards. If 16 cards have already been played, how many are left? _____

3. James was reading a 342 page book. He has read through page 128. How many pages has he left to complete the book? _____

4. If I have 628 jujubes and 379 jelly beans, how many more jujubes than jelly beans do I have? _____

5. There were 364,521 pinto beans in a very large container. In another large container there were 215,987 kidney beans. How many more pinto beans are there than kidney beans? _____

6. St. Ambrose fourth graders collected 2564 labels in March and 5739 labels in April. How many more labels did they collect in April than in March? _____

7. The River Blue is 3,850 kilometers long. Its main tributary is 2,465 kilometers long. How much longer is the River Blue than its tributary? _____

8. A small pickup could carry 1,986 pounds of cargo. A larger truck could carry 7,123 pounds of cargo. How much more could the larger truck carry? _____

9. The apple pickers were divided into two groups, one to pick Red Delicious and one to pick Golden Delicious. The Red Delicious group picked 5432 apples and the Golden Delicious group picked 3678 apples. How many more red apples were picked than golden apples? _____

10. What is the difference between a minuend of 513 and a subtrahend of 279? _____

Adding and Subtracting Money

Adding and subtracting money is just like subtracting whole numbers. The only difference is the $ and the . , which we simply write in the answer after we have completed the problem. Be especially careful to line up the dollars and cents when you rewrite the problem vertically. Here are two examples.

Add: $57.59 + $33.46

```
    1
 $ 57.59
+$ 33.46
────────
       5
```

The first thing that we do is rewrite the problem vertically, making sure that the places and decimal points are lined up correctly. Then we proceed just like in adding whole numbers. Start at the right and move left. The first place on the right is the pennies place. We add the pennies place and regroup if necessary.

```
  1 1  1
 $ 57.59
+$ 33.46
────────
    1 05
```

Then we move on to the dimes place and add and regroup as necessary. Then we pass over the decimal and move to the dollars and add the ones place. Regroup if necessary.

```
  1 1  1
 $ 57.59
+$ 33.46
────────
 $ 91.05
```

Finally, we move to the tens place and add. Then we put in the dollar sign ($) and the decimal (.) in the proper places.

Study the example carefully.

Subtract: $57.56 – $33.59

```
     4 16
 $ 57.56
-$ 33.59
────────
       7
```

Again, we begin by rewriting the problem vertically, lining up the decimal points. Then we proceed beginning on the right, just like in subtracting whole numbers. The first place on the right is the pennies place. We check and see if we have enough pennies to subtract. If we don't, we regroup one of the dimes into 10 pennies and then subtract.

```
      14
   6  X 16
 $ 57.56
-$ 33.59
────────
      97
```

Then we move on to the dimes place and check to see if we have enough dimes to subtract. If not, then we must regroup one of the dollars into 10 dimes and then subtract.

```
      14
   6  X 16
 $ 57.56
-$ 33.59
────────
 $ 23.97
```

Then we pass over the decimal and move to the dollars and check if we have enough one dollars to subtract. If not, we regroup the ten dollar column and then subtract. Then we move left and finish up and put in the dollar sign ($) and the decimal (.).

Study the example.

Exercise

Add or subtract.

1. $ 23.92
 +$ 68.75

2. $ 83.79
 −$ 52.49

3. $ 87.55
 −$ 38.62

4. $ 59.16
 +$ 23.06

5. $ 23.29
 −$ 14.62

6. $ 93.26
 +$ 87.42

7. $ 52.34
 −$ 28.71

8. $ 75.85
 +$ 43.96

9. $ 31.64
 +$ 28.95

10. $ 31.64
 −$ 28.95

11. $ 30.19
 +$ 28.71

12. $ 30.19
 −$ 28.71

13. $ 20.00
 −$ 16.51

14. $ 35.16
 +$ 67.29

15. $ 60.24
 −$ 29.83

16. $ 93.24
 +$ 18.52

17. $ 13.27
 +$ 49.58

18. $ 93.14
 −$ 87.01

19. $ 75.42
 −$ 18.95

20. $ 31.66
 +$ 24.41

21. $ 58.45
 −$ 27.04

22. $ 72.02
 +$ 16.95

23. $ 45.06
 −$ 26.17

24. $ 58.06
 +$ 24.47

25. $ 87.53
 +$ 14.61

26. $ 53.64
 −$ 34.74

27. $ 27.49
 +$ 35.47

28. $ 27.40
 −$ 15.41

29. $ 75.23
 −$ 34.14

30. $ 33.66
 +$ 45.81

31. $ 67.33
 −$ 42.43

32. $ 37.78
 +$ 67.64

What is the value of the underlined digit?

1. 42,<u>5</u>70 _____
2. 3,<u>4</u>56 _____
3. 2,34<u>5</u> _____

Write the word name for each number.

4. 265,325 _____

5. 412,133 _____

6. 391,055,102 _____

_____

Write each number in expanded notation.

7. 33,089,211

_____

8. 8,354,623

_____

Round each number to the indicated place.

9. 857,327,549 to the nearest million _____

10. 723,294,347 to the nearest hundred _____

11. 483,756,693 to the nearest thousand _____

12. 901,875,432 to the nearest ten _____

Write each of the following in standard form.

13. MCMLXVI _____

14. LXV _____

15. DCVII _____

16. MMXC _____

17. XIV _____

18. MMVIII _____

Write a number sentence for each word sentence.

19. The sum of eight and seven is fifteen. _____

20. Nine is the sum of four and five. _____

Write a number sentence for each word sentence, then find the solution.

21. The sum of eight and three is what? _____

22. What is the sum of seven and six? _____

23. What number, when added to five, will give a sum of nine?

_____   _____

24. What number, when you add three to it, is seven?

_____   _____

25. In order to get a sum of sixteen, what number should you add to eight?

_____   _____

26. What number do you add to six to get fourteen?

_____   _____

Find the solution to each number sentence.

27. 8 + 8 = n   28. 1 + n = 9   29. n + 4 = 10

    n = _____   n = _____   n = _____

30. 15 − 9 = n   31. 7 − n = 5   32. n − 8 = 8

    n = _____   n = _____   n = _____

Add or subtract.

33. $\begin{array}{r} 1785 \\ + 1024 \\ \hline \end{array}$ 34. $\begin{array}{r} 3542 \\ + 1690 \\ \hline \end{array}$ 35. $\begin{array}{r} 7605 \\ + 3517 \\ \hline \end{array}$ 36. $\begin{array}{r} 3456 \\ + 2497 \\ \hline \end{array}$

37. $\begin{array}{r} 6976 \\ - 2487 \\ \hline \end{array}$ 38. $\begin{array}{r} 9796 \\ - 4518 \\ \hline \end{array}$ 39. $\begin{array}{r} 7211 \\ - 3842 \\ \hline \end{array}$ 40. $\begin{array}{r} 4182 \\ - 1195 \\ \hline \end{array}$

41. $\begin{array}{r} \$\,60.56 \\ +\$\,32.98 \\ \hline \end{array}$ 42. $\begin{array}{r} \$\,58.35 \\ -\$\,19.39 \\ \hline \end{array}$ 43. $\begin{array}{r} \$\,76.50 \\ -\$\,48.92 \\ \hline \end{array}$ 44. $\begin{array}{r} \$\,39.24 \\ +\$\,11.63 \\ \hline \end{array}$

45. $\begin{array}{r} 6324 \\ - 4851 \\ \hline \end{array}$ 46. $\begin{array}{r} 6184 \\ + 4023 \\ \hline \end{array}$ 47. $\begin{array}{r} 7270 \\ + 1645 \\ \hline \end{array}$ 48. $\begin{array}{r} 3851 \\ - 2573 \\ \hline \end{array}$

Checking Addition and Subtraction

It is always a good idea to check your work for mistakes. We know that addition and subtraction are inverse operations. We can check addition by using subtraction and we can check subtraction by using addition.

Look at the examples.   Add: 473 + 639, then check your answer.

```
    473          1112
  + 639         − 639
  ─────         ─────
   1112           473
```

We check addition by taking the sum and subtracting either one of the addends. The difference will be the other addend. If the difference is not the other addend, then we know we've made a mistake.

Subtract: 1112 − 473 and check your answer.

```
   1112           639
  − 473         + 473
  ─────         ─────
    639          1112
```

To check subtraction, we take the difference and add the subtrahend. The answer will be the minuend. If the answer is not the minuend, we know that we have made a mistake.

Exercise

Perform each operation and then check using the inverse operation.

1. 763 + 762

2. 1637 − 439

```
    +              −              −              +
  ─────          ─────          ─────          ─────
```

3. 1542 − 286

4. 423 + 798

5. 358 + 759

6. 1345 − 629

7. 1764 − 925

8. 816 + 395

9. 926 + 178

10. 1574 − 923

Check each answer. If the answer is incorrect, write the correct answer.

11.
$$
\begin{array}{r}
927 \\
-405 \\
\hline
522
\end{array}
$$

12.
$$
\begin{array}{r}
542 \\
+318 \\
\hline
850
\end{array}
$$

13.
$$
\begin{array}{r}
542 \\
-314 \\
\hline
238
\end{array}
$$

14.
$$
\begin{array}{r}
265 \\
+429 \\
\hline
684
\end{array}
$$

15.
$$
\begin{array}{r}
765 \\
-238 \\
\hline
533
\end{array}
$$

16.
$$
\begin{array}{r}
553 \\
+274 \\
\hline
727
\end{array}
$$

17.
$$
\begin{array}{r}
926 \\
-341 \\
\hline
625
\end{array}
$$

18.
$$
\begin{array}{r}
629 \\
+280 \\
\hline
809
\end{array}
$$

19.
$$
\begin{array}{r}
563 \\
-281 \\
\hline
382
\end{array}
$$

Facts Review

Complete each number sentence.

1. 9 + 8 = ____   2. 8 + 1 = ____   3. 3 + 9 = ____   4. 0 + 8 = ____

5. 6 + 4 = ____   6. 2 + 4 = ____   7. 4 + 9 = ____   8. 6 + 7 = ____

9. 5 + 8 = ____   10. 8 + 3 = ____   11. 6 + 6 = ____   12. 5 + 3 = ____

13. 5 − 3 = ____   14. 8 − 6 = ____   15. 8 − 3 = ____   16. 13 − 4 = ____

17. 4 − 3 = ____   18. 8 − 5 = ____   19. 14 − 5 = ____   20. 10 − 7 = ____

21. 6 − 4 = ____   22. 13 − 7 = ____   23. 9 − 5 = ____   24. 12 − 8 = ____

25. 6 × 5 = ____   26. 1 × 1 = ____   27. 2 × 7 = ____   28. 2 × 9 = ____

29. 0 × 8 = ____   30. 5 × 2 = ____   31. 5 × 4 = ____   32. 2 × 4 = ____

33. 3 × 5 = ____   34. 2 × 8 = ____   35. 5 × 3 = ____   36. 2 × 3 = ____

37. 18 ÷ 2 = ____   38. 6 ÷ 1 = ____   39. 8 ÷ 2 = ____   40. 15 ÷ 3 = ____

41. 40 ÷ 5 = ____   42. 16 ÷ 2 = ____   43. 3 ÷ 3 = ____   44. 12 ÷ 2 = ____

45. 9 ÷ 1 = ____   46. 0 ÷ 4 = ____   47. 45 ÷ 5 = ____   48. 12 ÷ 3 = ____

Multiplication Facts

Let's test how well you remember your multiplication facts. If you find that you have gotten rusty, then take some time and practice your times table.

Facts Check

Multiply.

1. $\begin{array}{r} 9 \\ \times\, 9 \\ \hline \end{array}$
2. $\begin{array}{r} 5 \\ \times\, 5 \\ \hline \end{array}$
3. $\begin{array}{r} 4 \\ \times\, 6 \\ \hline \end{array}$
4. $\begin{array}{r} 2 \\ \times\, 8 \\ \hline \end{array}$

5. $\begin{array}{r} 5 \\ \times\, 4 \\ \hline \end{array}$
6. $\begin{array}{r} 3 \\ \times\, 7 \\ \hline \end{array}$
7. $\begin{array}{r} 4 \\ \times\, 5 \\ \hline \end{array}$
8. $\begin{array}{r} 0 \\ \times\, 8 \\ \hline \end{array}$
9. $\begin{array}{r} 6 \\ \times\, 6 \\ \hline \end{array}$
10. $\begin{array}{r} 9 \\ \times\, 8 \\ \hline \end{array}$

11. $0 \times 0 =$ _____
12. $2 \times 3 =$ _____
13. $3 \times 0 =$ _____

14. $2 \times 6 =$ _____
15. $3 \times 8 =$ _____
16. $5 \times 3 =$ _____

17. $\begin{array}{r} 6 \\ \times\, 4 \\ \hline \end{array}$
18. $\begin{array}{r} 5 \\ \times\, 2 \\ \hline \end{array}$
19. $\begin{array}{r} 3 \\ \times\, 9 \\ \hline \end{array}$
20. $\begin{array}{r} 4 \\ \times\, 3 \\ \hline \end{array}$
21. $\begin{array}{r} 4 \\ \times\, 9 \\ \hline \end{array}$
22. $\begin{array}{r} 3 \\ \times\, 5 \\ \hline \end{array}$

23. $\begin{array}{r} 0 \\ \times\, 6 \\ \hline \end{array}$
24. $\begin{array}{r} 1 \\ \times\, 7 \\ \hline \end{array}$
25. $\begin{array}{r} 2 \\ \times\, 5 \\ \hline \end{array}$
26. $\begin{array}{r} 3 \\ \times\, 2 \\ \hline \end{array}$
27. $\begin{array}{r} 5 \\ \times\, 1 \\ \hline \end{array}$
28. $\begin{array}{r} 6 \\ \times\, 0 \\ \hline \end{array}$

29. $7 \times 2 =$ _____
30. $8 \times 6 =$ _____
31. $4 \times 4 =$ _____

32. $0 \times 7 =$ _____
33. $3 \times 6 =$ _____
34. $4 \times 8 =$ _____

35. $5 \times 7 =$ _____
36. $2 \times 9 =$ _____
37. $8 \times 4 =$ _____

Sequences

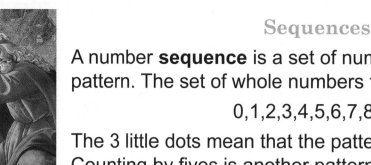

A number **sequence** is a set of numbers that follow a pattern. The set of whole numbers follows a pattern.

0,1,2,3,4,5,6,7,8, ...

The 3 little dots mean that the pattern continues. Counting by fives is another pattern.

5,10,15,20,25,30,35, ...

We can study a sequence and determine its pattern. Its pattern is the rule for the sequence. If we know the rule for the sequence, then we can find additional numbers in the sequence.

Try to find the rule for this sequence: 2, 4, 6, 8, 10, 12, 14, ...

Were you able to find the rule? The rule is counting by twos. Knowing the rule, we could say what the next numbers were in the sequence.

Find the pattern of this sequence and determine what the next three numbers are.   3, 6, 9, 12, 15, ___, ___, ___, ...

The pattern is counting by 3s and the next three numbers are:

18, 21, and 24.

Find the missing number in this sequence:

30, 27, 24, 21, 18, ___, 12, 9, ...

The rule is counting down by 3s and the missing number is 15.

Try These

Find the missing numbers in each sequence.

1. 4, 8, 12, 16, _____, 24, 28, ...   2. 49, 42, 35, _____, 21, 14, ...

3. 1, 3, 5, 7, _____, 11, 13, ...   4. 10, 20, 30, _____, 50, 60, ...

5. 12, 18, 24, 30, _____, _____, _____, 54, 60, 66, ...

6. 1, 1, 2, 3, 5, 8, 13, _____, ...   7. 81, 72, 63, 54, _____, ...

8. 1, 2, 4, 7, 11, _____, 22, 29, _____, 46, _____, ...

We have learned the basic multiplication table up through 9 × 9.
Now we are going to learn the multiplication facts for 10, 11 and 12.
First, complete the list of facts below and then do the exercise.

10 × 0 = 0	11 × 0 = 0	12 × 0 = 0
10 × 1 = 10	11 × 1 = 11	12 × 1 = 12
10 × 2 = _____	11 × 2 = _____	12 × 2 = _____
10 × 3 = _____	11 × 3 = _____	12 × 3 = _____
10 × 4 = _____	11 × 4 = _____	12 × 4 = _____
10 × 5 = _____	11 × 5 = _____	12 × 5 = _____
10 × 6 = _____	11 × 6 = _____	12 × 6 = _____
10 × 7 = _____	11 × 7 = _____	12 × 7 = _____
10 × 8 = _____	11 × 8 = _____	12 × 8 = _____
10 × 9 = _____	11 × 9 = _____	12 × 9 = _____
10 × 10 = _____	11 × 10 = _____	12 × 10 = _____
10 × 11 = _____	11 × 11 = _____	12 × 11 = _____
10 × 12 = _____	11 × 12 = _____	12 × 12 = _____

Multiply.

1. 10 × 10 = _____   2. 11 × 11 = _____   3. 12 × 12 = _____

4. 10 × 12 = _____   5. 12 × 11 = _____   6. 11 × 10 = _____

7. 11 × 12 = _____   8. 10 × 11 = _____   9. 12 × 10 = _____

10. 11 × 9 = _____   11. 10 × 9 = _____   12. 12 × 9 = _____

Properties of Multiplication

Commutative Property of Multiplication (Order)

Changing the order of the factors does not change the product.

$$a \times b = b \times a$$

Study these examples.

2 × 4 = 8	4 × 2 = 8	2 × 5 = 10	5 × 2 = 10
3 × 2 = 6	2 × 3 = 6	6 × 3 = 18	3 × 6 = 18

We can multiply in any order.

Identity Property of Multiplication (One)

Multiplying a number by 1 does not change the number.
The product of any number and 1 is that number.

$$n \times 1 = n$$

Study these examples.

3 × 1 = 3   999,999 × 1 = 999,999

345,678 × 1 = 345,678   5 × 1 = 5

We can multiply any number by 1 without changing the number.

Zero Property of Multiplication

The product of any number and 0 is always 0.

$$n \times 0 = 0$$

Study these examples.

8 × 0 = 0	0 × 9 = 0	12 × 0 = 0
0 × 3 = 0	5 × 0 = 0	0 × 7 = 0

The Zero Property of Multiplication tells us that when we multiply any number by zero (0), we will always get a product of zero (0).

Anything multiplied by 0 is always going to be 0.

Try These

Find the products.

1. 6 × 8 = _____   8 × 6 = _____   2. 3 × 4 = _____   4 × 3 = _____

3.   4   2
   × 2   × 4

4.   8   2
   × 2   × 8

5.   3   8
   × 8   × 3

6. 6 × 1 = _____   7. 3 × 1 = _____   8. 5 × 1 = _____

9.   4   1
   × 1   × 4

10.   1   2
   × 2   × 1

11.   1   8
   × 8   × 1

12. 6 × 0 = _____   13. 3 × 0 = _____   14. 5 × 0 = _____

15.   4   0
   × 0   × 4

16.   0   2
   × 2   × 0

17.   0   8
   × 8   × 0

Multiples

A **multiple** of a number is a *product* that has that number *for at least one of its factors*. In other words, you can find a multiple of a number by multiplying it by some other number. If, for example, I wanted to find some multiples of 5, I could multiply 5 by 4 to get 20. Twenty is a multiple of 5. Twenty is also a multiple of 4 because it has 4 *for at least one of its factors*. Twenty is also a multiple of what other numbers? If I multiply 10 by 2, the product is 20. So, 20 is a multiple of both 10 and 2. Is 20 a multiple of 1? Yes, it is because 1 × 20 = 20. The product 20 has 1 *for at least one of its factors*. Is the number 0 a multiple of anything? Think about it.

Try These

**Find the first thirteen multiples of each number.
The first one is started for you.**

1. 2 ___0___ , ___2___ , ___4___ , _____ , _____ , _____ , _____ , _____ , _____ , _____ , _____ , _____ , _____

2. 5 _____ , _____ , _____ , _____ , _____ , _____ , _____ , _____ , _____ , _____ , _____ , _____ , _____

3. 12 _____ , _____ , _____ , _____ , _____ , _____ , _____ , _____ , _____ , _____ , _____ , _____ , _____

4. 7 _____ , _____ , _____ , _____ , _____ , _____ , _____ , _____ , _____ , _____ , _____ , _____ , _____

5. 6 _____ , _____ , _____ , _____ , _____ , _____ , _____ , _____ , _____ , _____ , _____ , _____ , _____

6. 11 _____ , _____ , _____ , _____ , _____ , _____ , _____ , _____ , _____ , _____ , _____ , _____ , _____

7. 10 _____ , _____ , _____ , _____ , _____ , _____ , _____ , _____ , _____ , _____ , _____ , _____ , _____

When a problem has more than one operation, we solve it using what is called the **order of operations**. The order of operations tells us in what order to work the problem. For example, if we have a problem like 6 + 8 × 2, we have to have a rule that tells us which operation we do first. If we do 6 + 8 first to get 14 and then multiply by 2, we get an answer of 28. On the other hand, if we multiply 8 × 2 first to get 16 and then we add 6, we get an answer of 22. Without an order of operation, there would be confusion, so the rule tells us how to go about solving so that everyone will get the same answer. The rule for the order of operations is that we first do any multiplication or division before we do addition and subtraction and that we perform the operation going from left to right. In the above problem, the correct answer is 22. We do the multiplication first and then the addition. Also, in the order of operations, operations within parentheses should be worked before any others.

Order of Operations

First multiply or divide from left to right.

Then add or subtract in order from left to right.

Operations within parentheses should be worked before any others.

Study these examples.

2 × 4 + 8	7 + 6 × 6	5 − 2 × 2
8 + 8	7 + 36	5 − 4
16	43	1
3 + 2 × 6	6 × 3 − 18	3 × 5 + 6
3 + 12	18 − 18	15 + 6
15	0	21
(3 + 2) × 6	2 × (4 + 8)	3 × (5 + 6)
5 × 6	2 × 12	3 × 11
30	24	33

Just as subtraction is the inverse operation of addition, so division is the inverse operation of multiplication. Subtraction is the opposite of and "undoes" addition. Division is the opposite of and "undoes" multiplication. When we are missing a factor in multiplication, we have two ways to solve for the missing factor. We represent the missing factor as n. If we know our basic facts and the numbers are 0-12, then we simply remember the facts and decide the missing factor. For example, find the missing factor in :

$$3 \times n = 12$$

We know our multiplication facts and remember that $3 \times 4 = 12$, so we can discover that the missing factor is 4. $n = 4$ Problem solved.

We could also use division to "undo" the multiplication and thus solve for n:

$$3 \times n = 12 \qquad 12 \div 3 = n \qquad 12 \div 3 = 4 \qquad n = 4$$

$$\text{if} \quad a \times b = c \quad \text{then} \quad c \div a = b \quad \text{and} \quad c \div b = a$$

Study these examples.

$4 \times n = 12$	$n \times 5 = 15$	$n \times 6 = 24$
$4 \times 3 = 12$	$3 \times 5 = 15$	$4 \times 6 = 24$
$n = 3$	$n = 3$	$n = 4$
or	or	or
$12 \div 4 = n$	$15 \div 5 = n$	$24 \div 6 = n$
$n = 3$	$n = 3$	$n = 4$

Try These

Solve for n.

1. $2 \times n = 14$

    $n = $ _____

2. $n \times 7 = 21$

    $n = $ _____

3. $n \times 9 = 45$

    $n = $ _____

4. $n \times 11 = 121$

    $n = $ _____

5. $12 \times n = 144$

    $n = $ _____

6. $10 \times n = 120$

    $n = $ _____

68

More Properties of Multiplication

Associative Property of Multiplication (Grouping)
Changing the grouping of the factors does not change the product.

$$(a \times b) \times c = a \times (b \times c)$$

Study these examples.

$(2 \times 3) \times 5 = 2 \times (3 \times 5)$	$(6 \times 2) \times 4 = 6 \times (2 \times 4)$
$6 \times 5 = 2 \times 15$	$12 \times 4 = 6 \times 8$
$30 = 30$	$48 = 48$

Distributive Property of Multiplication
Multiplication can be distributed over addition.

$$a \times (b + c) = (a \times b) + (a \times c)$$

Study these examples.

$4 \times (2 + 3) = (4 \times 2) + (4 \times 3)$	$6 \times (5 + 7) = (6 \times 5) + (6 \times 7)$
$4 \times 5 = 8 + 12$	$6 \times 12 = 30 + 42$
$20 = 20$	$72 = 72$

Try These

Simplify each expression as in the examples. Show your work.

1. $(2 \times 5) \times 6 = 2 \times (5 \times 6)$

2. $5 \times (4 + 3) = (5 \times 4) + (5 \times 3)$

3. $3 \times (3 + 3) = (3 \times 3) + (3 \times 3)$

4. $(4 \times 5) \times 5 = 4 \times (5 \times 5)$

5. $(6 \times 2) \times 10 = 6 \times (2 \times 10)$

6. $7 \times (4 + 5) = (7 \times 4) + (7 \times 5)$

Multiplying by Powers of 10 – Tens, Hundreds, Thousands

Examine the patterns below.

$10^0 = 1$ $1 \times 5 = 5$

$10^1 = 10$ $10 \times 5 = 50$

$10^2 = 10 \times 10 = 100$ $100 \times 5 = 500$

$10^3 = 10 \times 10 \times 10 = 1000$ $1000 \times 5 = 5000$

$10^4 = 10 \times 10 \times 10 \times 10 = 10{,}000$ $10{,}000 \times 5 = 50{,}000$

$10^5 = 10 \times 10 \times 10 \times 10 \times 10 = 100{,}000$ $100{,}000 \times 5 = 500{,}000$

$1 \times 6 = 6$	$1 \times 3 = 3$	$1 \times 7 = 7$
$10 \times 6 = 60$	$10 \times 3 = 30$	$10 \times 7 = 70$
$100 \times 6 = 600$	$100 \times 3 = 300$	$100 \times 7 = 700$
$1000 \times 6 = 6000$	$1000 \times 3 = 3000$	$1000 \times 7 = 7000$

To multiply tens, hundreds, thousands, we multiply the nonzero digits and then write the product with 1, 2, or 3 zeros. The product has the same number of zeros as there are in the factors.

This pattern applies to multiplying all the powers of ten.

Try These

Multiply.

1. $10 \times 6 = $ _____

2. $100 \times 9 = $ _____

3. $1000 \times 2 = $ _____

4. $100 \times 10 = $ _____

5. $10 \times 11 = $ _____

6. $1000 \times 5 = $ _____

7. $1000 \times 1 = $ _____

8. $100 \times 8 = $ _____

9. $10 \times 12 = $ _____

10. $10 \times 2 = $ _____

11. $1000 \times 7 = $ _____

12. $100 \times 6 = $ _____

Exercise

Find the missing numbers in each sequence.

1. 3, 6, 9, _____, 15, 18, ...

2. 48, 42, 36, _____, 24, ...

3. 10, 20, 30, _____, 50, ...

4. 5, 10, 15, _____, 25, ...

5. 1, 1, 2, 3, _____, 8, 13, 21, _____, 55, 89, ...

Multiply.

6. $10 \times 9 =$ _____

7. $11 \times 5 =$ _____

8. $12 \times 6 =$ _____

9. $10 \times 11 =$ _____

10. $12 \times 12 =$ _____

11. $11 \times 11 =$ _____

12. $11 \times 5 =$ _____

13. $7 \times 11 =$ _____

14. $12 \times 4 =$ _____

15. $11 \times 3 =$ _____

16. $10 \times 8 =$ _____

17. $12 \times 9 =$ _____

Find the first ten multiples of each number.

18. 3 ____, ____, ____, ____, ____, ____, ____, ____, ____, ____,

19. 6 ____, ____, ____, ____, ____, ____, ____, ____, ____, ____,

20. 8 ____, ____, ____, ____, ____, ____, ____, ____, ____, ____,

Solve using the order of operations.

21. $9 \times 5 + 3$

22. $7 + 3 \times 8$

23. $38 - 5 \times 7$

24. $9 - 1 \times 4$

25. $10 \times 6 - 5$

26. $22 + 3 \times 11$

27. $5 \times 9 + 6$

28. $10 \times (7 + 3)$

29. $(9 + 3) \times 12$

30. $(20 - 8) \times 5$

31. $938 \times (3 - 3)$

32. $1 + 3 \times 5$

33. $4 \times 7 + 10$

34. $3 + 8 \times 9$

35. $69 - 6 \times 5$

36. $41 - 1 \times 2$

37. $10 \times 5 - 15$

38. $6 + 9 \times 6$

39. $3 \times 7 + 9$

40. $12 \times (8 + 4)$

41. $(1 + 2) \times 3$

42. $(54 - 45) \times 9$

43. $11 \times (10 - 5)$

44. $7 + 7 \times 2$

Solve for n.

45. $5 \times n = 45$

n = _____

46. $n \times 6 = 66$

n = _____

47. $n \times 4 = 28$

n = _____

48. $n \times 7 = 35$

n = _____

49. $12 \times n = 120$

n = _____

50. $8 \times n = 48$

n = _____

51. $7 \times n = 49$

n = _____

52. $n \times 9 = 81$

n = _____

53. $n \times 9 = 99$

n = _____

54. n × 2 = 24   55. 3 × n = 21   56. 5 × n = 25

n = _____   n = _____   n = _____

Simplify each expression. Show your work.

57. (1 × 3) × 4 = 1 × (3 × 4)   58. 9 × (5 + 4) = (9 × 5) + (9 × 4)

59. 4 × (3 + 7) = (4 × 3) + (4 × 7)   60. 3 × (2 × 6) = (3 × 2) × 6

61. (3 × 5) × 2 = 3 × (5 × 2)   62. 7 × (4 + 2) = (7 × 4) + (7 × 2)

63. 3 × (3 + 9) = (3 × 3) + (3 × 9)   64. 2 × (4 × 4) = (2 × 4) × 4

65. (1 × 7) × 3 = 1 × (7 × 3)   66. 9 × (6 + 4) = (9 × 6) + (9 × 4)

Multiply.

67. 10 × 7 = _____   68. 100 × 8 = _____   69. 1000 × 3 = _____

70. 100 × 11 = _____   71. 10 × 12 = _____   72. 1000 × 6 = _____

73. 1000 × 1 = _____   74. 100 × 8 = _____   75. 10 × 15 = _____

76. 10 × 4 = _____   77. 1000 × 10 = _____   78. 100 × 9 = _____

Problem Solving

Solve each problem.

1. A dozen is 12. How many eggs is 5 dozen? _____

2. The marching band lined up in 5 rows of 11 each.
   How many marchers were there? _____

3. The classroom had 5 rows of desks and there
   were 4 desks in each row.
   How many students could be seated? _____

4. A chessboard has 8 rows of 8 squares each.
   How many squares are on a chessboard? _____

5. When David was memorizing the multiplication table,
   he practiced for 8 minutes, four times a day.
   How many minutes did he practice each day? _____

6. A box of chocolates is arranged in 5 rows with 7 chocolates
   in each row. How many chocolates are in the box? _____

7. If you plant 7 rows of tomatoes with 7 plants
   in each row, how many plants will you have
   planted altogether? _____

8. If 42 is the product and 6 is one of the factors,
   what is the other factor? _____

9. If Mary works 4 hours a day and 5 days a week,
   how many hours does she work in a week? _____

10. Nine runners each ran a thousand meters.
    How many meters did the runners run altogether? _____

Facts Review

Complete each number sentence.

1. $4 + 1 =$ _____   2. $9 + 7 =$ _____   3. $3 + 3 =$ _____   4. $5 + 5 =$ _____

5. $5 + 8 =$ _____   6. $8 + 3 =$ _____   7. $6 + 6 =$ _____   8. $2 + 9 =$ _____

9. $4 + 8 =$ _____   10. $5 + 6 =$ _____   11. $2 + 5 =$ _____   12. $7 + 4 =$ _____

13. $11 - 3 =$ _____   14. $18 - 9 =$ _____   15. $9 - 6 =$ _____   16. $11 - 7 =$ _____

17. $10 - 2 =$ _____   18. $9 - 7 =$ _____   19. $11 - 6 =$ _____   20. $14 - 8 =$ _____

21. $7 - 4 =$ _____   22. $15 - 9 =$ _____   23. $8 - 2 =$ _____   24. $12 - 5 =$ _____

25. $0 \times 5 =$ _____   26. $7 \times 2 =$ _____   27. $4 \times 0 =$ _____   28. $8 \times 2 =$ _____

29. $7 \times 0 =$ _____   30. $5 \times 6 =$ _____   31. $2 \times 1 =$ _____   32. $4 \times 2 =$ _____

33. $0 \times 0 =$ _____   34. $2 \times 6 =$ _____   35. $5 \times 9 =$ _____   36. $4 \times 5 =$ _____

37. $5 \div 1 =$ _____   38. $45 \div 9 =$ _____   39. $7 \div 7 =$ _____   40. $30 \div 6 =$ _____

41. $8 \div 4 =$ _____   42. $36 \div 4 =$ _____   43. $16 \div 4 =$ _____   44. $24 \div 3 =$ _____

45. $21 \div 3 =$ _____   46. $42 \div 6 =$ _____   47. $48 \div 6 =$ _____   48. $56 \div 7 =$ _____

Multiplication with Multiples of Ten

As with multiplying by powers of 10, we simply multiply the nonzero digits and then write the product with 1, 2, or 3 zeros. The product has the same number of zeros as there are in the factors. This pattern applies to multiplying all the multiples of ten.

Examine the patterns below.

2 × 6 = 12	5 × 3 = 15	3 × 7 = 21
20 × 6 = 120	50 × 3 = 150	30 × 7 = 210
200 × 6 = 1200	500 × 3 = 1500	300 × 7 = 2100
2000 × 6 = 12,000	5000 × 3 = 15,000	3000 × 7 = 21,000

Try These

Multiply.

1. 20 × 8 = _____   2. 600 × 9 = _____   3. 2000 × 2 = _____

4. 300 × 10 = _____   5. 70 × 11 = _____   6. 6000 × 5 = _____

7. 5000 × 1 = _____   8. 900 × 8 = _____   9. 90 × 12 = _____

10. 40 × 2 = _____   11. 1100 × 7 = _____   12. 1200 × 6 = _____

Multiplication Beyond the Facts

We have studied expanded notation and the distributive property of multiplication. We will use these as we continue to explore multiplication.

Use expanded notation and the distributive property to solve: 349 × 7

First, write in expanded notation.

349 × 7 =   (300 + 40 + 9) × 7 =

Then rewrite using the distributive property.

(300 × 7) + (40 × 7) + (9 × 7) =

Then simplify and add.   2100 + 280 + 63 =

$$
\begin{array}{r}
\overset{1}{2100} \\
280 \\
+\;\;\; 63 \\
\hline
2443
\end{array}
$$

Study these examples.

295 × 5	415 × 8
(200 + 90 + 5) × 5	(400 + 10 + 5) × 8
(200 × 5) + (90 × 5) + (5 × 5)	(400 × 8) + (10 × 8) + (5 × 8)
1000 + 450 + 25	3200 + 80 + 40
1475	3320

Try These

Rewrite in expanded notation, then rewrite using the distributive property, then simplify and add.

1. 123 × 4

2. 198 × 7

3. 546 × 6

4. 362 × 3

Multiplying Ones, Tens, Hundreds

As with addition, when multiplying, we start at the right with the ones and move left until finished.

Multiply 313 × 3

First we rewrite vertically.

$$\begin{array}{r} 313 \\ \times \quad 3 \\ \hline \end{array} \qquad \begin{array}{r} 313 \\ \times \quad 3 \\ \hline 9 \end{array}$$

Then multiply the ones.

Then we multiply the tens.

And then the hundreds.

Then we add them up.

$$\begin{array}{r} 313 \\ \times \quad 3 \\ \hline 9 \\ 30 \end{array} \qquad \begin{array}{r} 313 \\ \times \quad 3 \\ \hline 9 \\ 30 \\ 900 \end{array} \qquad \begin{array}{r} 313 \\ \times \quad 3 \\ \hline 9 \\ 30 \\ 900 \\ \hline 939 \end{array}$$

Study this example.

Multiply 123 × 2

$$\begin{array}{r} 123 \\ \times \quad 2 \\ \hline \end{array}$$
Rewrite
vertically

$$\begin{array}{r} 123 \\ \times \quad 2 \\ \hline 6 \end{array}$$
Multiply
the ones

$$\begin{array}{r} 123 \\ \times \quad 2 \\ \hline 6 \\ 40 \end{array}$$
Multiply
the tens

$$\begin{array}{r} 123 \\ \times \quad 2 \\ \hline 6 \\ 40 \\ 200 \end{array}$$
Multiply the
hundreds

$$\begin{array}{r} 123 \\ \times \quad 2 \\ \hline 6 \\ 40 \\ 200 \\ \hline 246 \end{array}$$
Add them up

Try These

Multiply.

1. 24 × 2 = _____

2. 123 × 3 = _____

3. 321 × 2 = _____

4. 13 × 2 = _____

5. 12 × 4 = _____

6. 341 × 2 = _____

7. 121 × 3 = _____

8. 221 × 4 = _____

9. 132 × 3 = _____

Multiplying (Shortened Form)

There is a shortened form that we can use in multiplying. The steps are the same, but we write all the products on the same line.

Multiply 313 × 3

First we rewrite vertically.

$$\begin{array}{r} 313 \\ \times3 \\ \hline \end{array} \qquad \begin{array}{r} 313 \\ \times3 \\ \hline 9 \end{array}$$

Then multiply the ones.

Then we multiply the tens and the hundreds, but we keep them on the same line.

$$\begin{array}{r} 313 \\ \times3 \\ \hline 39 \end{array} \qquad \begin{array}{r} 313 \\ \times3 \\ \hline 939 \end{array}$$

Because we have the shortened form, there is no need to add at the end. We have used place value for our tens and hundreds.

Study this example.

Multiply 123 × 2

$$\begin{array}{r} 123 \\ \times2 \\ \hline \end{array} \qquad \begin{array}{r} 123 \\ \times2 \\ \hline 6 \end{array} \qquad \begin{array}{r} 123 \\ \times2 \\ \hline 46 \end{array} \qquad \begin{array}{r} 123 \\ \times2 \\ \hline 246 \end{array} \qquad \begin{array}{r} 123 \\ \times2 \\ \hline 246 \end{array}$$

| Rewrite vertically | Multiply the ones | Multiply the tens | Multiply the hundreds | We're done |

Try These

Multiply. Use the shortened form.

1. 24 × 2 = _____

2. 123 × 3 = _____

3. 321 × 2 = _____

4. 13 × 2 = _____

5. 12 × 4 = _____

6. 341 × 2 = _____

7. 121 × 3 = _____

8. 221 × 4 = _____

9. 132 × 3 = _____

Multiplying with Regrouping

As with addition, when multiplying, we start at the right with the ones and move left until finished.

Multiply 17 × 4

First we rewrite vertically.

$$\begin{array}{r} 17 \\ \times\ 4 \\ \hline \end{array} \qquad \begin{array}{r} \overset{2}{1}7 \\ \times\ 4 \\ \hline 8 \end{array}$$

Then multiply the ones.

$$4 \times 7 = 28$$

28 is 2 tens and 8 ones. We put the tens above the tens place and write the ones in the ones place.

Then we multiply the tens, and add the regrouped tens.

$$\begin{array}{r} \overset{2}{1}7 \\ \times\ 4 \\ \hline 68 \end{array}$$

$$4 \times 1 \text{ ten} = 4 \text{ tens}$$
$$4 \text{ tens} + 2 \text{ tens} = 6 \text{ tens}$$

$$17 \times 4 = 68$$

Study these examples.

Multiply 58 × 9

$$\begin{array}{r} 58 \\ \times\ 9 \\ \hline \end{array} \qquad \begin{array}{r} \overset{7}{5}8 \\ \times\ 9 \\ \hline 2 \end{array} \qquad \begin{array}{r} \overset{7}{5}8 \\ \times\ 9 \\ \hline 522 \end{array}$$

Rewrite vertically.
Multiply the ones.
Regroup.
Multiply the tens.
Add the regrouped tens.

Multiply 75 × 6

$$\begin{array}{r} 75 \\ \times\ 6 \\ \hline \end{array} \qquad \begin{array}{r} \overset{3}{7}5 \\ \times\ 6 \\ \hline 0 \end{array} \qquad \begin{array}{r} \overset{3}{7}5 \\ \times\ 6 \\ \hline 450 \end{array}$$

Try These

Multiply.

1. 24 × 5 = _____

2. 32 × 6 = _____

3. 48 × 3 = _____

4. 55 × 2 = _____

5. 14 × 4 = _____

6. 73 × 7 = _____

7. 89 × 3 = _____

8. 45 × 8 = _____

9. 96 × 5 = _____

More Multiplying with Regrouping

There is a shortened form that we can use in multiplying. The steps are the same, but we write all the products on the same line.

Multiply 362 × 6

Multiply the ones. Regroup.

$$\begin{array}{r} {}^{1} \\ 36\,2 \\ \times\ \ 6 \\ \hline 2 \end{array} \qquad \begin{array}{r} {}^{3\ 1} \\ 36\,2 \\ \times\ \ 6 \\ \hline 7\,2 \end{array}$$

Then we multiply the tens and add the regrouped tens. Regroup.

Then we multiply the hundreds and add the regrouped hundreds.

$$\begin{array}{r} {}^{3\ 1} \\ 362 \\ \times\ \ 6 \\ \hline 2172 \end{array}$$

Study these examples.

Multiply 272 × 7

$$\begin{array}{r} {}^{1} \\ 27\,2 \\ \times\ \ 7 \\ \hline 4 \end{array} \qquad \begin{array}{r} {}^{5\ 1} \\ 27\,2 \\ \times\ \ 7 \\ \hline 0\,4 \end{array} \qquad \begin{array}{r} {}^{5\ 1} \\ 272 \\ \times\ \ 7 \\ \hline 1904 \end{array}$$

Multiply the ones.
Regroup.
Multiply the tens.
Add the regrouped tens.
Multiply the hundreds.
Add the regrouped hundreds.

Multiply 435 × 5

$$\begin{array}{r} {}^{2} \\ 43\,5 \\ \times\ \ 5 \\ \hline 5 \end{array} \qquad \begin{array}{r} {}^{1\ 2} \\ 43\,5 \\ \times\ \ 5 \\ \hline 7\,5 \end{array} \qquad \begin{array}{r} {}^{1\ 2} \\ 435 \\ \times\ \ 5 \\ \hline 2175 \end{array}$$

Try These

Multiply. Regroup as necessary.

1.
$$\begin{array}{r} 174 \\ \times\ \ 6 \\ \hline \end{array}$$

2.
$$\begin{array}{r} 287 \\ \times\ \ 4 \\ \hline \end{array}$$

3.
$$\begin{array}{r} 718 \\ \times\ \ 7 \\ \hline \end{array}$$

4.
$$\begin{array}{r} 363 \\ \times\ \ 9 \\ \hline \end{array}$$

5.
$$\begin{array}{r} 457 \\ \times\ \ 2 \\ \hline \end{array}$$

6.
$$\begin{array}{r} 843 \\ \times\ \ 3 \\ \hline \end{array}$$

7.
$$\begin{array}{r} 838 \\ \times\ \ 6 \\ \hline \end{array}$$

8.
$$\begin{array}{r} 238 \\ \times\ \ 4 \\ \hline \end{array}$$

9.
$$\begin{array}{r} 126 \\ \times\ \ 7 \\ \hline \end{array}$$

10.
$$\begin{array}{r} 812 \\ \times\ \ 9 \\ \hline \end{array}$$

11.
$$\begin{array}{r} 534 \\ \times\ \ 5 \\ \hline \end{array}$$

12.
$$\begin{array}{r} 445 \\ \times\ \ 6 \\ \hline \end{array}$$

Exercise

Multiply. Regroup as necessary.

1. 296×4

2. 18×9

3. 193×5

4. 52×7

5. 19×5

6. 157×4

7. 22×7

8. 465×8

9. 149×8

10. 745×9

11. 164×5

12. 297×7

13. 23×5

14. 36×6

15. 23×8

16. 47×7

17. 366×6

18. 33×4

19. 535×9

20. 29×6

21. 73×4

22. 229×7

23. 85×2

24. 287×9

25. 159×5

26. 448×6

27. 423×8

28. 378×5

29. 62×8

30. 14×6

31. 98×5

32. 89×7

Find the missing numbers in each sequence.

33. 5, 10, 15, _____, 25, 30, ...   34. 48, 44, 40, _____, 32, ...

35. 11, 22, 33, _____, 55, ...   36. 30, 25, 20, _____, 10, ...

Multiply.

37. $10 \times 10 =$ _____   38. $11 \times 7 =$ _____   39. $12 \times 8 =$ _____

40. $10 \times 11 =$ _____   41. $12 \times 12 =$ _____   42. $11 \times 11 =$ _____

Solve using the order of operations.

43. $9 \times 6 + 5$ 44. $7 + 3 \times 5$ 45. $38 - 5 \times 2$

46. $9 - 1 \times 7$ 47. $11 \times 6 - 5$ 48. $22 + 5 \times 11$

49. $3 \times 6 + 9$ 50. $11 \times (7 + 4)$ 51. $(1 + 2) \times 4$

52. $(63 - 13) \times 9$ 53. $12 \times (10 - 5)$ 54. $7 + 6 \times 2$

Solve for n.

55. $6 \times n = 48$ 56. $n \times 5 = 55$ 57. $n \times 3 = 21$

n = _____   n = _____   n = _____

58. $n \times 9 = 45$ 59. $11 \times n = 121$ 60. $8 \times n = 72$

n = _____   n = _____   n = _____

Rounding Factors and Estimating Products

When we multiply larger or more complicated numbers, sometimes it is helpful to do an estimate of what the correct answer might be and then when we actually perform the multiplication, we can check to see if it makes sense.

In this lesson we want to practice rounding factors and then estimating products. Study the pattern.

2 × 6 = 12	5 × 30 = 150	5 × 70 = 350
20 × 6 = 120	50 × 30 = 1500	30 × 70 = 2100
200 × 6 = 1200	500 × 30 = 15,000	400 × 70 = 28,000
2000 × 6 = 12,000	5000 × 30 = 150,000	60 × 70 = 4200

As you can see, we multiply the nonzero digits and then write the product with the same number of zeros that are in the factors.

Round the factor that has more than one digit and then rewrite the multiplication expression with the rounded factor and solve the estimate.

276 × 4   276 rounds to 300.   300 × 4 = 1200

Study these examples.

Round the factors that have more than one digit, rewrite the problem with the rounded factors, and find the estimated product.

Example: 249 × 5	Example: $3.56 × 7	Example: 584 × 56
200 × 5	$4.00 × 7	600 × 60
1000	$28.00	36,000

Try These

1. 34 × 8

2. 432 × 9

3. $5.49 × 2

4. 452 × 10

5. 42 × 24

6. 375 × 69

Exercise

Round each number to the indicated place.

1. **7,549** to the nearest thousand _____

2. **347** to the nearest hundred _____

3. **693** to the nearest hundred _____

4. **32** to the nearest ten _____

Round the factors that have more than one digit, rewrite the problem with the rounded factors, and find the estimated product.

5. 53 × 7

6. 638 × 3

7. $7.93 × 6

8. 345 × 92

9. $4.32 × 4

10. 1452 × 5

11. $9.99 × 31

12. $.57 × 87

13. 3341 × 8

14. 89 × 3

15. 283 × 4

16. $5.51 × 7

17. 198 × 25

18. $74.41 × 6

19. 2177 × 9

20. $3.48 × 39

21. $.49 × 51

22. 9412 × 8

When we multiply larger numbers, sometime it is helpful to do an estimate of what the correct answer might be and then when we actually perform the multiplication, we can check to see if it makes sense.

Estimate the product of 3468 and 7. We see that 3468 is between 3000 and 4000, so our answer should be between 21,000 and 28,000, but a little closer to 21,000 than 28,000. Let's check.   Multiply 3468 × 7.

Rewrite vertically.
Multiply the ones.
  Regroup.
Multiply the tens.
Add the regrouped tens.
  Regroup
Multiply the hundreds.
Add the regrouped hundreds.
  Regroup.
Multiply the thousands.
Add the regrouped thousands.

$$\begin{array}{r}\overset{5}{346}8\\ \times\quad 7\\ \hline 24{,}276\end{array}\qquad \begin{array}{r}\overset{45}{346}8\\ \times\quad 7\\ \hline 24{,}276\end{array}$$

$$\begin{array}{r}\overset{345}{3}468\\ \times\quad 7\\ \hline 24{,}276\end{array}\qquad \begin{array}{r}\overset{345}{3}468\\ \times\quad 7\\ \hline 24{,}276\end{array}$$

We see that the product is between 21,000 and 28,000 and is a little closer to 21,000, so our answer is reasonable.

Study these examples.

Multiply 5863 × 9

Multiply 7504 × 6

First estimate.

5863 is a little less than 6000.
6000 × 9 = 54,000
Our answer should be
a little less than 54,000.

7504 is between 7000 and 8000.
7000 × 6 = 42,000
8000 × 6 = 48,000
Our answer should be
between 42,000 and 48,000

$$\begin{array}{r}\overset{2}{586}3\\ \times\quad 9\\ \hline 7\end{array}\qquad \begin{array}{r}\overset{52}{586}3\\ \times\quad 9\\ \hline 67\end{array}$$

Rewrite vertically.
Multiply the ones.
  Regroup.
Multiply the tens.
Add the regrouped tens.
  Regroup
Multiply the hundreds.
Add the regrouped hundreds.
  Regroup.
Multiply the thousands.
Add the regrouped thousands.

$$\begin{array}{r}\overset{2}{750}4\\ \times\quad 6\\ \hline 4\end{array}\qquad \begin{array}{r}\overset{2}{750}4\\ \times\quad 6\\ \hline 24\end{array}$$

$$\begin{array}{r}\overset{752}{5}863\\ \times\quad 9\\ \hline 767\end{array}\qquad \begin{array}{r}\overset{752}{5}863\\ \times\quad 9\\ \hline 52{,}767\end{array}$$

$$\begin{array}{r}\overset{3\ 2}{75}04\\ \times\quad 6\\ \hline 024\end{array}\qquad \begin{array}{r}\overset{3\ 2}{75}04\\ \times\quad 6\\ \hline 45{,}024\end{array}$$

Multiplying money is the same as multiplying whole numbers. We simply multiply as usual and then put in the decimal point (.) in the product two places from the right and add the dollar sign ($). It can also be helpful to estimate the product before multiplying and then, after finding the actual product, checking with the estimate to make sure the product is reasonable.

Multiply $34.68 × 7.

Estimate the product of $34.68 and 7. We see that $34.68 is between $30.00 and $40.00, so our answer should be between $210.00 and $280.00, but a little closer to $210.00 than $280.00.

$$\begin{array}{r} \overset{5}{\$34.68} \\ \times\ \ \ \ 7 \\ \hline 6 \end{array} \qquad \begin{array}{r} \overset{4\ 5}{\$34.68} \\ \times\ \ \ \ 7 \\ \hline 76 \end{array}$$

Rewrite vertically. Start at the right and multiply. Regroup and move left. Continue to multiply and add as in whole numbers. When finished, add the dollar sign ($) and place the decimal point (.) two places from the right.

$$\begin{array}{r} \overset{3\ 4\ 5}{\$34.68} \\ \times\ \ \ \ 7 \\ \hline 276 \end{array} \qquad \begin{array}{r} \overset{3\ 4\ 5}{\$34.68} \\ \times\ \ \ \ 7 \\ \hline \$242.76 \end{array}$$

We see that the product is between $210.00 and $280.00 and is a little closer to $210.00, so our answer is reasonable.

Study these examples.

Multiply $42.49 × 8

$42.49 is a little more than $40.00.
$40.00 × 8 = $320.00
Our answer should be
a little more than $320.00.

$$\begin{array}{r} \overset{7}{\$42.49} \\ \times\ \ \ \ 8 \\ \hline 2 \end{array} \qquad \begin{array}{r} \overset{3\ 7}{\$42.49} \\ \times\ \ \ \ 8 \\ \hline 92 \end{array}$$

$$\begin{array}{r} \overset{1\ 3\ 7}{\$42.49} \\ \times\ \ \ \ 8 \\ \hline 992 \end{array} \qquad \begin{array}{r} \overset{1\ 3\ 7}{\$42.49} \\ \times\ \ \ \ 8 \\ \hline \$339.92 \end{array}$$

Multiply $64.99 × 5

$64.99 is between $60.00 and $70.00.
$60.00 × 5 = $300.00
$70.00 × 5 = $350.00
Our answer should be
between $300.00 and $350.00

$$\begin{array}{r} \overset{4}{\$64.99} \\ \times\ \ \ \ 5 \\ \hline 5 \end{array} \qquad \begin{array}{r} \overset{4\ 4}{\$64.99} \\ \times\ \ \ \ 5 \\ \hline 95 \end{array}$$

$$\begin{array}{r} \overset{2\ 4\ 4}{\$64.99} \\ \times\ \ \ \ 5 \\ \hline 495 \end{array} \qquad \begin{array}{r} \overset{2\ 4\ 4}{\$64.99} \\ \times\ \ \ \ 5 \\ \hline \$324.95 \end{array}$$

87

Exercise

Multiply. Regroup as necessary.

1. 399×6

2. 42×5

3. 454×8

4. 19×3

5. 9487×2

6. 6125×4

7. 8312×6

8. 3245×5

9. $\$.48 \times 4$

10. $\$1.78 \times 4$

11. $\$47.32 \times 9$

12. $\$27.43 \times 5$

13. 9956×3

14. 4527×9

15. 7549×7

16. 6893×8

17. $\$.27 \times 7$

18. $\$2.78 \times 6$

19. $\$88.31 \times 8$

20. $\$51.15 \times 5$

21. 438×4

22. 38×9

23. 272×8

24. 75×8

25. 1436×7

26. 5386×6

27. 4925×2

28. 6287×3

29. $\$.63 \times 6$

30. $\$6.26 \times 9$

31. $\$59.95 \times 2$

32. $\$74.87 \times 4$

Solve each problem.

1. The hamburgers were $ .89 each.
    If we bought 9, how much would it cost?   _____

2. There are 365 days in a year.
    How many days are there in 3 years?   _____

3. There are 5280 feet in one mile.
    How many feet are there in 5 miles?   _____

4. There are 1760 yards in one mile.
    How many yards are there in 7 miles?   _____

5. There are 60 minutes in one hour. How many
    minutes are in 8 hours?   _____

6. There are 3600 seconds in one hour.
    How many seconds are in 9 hours?   _____

7. If the vegetable farmer planted 7 long rows
    of tomato plants with 39 plants in each row,
    then how many tomato plants does he have planted?   _____

8. If there are 52 cards in a regular deck of playing cards,
    how many cards would there be in 6 decks?   _____

9. If one lap on a track is 440 yards long, then how
    many yards would a person run if he ran 4 laps?   _____

10. If tickets to the amusement park cost
    $15.49 each and the family bought 7 tickets,
    how much did they spend on the tickets?   _____

11. If the tires for my car cost $59.95 each and
    I need four, how much will I have to spend?   _____

Multiplying by Two-Digit Numbers

As multiplication problems become more complicated, it can be useful to keep in mind the basic properties of multiplication. Take a moment and review them.

Commutative Property of Multiplication (Order)

Changing the order of the factors does not change the product.

$$a \times b = b \times a$$
We can multiply in any order.

Associative Property of Multiplication (Grouping)

Changing the grouping of the factors does not change the product.

$$(a \times b) \times c = a \times (b \times c)$$

Distributive Property of Multiplication

Multiplication can be distributed over addition.

$$a \times (b + c) = (a \times b) + (a \times c)$$

Examine these expressions.

24×27 $(20 + 7) \times (20 + 4)$ $(20 + 4) \times 27$ $(20 \times 27) + (4 \times 27)$

$(27 \times 4) + (27 \times 20)$ $(20 \times 20) + (20 \times 4) + (7 \times 20) + (7 \times 4)$

They all express the number 648 in different ways.

When we multiply by a two-digit number we can think of it as two problems.

$24 \times 27 = (24 \times 20) + (24 \times 7)$

$$\begin{array}{r} 24 \\ \times\ 20 \\ \hline 480 \end{array} \qquad \begin{array}{r} ^2\ \\ 24 \\ \times\ 7 \\ \hline 168 \end{array}$$

If we add the product from the two problems, we get the total product. $480 + 168 = 648$

Let's estimate some products of some two-digit problems. 52×35

First, let's round each number.

$$50 \times 40$$

Then we multiply the nonzero numbers and add the zeros. $5 \times 4 = 20$ 2000

Estimate the product of 23 and 44.

First we round: 20 and 40

Then multiply and add zeros.   800

The estimated product of 23 and 44 is 800.

Try These

Estimate the products.

1. 34 × 61

2. 19 × 81

3. 72 × 75

4. 22 × 69

5. 41 × 56

6. 29 × 56

When we multiply by a two-digit number, we first multiply by the ones' digit. We then multiply by the tens' digit and then we add the two products together.

Example:
$$\begin{array}{r} 44 \\ \times\ 23 \\ \hline \end{array} = \begin{array}{r} 44 \\ \times\ 3 \\ \hline 132 \end{array} + \begin{array}{r} 44 \\ \times\ 20 \\ \hline 880 \end{array} \quad \begin{array}{r} 132 \\ +\ 880 \\ \hline 1012 \end{array}$$

Try These

Rewrite each problem as two problems, then find the answer.

1.
$$\begin{array}{r} 23 \\ \times\ 14 \\ \hline \end{array} = \underline{} \times \underline{} + \underline{} \times \underline{} + \underline{} \qquad \underline{}$$

2.
$$\begin{array}{r} 34 \\ \times\ 21 \\ \hline \end{array} = \underline{} \times \underline{} + \underline{} \times \underline{} + \underline{} \qquad \underline{}$$

3.
$$\begin{array}{r} 12 \\ \times\ 17 \\ \hline \end{array} = \underline{} \times \underline{} + \underline{} \times \underline{} + \underline{} \qquad \underline{}$$

Multiplying by Two-Digit Numbers

We've looked at multiplying by two-digit numbers with estimating and separating into two problems. Now let's look at the way we actually will be performing the operation. Basically there are three steps. The first step is to multiply by the ones' digit. We already know how to do that. The second step is to multiply by the tens' digit, writing the product below the product we already have from the ones' digit. The final step is to draw a line under the two products and add them and write that sum below the line. Let's look at some examples to show the procedure.

Example   Multiply:

$$\begin{array}{r} 23 \\ \times\,21 \\ \hline \end{array}$$

Multiply by the ones.

$$\begin{array}{r} 23 \\ \times\,21 \\ \hline 23 \end{array}$$

Multiply by the tens.

$$\begin{array}{r} 23 \\ \times\,21 \\ \hline 23 \\ 460 \end{array}$$

Now add the partial products.

$$\begin{array}{r} 23 \\ \times\,21 \\ \hline 23 \\ 460 \\ \hline 483 \end{array}$$

Example   Multiply:

$$\begin{array}{r} 12 \\ \times\,24 \\ \hline \end{array}$$

Multiply by the ones.

$$\begin{array}{r} 12 \\ \times\,24 \\ \hline 48 \end{array}$$

Multiply by the tens.

$$\begin{array}{r} 12 \\ \times\,24 \\ \hline 48 \\ 240 \end{array}$$

Add the partial products.

$$\begin{array}{r} 12 \\ \times\,24 \\ \hline 48 \\ 240 \\ \hline 288 \end{array}$$

Example   Multiply:

$$\begin{array}{r} 32 \\ \times\,13 \\ \hline \end{array}$$

Multiply by the ones.

$$\begin{array}{r} 32 \\ \times\,13 \\ \hline 96 \end{array}$$

Multiply by the tens.

$$\begin{array}{r} 32 \\ \times\,13 \\ \hline 96 \\ 320 \end{array}$$

Add the partial products.

$$\begin{array}{r} 32 \\ \times\,13 \\ \hline 96 \\ 320 \\ \hline 416 \end{array}$$

Multiply.

1. $\begin{array}{r} 44 \\ \times 22 \\ \hline \end{array}$

2. $\begin{array}{r} 24 \\ \times 12 \\ \hline \end{array}$

3. $\begin{array}{r} 64 \\ \times 11 \\ \hline \end{array}$

4. $\begin{array}{r} 32 \\ \times 32 \\ \hline \end{array}$

5. $\begin{array}{r} 42 \\ \times 12 \\ \hline \end{array}$

6. $\begin{array}{r} 45 \\ \times 11 \\ \hline \end{array}$

7. $\begin{array}{r} 21 \\ \times 41 \\ \hline \end{array}$

8. $\begin{array}{r} 13 \\ \times 12 \\ \hline \end{array}$

9. $\begin{array}{r} \$ \ .52 \\ \times \quad 7 \\ \hline \end{array}$

10. $\begin{array}{r} \$ \ 4.41 \\ \times \quad 5 \\ \hline \end{array}$

11. $\begin{array}{r} \$ \ 53.72 \\ \times \quad 9 \\ \hline \end{array}$

12. $\begin{array}{r} \$ \ 29.95 \\ \times \quad 7 \\ \hline \end{array}$

13. $\begin{array}{r} 6893 \\ \times \quad 8 \\ \hline \end{array}$

14. $\begin{array}{r} 2995 \\ \times \quad 6 \\ \hline \end{array}$

15. $\begin{array}{r} 4726 \\ \times \quad 4 \\ \hline \end{array}$

16. $\begin{array}{r} 8475 \\ \times \quad 5 \\ \hline \end{array}$

17. $\begin{array}{r} 43 \\ \times 11 \\ \hline \end{array}$

18. $\begin{array}{r} 14 \\ \times 22 \\ \hline \end{array}$

19. $\begin{array}{r} 32 \\ \times 12 \\ \hline \end{array}$

20. $\begin{array}{r} 42 \\ \times 21 \\ \hline \end{array}$

21. $\begin{array}{r} 21 \\ \times 32 \\ \hline \end{array}$

22. $\begin{array}{r} 22 \\ \times 34 \\ \hline \end{array}$

23. $\begin{array}{r} 23 \\ \times 12 \\ \hline \end{array}$

24. $\begin{array}{r} 33 \\ \times 22 \\ \hline \end{array}$

25. $\begin{array}{r} \$ \ .39 \\ \times \quad 5 \\ \hline \end{array}$

26. $\begin{array}{r} \$ \ 5.95 \\ \times \quad 8 \\ \hline \end{array}$

27. $\begin{array}{r} \$ \ 24.93 \\ \times \quad 7 \\ \hline \end{array}$

28. $\begin{array}{r} \$ \ 68.65 \\ \times \quad 8 \\ \hline \end{array}$

Simplify.

29. $9 \times 5 + 5$

30. $7 + 2 \times 5$

31. $28 - 5 \times 2$

32. $9 - 1 \times 6$

33. $11 \times 6 - 5$

34. $22 + 5 \times 11$

35. $3 \times 4 + 9$

36. $11 \times 7 + 4$

37. $1 + 2 \times 4$

Solve.

38. $6 \times n = 42$

39. $n \times 6 = 66$

40. $n \times 4 = 28$

41. $n \times 9 = 54$

42. $12 \times n = 144$

43. $8 \times n = 64$

Multiply.

44. $100 \times 12 =$ _____

45. $10 \times 20 =$ _____

46. $1000 \times 5 =$ _____

Add or subtract.

47.
$$\begin{array}{r} 2193 \\ + 1024 \\ \hline \end{array}$$

48.
$$\begin{array}{r} 2294 \\ + 1690 \\ \hline \end{array}$$

49.
$$\begin{array}{r} 5607 \\ + 3517 \\ \hline \end{array}$$

50.
$$\begin{array}{r} 6534 \\ + 2497 \\ \hline \end{array}$$

51.
$$\begin{array}{r} 7695 \\ - 2487 \\ \hline \end{array}$$

52.
$$\begin{array}{r} 5478 \\ - 4518 \\ \hline \end{array}$$

53.
$$\begin{array}{r} 9311 \\ - 3842 \\ \hline \end{array}$$

54.
$$\begin{array}{r} 3194 \\ - 1195 \\ \hline \end{array}$$

In this lesson, we will practice more multiplication, remembering the three steps we have used. These problems will require regrouping, but the steps still remain the same.

Step 1   Multiply by the ones digit and write the partial product, regrouping as necessary.

Step 2   Multiply by the tens digit and write the partial product, regrouping as necessary.   We will have to be careful not to get confused by any of the first regroupings.

Step 3   Add the partial products

Example   Multiply: 24
                                × 58   Multiply by the ones.

$$
\begin{array}{r}
\overset{3}{2}4 \\
\times\ 58 \\
\hline
192
\end{array}
$$

Multiply by the tens.

$$
\begin{array}{r}
\overset{2}{\cancel{8}} \\
24 \\
\times\ 58 \\
\hline
192 \\
1200
\end{array}
$$

Now add the partial products.

$$
\begin{array}{r}
24 \\
\times\ 58 \\
\hline
192 \\
1200 \\
\hline
1392
\end{array}
$$

Example   Multiply: 34
                                × 89

Multiply by the ones.

$$
\begin{array}{r}
\overset{3}{3}4 \\
\times\ 89 \\
\hline
306
\end{array}
$$

Multiply by the tens.

$$
\begin{array}{r}
\overset{3}{\cancel{8}} \\
34 \\
\times\ 89 \\
\hline
306 \\
2720
\end{array}
$$

Add the partial products.

$$
\begin{array}{r}
34 \\
\times\ 89 \\
\hline
306 \\
2720 \\
\hline
3026
\end{array}
$$

Try These

Multiply using the steps, regrouping as necessary.

1. $\begin{array}{r} 36 \\ \times 18 \\ \hline \end{array}$
2. $\begin{array}{r} 16 \\ \times 52 \\ \hline \end{array}$
3. $\begin{array}{r} 55 \\ \times 27 \\ \hline \end{array}$
4. $\begin{array}{r} 56 \\ \times 73 \\ \hline \end{array}$

Example   Multiply: 76
                        × 39

Multiply by the ones.   Multiply by the tens.   Add the partial products.

$$
\begin{array}{r}
\overset{5}{7}6 \\
\times\, 39 \\
\hline
684
\end{array}
$$

$$
\begin{array}{r}
\overset{1}{\overset{5}{7}}6 \\
\times\;\, 39 \\
\hline
684 \\
2280
\end{array}
$$
← This zero does not have to be written.

$$
\begin{array}{r}
76 \\
\times\; 39 \\
\hline
684 \\
2280 \\
\hline
2964
\end{array}
$$

Example   Multiply: 82
                        × 56

Multiply by the ones.   Multiply by the tens.   Add the partial products.

$$
\begin{array}{r}
\overset{1}{8}2 \\
\times\, 56 \\
\hline
492
\end{array}
$$

$$
\begin{array}{r}
\overset{1}{\overset{\cancel{1}}{8}}2 \\
\times\;\, 56 \\
\hline
492 \\
4100
\end{array}
$$

$$
\begin{array}{r}
82 \\
\times\; 56 \\
\hline
492 \\
4100 \\
\hline
4592
\end{array}
$$

Exercise

Multiply.

1.
$$
\begin{array}{r}
47 \\
\times 68 \\
\hline
\end{array}
$$

2.
$$
\begin{array}{r}
58 \\
\times 72 \\
\hline
\end{array}
$$

3.
$$
\begin{array}{r}
74 \\
\times 56 \\
\hline
\end{array}
$$

4.
$$
\begin{array}{r}
35 \\
\times 25 \\
\hline
\end{array}
$$

5.
$$
\begin{array}{r}
76 \\
\times 54 \\
\hline
\end{array}
$$

6.
$$
\begin{array}{r}
27 \\
\times 36 \\
\hline
\end{array}
$$

7.
$$
\begin{array}{r}
39 \\
\times 42 \\
\hline
\end{array}
$$

8.
$$
\begin{array}{r}
82 \\
\times 38 \\
\hline
\end{array}
$$

9.   95
   ×76

10.   39
   ×55

11.   47
   ×63

12.   25
   ×92

13.   23
   ×36

14.   83
   ×65

15.   67
   ×42

16.   79
   ×53

17.   68
   ×73

18.   36
   ×24

19.   41
   ×48

20.   23
   ×42

21.   38
   ×74

22.   42
   ×58

23.   56
   ×39

24.   49
   ×86

25.   48
   ×62

26.   86
   ×58

27.   37
   ×94

28.   73
   ×66

29.   40
   ×55

30.   45
   ×51

31.   87
   ×39

32.   27
   ×27

Multiplying Three-Digit Numbers by Two-Digit Numbers

In this lesson, we will multiply 3-digit numbers by 2-digit numbers. The steps are the same and regrouping will be required. Study the examples.

Multiply:
```
  286
× 32
```

Multiply by the ones.
```
 1 1
 286
×  32
 572
```

Multiply by the tens.
```
 2 1
 ₓ ₓ
 286
×  32
 572
8580
```
This zero does not have to be written.

Add the partial products.
```
  286
×  32
  572
 8580
 9152
```

Example   Multiply:
```
 375
× 89
```

Multiply by the ones.
```
 6 4
 375
×  89
3375
```

Multiply by the tens.
```
 6 4
 8 4
 375
×  89
 3375
30000
```
This zero does not have to be written.

Add the partial products.
```
  375
×  89
 3375
30000
33,375
```

Try These

Multiply using the steps, regrouping as necessary.

1.
```
 915
× 67
```

2.
```
 924
× 27
```

3.
```
 639
× 82
```

4.
```
 823
× 92
```

5.
```
 738
× 29
```

6.
```
 825
× 78
```

7.
```
 467
× 54
```

8.
```
 937
× 83
```

Multiplying money works the same way. We just add the dollar sign and the decimal. The decimal is two places from the right. Study the examples.

Example   Multiply: $ 4.99
                        ×   76

Multiply by the ones.
Add any extra dimes
and dollars.

$$\begin{array}{r}\overset{5\ 5}{\$\ 4.99} \\ \times\ \ 76 \\ \hline 29\,94 \end{array}$$

Multiply by the tens.
Add any extra dimes
and dollars.

$$\begin{array}{r}\overset{6\ 6}{\underset{}{\$\ 4.99}} \\ \times\ \ 76 \\ \hline 29\,94 \\ 349\,30 \end{array}$$

Add the partial
products. Place
the dollar sign and
decimal point.

$$\begin{array}{r}\$\ 4.99 \\ \times\ \ 76 \\ \hline 29\,94 \\ 349\,30 \\ \hline \$379.24 \end{array}$$

Example   Multiply: $ 3.98
                        ×   62

$$\begin{array}{r}\overset{1\ 1}{\$\ 3.98} \\ \times\ \ 62 \\ \hline 7\,96 \end{array}$$

$$\begin{array}{r}\overset{5\ 4}{\$\ 3.98} \\ \times\ \ 62 \\ \hline 7\,96 \\ 238\,80 \end{array}$$

$$\begin{array}{r}\$\ 3.98 \\ \times\ \ 62 \\ \hline 7\,96 \\ 238\,80 \\ \hline \$246.76 \end{array}$$

Try These

Multiply.

1. $ 5.40
    ×   63

2. $ 8.09
    ×   53

3. $ 5.48
    ×   91

4. $ 5.85
    ×   35

5. $ 2.55
    ×   82

6. $ 3.27
    ×   48

7. $ 8.59
    ×   76

8. $ 4.78
    ×   82

Facts Review

Complete each number sentence.

1. $4 + 8 = $ _____
2. $5 + 6 = $ _____
3. $2 + 5 = $ _____
4. $7 + 4 = $ _____

5. $8 + 9 = $ _____
6. $3 + 7 = $ _____
7. $7 + 7 = $ _____
8. $8 + 8 = $ _____

9. $4 + 2 = $ _____
10. $6 + 8 = $ _____
11. $1 + 6 = $ _____
12. $5 + 9 = $ _____

13. $7 - 7 = $ _____
14. $10 - 5 = $ _____
15. $10 - 3 = $ _____
16. $9 - 4 = $ _____

17. $15 - 6 = $ _____
18. $8 - 4 = $ _____
19. $11 - 9 = $ _____
20. $16 - 7 = $ _____

21. $13 - 6 = $ _____
22. $4 - 4 = $ _____
23. $17 - 8 = $ _____
24. $7 - 3 = $ _____

25. $1 \times 3 = $ _____
26. $8 \times 5 = $ _____
27. $4 \times 8 = $ _____
28. $8 \times 7 = $ _____

29. $9 \times 7 = $ _____
30. $6 \times 7 = $ _____
31. $4 \times 9 = $ _____
32. $3 \times 7 = $ _____

33. $9 \times 6 = $ _____
34. $7 \times 4 = $ _____
35. $9 \times 2 = $ _____
36. $7 \times 7 = $ _____

37. $27 \div 3 = $ _____
38. $24 \div 4 = $ _____
39. $72 \div 9 = $ _____
40. $24 \div 6 = $ _____

41. $36 \div 9 = $ _____
42. $48 \div 8 = $ _____
43. $32 \div 8 = $ _____
44. $81 \div 9 = $ _____

45. $25 \div 5 = $ _____
46. $21 \div 7 = $ _____
47. $42 \div 7 = $ _____
48. $27 \div 9 = $ _____

Exercise

Multiply.

1.
```
  324
×  26
```

2.
```
  584
×  67
```

3.
```
  746
×  53
```

4.
```
  312
×  37
```

5.
```
$ 3.64
×   45
```

6.
```
$ 5.75
×   47
```

7.
```
$ 4.67
×   54
```

8.
```
$ 6.81
×   49
```

9.
```
  729
×  84
```

10.
```
  342
×  82
```

11.
```
  296
×  88
```

12.
```
  321
×  73
```

13.
```
$ 7.84
×   96
```

14.
```
$ 3.65
×   28
```

15.
```
$ 3.57
×   85
```

16.
```
$ 8.28
×   56
```

17.
```
  423
×  29
```

18.
```
  951
×  79
```

19.
```
  682
×  57
```

20.
```
  923
×  37
```

21.
```
$ 5.37
×   49
```

22.
```
$ 4.28
×   96
```

23.
```
$ 4.03
×   56
```

24.
```
$ 6.32
×   99
```

Simplify.

25. 3 × 4 + 8

26. 9 + 7 × 5

27. 22 − 2 × 11

28. 3 × (4 + 8)

29. 2 × 4 − 3

30. (2 + 4) × 10

Solve.

31. 8 × n = 72

32. n × 8 = 64

33. n × 11 = 121

34. n × 3 = 24

35. 6 × n = 36

36. 8 × n = 48

Add or subtract.

37.
```
  3142
+ 4987
```

38.
```
  7193
+ 1456
```

39.
```
  5607
− 3517
```

40.
```
  6534
− 2497
```

41.
```
  6695
− 2497
```

42.
```
  3478
+ 4568
```

43.
```
  6221
− 3842
```

44.
```
  3194
+ 1195
```

45.
```
  124
  541
+ 262
```

46.
```
  470
  322
   87
+  22
```

Problem Solving

Solve each problem.

1. The hamburgers were $ .89 each.
   If we bought 12, how much would it cost?   _____

2. There are 365 days in a year.
   How many days are there in 15 years?   _____

3. The car can travel 34 miles on one
   gallon of gasoline. How many miles
   can it travel on 25 gallons of gasoline?   _____

4. If a gallon of gasoline costs $ 3.45,
   then how much would 27 gallons cost?   _____

5. There are 60 minutes in one hour.
   How many minutes are in 24 hours?   _____

6. There are 36 rows of seats in the auditorium.
   There are 33 seats in each row. How many
   seats are there in the auditorium?   _____

7. If each row of corn is 45 feet long
   and there are 42 rows, then how
   many feet of corn are there altogether?   _____

8. There are 52 weeks in a year.
   How many weeks are there in 26 years?   _____

9. Maria studied for 36 weeks. If she studied
   for 22 hours each of the weeks, then how
   many hours had she studied in the 36 weeks?   _____

10. There are 365 days in a normal year and each
    day is 24 hours long. How many hours are in a year?   _____

Reviewing the Division Facts

Divide.

1. $18 \div 2 =$ _____   2. $7\overline{)21}$ 3. $20 \div 4 =$ _____   4. $2\overline{)10}$

5. $5 \div 5 =$ _____   6. $1\overline{)0}$ 7. $0 \div 3 =$ _____   8. $2\overline{)6}$

9. $12 \div 2 =$ _____   10. $9\overline{)81}$ 11. $42 \div 6 =$ _____   12. $9\overline{)27}$

13. $54 \div 9 =$ _____   14. $1\overline{)9}$ 15. $18 \div 6 =$ _____   16. $7\overline{)7}$

17. $0 \div 4 =$ _____   18. $4\overline{)12}$ 19. $30 \div 5 =$ _____   20. $5\overline{)30}$

21. $18 \div 3 =$ _____   22. $7\overline{)49}$ 23. $72 \div 9 =$ _____   24. $3\overline{)27}$

25. $6 \div 2 =$ _____   26. $1\overline{)7}$ 27. $36 \div 9 =$ _____   28. $9\overline{)0}$

29. $16 \div 4 =$ _____   30. $9\overline{)36}$ 31. $40 \div 5 =$ _____   32. $4\overline{)28}$

33. $35 \div 5 =$ _____   34. $2\overline{)8}$ 35. $18 \div 9 =$ _____   36. $4\overline{)0}$

37. $8 \div 1 =$ _____   38. $3\overline{)15}$ 39. $36 \div 4 =$ _____   40. $7\overline{)14}$

41. $35 \div 7 =$ _____   42. $1\overline{)6}$ 43. $24 \div 6 =$ _____   44. $6\overline{)0}$

45. $100 \div 10 =$_____   46. $1\overline{)121}$ 47. $64 \div 8 =$ _____   48. $6\overline{)144}$

Division as the Inverse of Multiplication

Do you remember the four operations?

Addition   Subtraction   Multiplication   Division

Subtraction is the inverse operation of addition and division is the inverse operation of multiplication. For every multiplication sentence, there are two related division sentences.

What would be the related division sentences for:

$$3 \times 4 = 12 \ ?$$

The related division sentences are: $12 \div 3 = 4$ and $12 \div 4 = 3$

If $a \times b = c$ then $c \div a = b$ and $c \div b = a$

The form of a multiplication sentence is:

factor × factor = product

The form of a division sentence is:

dividend ÷ divisor = quotient

If we use the the multiplication terms in the division sentence, it would look like this:

product ÷ factor = factor

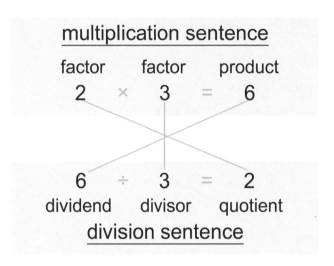

multiplication sentence

factor		factor		product
2	×	3	=	6

6	÷	3	=	2
dividend		divisor		quotient

division sentence

Try These

Write two related division sentences for each multiplication sentence.

1. 12 × 4 = 48   _____   _____

2. 7 × 5 = 35   _____   _____

3. 6 × 11 = 66   _____   _____

4. 5 × 10 = 50   _____   _____

Division and the Missing Factor

As we studied earlier, we can use division to find the missing factor. If we have a multiplication sentence with a missing or unknown factor, we write a related division sentence to solve for the missing factor. The product will be the dividend, the known factor will be the divisor, and the missing factor will be the quotient.

$n \times$ known factor = product
known factor $\times n$ = product

n = product $\div$ known factor

Study these examples.

We write the division sentence that will find the missing factor and solve.

$8 \times n = 48$	$n \times 9 = 54$	$12 \times n = 144$
$n = 48 \div 8$	$n = 54 \div 9$	$n = 144 \div 12$
$n = 6$	$n = 6$	$n = 12$

Try These

Write the division sentence that will find the missing factor and solve.

1. $8 \times n = 72$

2. $n \times 8 = 64$

3. $n \times 11 = 121$

4. $n \times 3 = 24$

5. $6 \times n = 36$

6. $8 \times n = 48$

7. $n \times 4 = 24$

8. $9 \times n = 63$

Write two related division sentences for each multiplication sentence.

1. $2 \times 3 = 6$ _____ _____

2. $4 \times 2 = 8$ _____ _____

3. $6 \times 8 = 48$ _____ _____

4. $5 \times 12 = 60$ _____ _____

Write the division sentence that will find the missing factor and solve.

5. $9 \times n = 54$　　　　　　　　6. $n \times 4 = 32$

7. $n \times 7 = 35$　　　　　　　　8. $n \times 5 = 20$

9. $8 \times n = 56$　　　　　　　10. $8 \times n = 16$

11. $n \times 9 = 54$　　　　　　　12. $9 \times n = 45$

13. $n \times 4 = 36$　　　　　　　14. $4 \times n = 12$

Multiply.

15.
$$\begin{array}{r} 48 \\ \times\ 36 \\ \hline \end{array}$$

16.
$$\begin{array}{r} \$4.08 \\ \times\ 7 \\ \hline \end{array}$$

17.
$$\begin{array}{r} 428 \\ \times\ 6 \\ \hline \end{array}$$

18.
$$\begin{array}{r} \$7.93 \\ \times\ 72 \\ \hline \end{array}$$

19.
$$\begin{array}{r} \$3.90 \\ \times\ 59 \\ \hline \end{array}$$

20.
$$\begin{array}{r} 368 \\ \times\ 47 \\ \hline \end{array}$$

21.
$$\begin{array}{r} \$6.38 \\ \times\ 85 \\ \hline \end{array}$$

22.
$$\begin{array}{r} 408 \\ \times\ 27 \\ \hline \end{array}$$

23.
$$\begin{array}{r} 867 \\ \times\ 84 \\ \hline \end{array}$$

24.
$$\begin{array}{r} \$5.47 \\ \times\ 34 \\ \hline \end{array}$$

25.
$$\begin{array}{r} 458 \\ \times\ 66 \\ \hline \end{array}$$

26.
$$\begin{array}{r} \$9.25 \\ \times\ 67 \\ \hline \end{array}$$

Simplify.

27. $7 \times 4 + 4$

28. $4 + 7 \times 8$

29. $(4 + 7) \times 8$

30. $7 \times (4 + 4)$

31. $9 \times 7 - 3$

32. $(5 + 3) + 6 \times 4$

Add or subtract.

33.
$$\begin{array}{r} 3795 \\ +\ 2289 \\ \hline \end{array}$$

34.
$$\begin{array}{r} 4245 \\ +\ 5866 \\ \hline \end{array}$$

35.
$$\begin{array}{r} 7841 \\ -\ 3265 \\ \hline \end{array}$$

36.
$$\begin{array}{r} 5467 \\ -\ 2559 \\ \hline \end{array}$$

Division in the Order of Operations

We have already learned about the order of operations. Let's look at some examples that include division.

> ## Order of Operations
>
> *First* multiply or divide from left to right.
>
> *Then* add or subtract in order from left to right.
>
> Operations within parentheses should be worked before any others.

Study these examples.

$4 \div 2 + 8$
$2 + 8$
10

$7 + 6 \div 6$
$7 + 1$
8

$5 - 2 \div 2$
$5 - 1$
4

$3 + 6 \div 2$
$3 + 3$
6

$15 \div 5 + 6$
$3 + 6$
9

$(3 + 9) \div 6$
$12 \div 6$
2

$12 \div (8 - 4) \times 4 \times 2 - 4 \times 4$
$12 \div 4 \times 8 - 16$
$3 \times 8 - 16 = 24 - 16$
8

$33 \div (5 + 6) + 4 \times 5 - 2$
$33 \div 11 + 20 - 2$
$3 + 20 - 2$
21

Try These

Solve using the order of operations.

1. $18 \div 2 + 1$

2. $9 + 9 \div 3$

3. $15 - 15 \div 3$

4. $3 + 12 \div 3$

5. $28 \div 4 + 3$

6. $(3 + 9) \times 2 \div 4$

7. $72 \div 8 \times 3 + 3 \times 3 + 12$

8. $64 \div 8 \times 2 + 2 \times 4 - 4 \times 5$

Some Things About Division

There are three different ways we can write division.
They all mean the same thing.

$$8 \div 4 = 2 \qquad\qquad 4\overline{)8}^{\,2} \qquad\qquad \frac{8}{4} = 2$$

Here are the terms we use in division.

$$\text{dividend} \div \text{divisor} = \text{quotient} \qquad \frac{\text{dividend}}{\text{divisor}} = \text{quotient} \qquad \text{divisor}\overline{)\text{dividend}}^{\,\text{quotient}}$$

Some other things you should know about division:

When you divide a number by itself, the quotient is 1.	$n \div n = 1$	Any number divided by itself is one.
When you divide a number by 1, the quotient is the number.	$n \div 1 = n$	Any number divided by one is that number.
When you divide 0 by a number, the quotient is 0.	$0 \div n = 0$	Zero divided by any number is still zero.
You CANNOT divide by zero.	~~$n \div 0 = ?$~~	Dividing by 0 is not allowed.

Try These

Answer the questions.

1. Is it possible to divide a number by zero? _____

2. What do you get for a quotient when you divide a number by itself?

   _____

3. What answer would you get if you divided zero by one million?

   _____

4. If you divide a number by 1, what is the quotient? _____

5. Write $18 \div 2 = 9$ in two other ways. _____

6. In $18 \div 2 = 9$, which number is the quotient? _____

7. In $18 \div 2 = 9$, which number is the dividend? _____

8. In $18 \div 2 = 9$, which number is the divisor? _____

Exercise

Divide.

1. $\dfrac{81}{9} =$ _____

2. $\dfrac{28}{7} =$ _____

3. $\dfrac{16}{4} =$ _____

4. $\dfrac{4}{4} =$ _____

5. $\dfrac{0}{4} =$ _____

6. $\dfrac{8}{1} =$ _____

7. $0 \div 3 =$ _____

8. $3 \div 1 =$ _____

9. $3 \div 3 =$ _____

10. $27 \div 3 =$ _____

11. $35 \div 7 =$ _____

12. $64 \div 8 =$ _____

13. $5\overline{)5}$

14. $1\overline{)9}$

15. $5\overline{)0}$

16. $6\overline{)6}$

17. $2\overline{)10}$

18. $3\overline{)15}$

19. $7\overline{)49}$

20. $8\overline{)56}$

21. $4\overline{)24}$

22. $12\overline{)0}$

23. $3\overline{)21}$

24. $5\overline{)30}$

Divisibility Rules and Remainders

When we say a number is **divisible** by a certain number, we mean that if we divide it by that number, it will come out evenly with nothing left over. It will not have what we call a remainder. For certain numbers, we can predict whether or not the division will come out evenly or whether the quotient will have a remainder. For example, every even number is divisible by two. If the number is odd, then the remainder will be one. Let's look at some examples.

We see that 234 is an even number, so we know that our quotient will not have a remainder.

$$2\overline{)234}$$

To divide, we start with the leftmost digit of the dividend, which is 2 in the hundreds place. Will the divisor 2 fit into the 2 in the hundreds place? Yes, it will. There is one 2 in 2 and 100 2s in 200, so we write the one in the hundreds place above. We don't need to write the zeros as long as we remember that the 1 represents 100. Then we multiply the divisor, 2, by the 100 and write the product below the dividend.

$$\begin{array}{r} 100 \\ 2\overline{)234} \\ 200 \end{array}$$

$$\begin{array}{r} 100 \\ 2\overline{)234} \\ \underline{200} \\ 34 \end{array}$$

Then we subtract that product from the original dividend and start the process all over again.

We could just use mental math and realize that 34 ÷ 2 is 17 and write that down, but let's go throught the steps.

$$\begin{array}{r} 110 \\ 2\overline{)234} \\ \underline{200} \\ 34 \\ \underline{20} \\ 14 \end{array}$$

2 will go into 3 one time. We write the 1 above the 3 in the dividend in the tens place, remembering that it is really 10 and not 1. Then we multiply the divisor, 2, by the 10 and write the product, 20, below. Then we subtract again and go through the steps one more time.

$$\begin{array}{r} 117 \\ 2\overline{)234} \\ \underline{200} \\ 34 \\ \underline{20} \\ 14 \end{array}$$

2 goes into 14 seven times.
We write it down and we are done!   234 ÷ 2 = 117

Let's review the steps. Moving from left to right, going through each place we:

    1. Divide   2. Multiply   3. Subtract   4. Repeat as necessary

We can then check our work by multiplying the quotient by the divisor. The product should be the dividend.

Study these examples:

$$
\begin{array}{r}
2\,)\overline{476}
\end{array}
\qquad
\begin{array}{r}
2 \\
2\,)\overline{476} \\
400
\end{array}
\qquad
\begin{array}{r}
2 \\
2\,)\overline{476} \\
400 \\
\hline
76
\end{array}
\qquad
\begin{array}{r}
23 \\
2\,)\overline{476} \\
400 \\
\hline
76 \\
60 \\
\hline
16
\end{array}
\qquad
\begin{array}{r}
238 \\
2\,)\overline{476} \\
400 \\
\hline
76 \\
60 \\
\hline
16
\end{array}
\qquad
\begin{array}{r}
238 \\
\times\ \ 2 \\
\hline
476
\end{array}
$$

$$
\begin{array}{r}
2\,)\overline{352}
\end{array}
\qquad
\begin{array}{r}
1 \\
2\,)\overline{352} \\
200
\end{array}
\qquad
\begin{array}{r}
1 \\
2\,)\overline{352} \\
200 \\
\hline
152
\end{array}
\qquad
\begin{array}{r}
17 \\
2\,)\overline{352} \\
200 \\
\hline
152 \\
140 \\
\hline
12
\end{array}
\qquad
\begin{array}{r}
176 \\
2\,)\overline{352} \\
200 \\
\hline
152 \\
140 \\
\hline
12
\end{array}
\qquad
\begin{array}{r}
176 \\
\times\ \ 2 \\
\hline
352
\end{array}
$$

Let's examine a case where the dividend is odd. Remember: when dividing by two, if the dividend is odd there will be a remainder of 1. Study the examples.

2 will not fit into 1, so we write 0 and the leftover becomes the remainder. We write it like this.

$$
\begin{array}{r}
2\,)\overline{421}
\end{array}
\qquad
\begin{array}{r}
2 \\
2\,)\overline{421} \\
400
\end{array}
\qquad
\begin{array}{r}
2 \\
2\,)\overline{421} \\
400 \\
\hline
21
\end{array}
\qquad
\begin{array}{r}
21 \\
2\,)\overline{421} \\
400 \\
\hline
21 \\
20 \\
\hline
1
\end{array}
\qquad
\begin{array}{r}
210 \\
2\,)\overline{421} \\
400 \\
\hline
21 \\
20 \\
\hline
1
\end{array}
\qquad
\begin{array}{r}
210\ R\ 1 \\
2\,)\overline{421} \\
400 \\
\hline
21 \\
20 \\
\hline
1
\end{array}
$$

$$
\begin{array}{r}
2\,)\overline{563}
\end{array}
\qquad
\begin{array}{r}
2 \\
2\,)\overline{563} \\
400
\end{array}
\qquad
\begin{array}{r}
2 \\
2\,)\overline{563} \\
400 \\
\hline
163
\end{array}
\qquad
\begin{array}{r}
28 \\
2\,)\overline{563} \\
400 \\
\hline
163 \\
160 \\
\hline
3
\end{array}
\qquad
\begin{array}{r}
281 \\
2\,)\overline{563} \\
400 \\
\hline
163 \\
160 \\
\hline
3 \\
2
\end{array}
\qquad
\begin{array}{r}
281\ R\ 1 \\
2\,)\overline{563} \\
400 \\
\hline
163 \\
160 \\
\hline
3 \\
2 \\
\hline
1
\end{array}
$$

Try These

Divide.

1. $2\,)\overline{298}$ 2. $2\,)\overline{397}$ 3. $2\,)\overline{654}$ 4. $2\,)\overline{563}$

Let's examine 3 as a divisor. How can we tell if a number is divisible by 3? A number is divisible by 3 if the sum of its digits is evenly divisible by 3. Is the number 123 divisible by 3? Find the sum of the digits.   1 + 2 + 3 = 6 Is 6 divisible by 3? Yes, it is, so 123 is divisible by 3. **There will be no remainder**. Is 575 divisible by 3? We check the sum of the digits: 5 + 7 + 5 = 17.   17 is not evenly divisible by 3, so 575 is not divisible by three. It will have a remainder of 1 or 2. Study the examples.

```
         1                1               19              192            192
3)576  3)576            3)576           3)576           3)576          ×   3
         300              300             300             300           576
                         276             276             276
                                         270             270
                                           6               6
```

```
3)252
```
We start at the left but 3 will not fit into 2 so we include the digit in the next place. 3 will go into 25 so we write the 8 above the tens place and proceed with the next step.

```
         8                8               84             84
      3)252            3)252           3)252          ×   3
         240              240             240           252
                          12              12
```

```
         1                1               14             140 R 1
3)421  3)421            3)421           3)421          3)421
         300              300             300            300
                         121             121            121
                                         120            120
                                           1              1
```

We only have 1 left over after the subtraction, so we are through dividing and we fill in the remaining place with 0 and write the remainder.

```
         1                1               18             187            187 R 2
3)563  3)563            3)563           3)563          3)563          3)563
         300              300             300            300            300
                         263             263             263            263
                                         240             240            240
                                          23              23             23
                                                          21             21
                                                                          2
```

Let's review the steps. Moving from left to right, going through each place we:

  1. Divide   2. Multiply   3. Subtract   4. Repeat as necessary

We can then check our work by multiplying the quotient by the divisor. The product should be the dividend.

Divisibility by 9:

How can we tell if a number is evenly divisible by 9? A number is divisible by 9 if the sum of its digits is divisible by 9. Is the number 423 divisible by 9? Find the sum of the digits.

$4 + 2 + 3 = 9$ Is 9 divisible by 9? Yes, it is, so 423 is divisible by 9. There will be no remainder.

Is 575 divisible by 9? We check the sum of the digits:

$5 + 7 + 5 = 17.$ 17 is not divisible by 9, so 575 is not divisible by 9. Study the examples.

$9\overline{)576}$

$$\begin{array}{r} 6 \\ 9\overline{)576} \\ 540 \end{array}$$

$$\begin{array}{r} 6 \\ 9\overline{)576} \\ 540 \\ \hline 36 \end{array}$$

$$\begin{array}{r} 64 \\ 9\overline{)576} \\ 540 \\ \hline 36 \end{array}$$

$$\begin{array}{r} 64 \\ \times\ \ 9 \\ \hline 576 \end{array}$$

$9\overline{)563}$

$$\begin{array}{r} 6 \\ 9\overline{)563} \\ 540 \end{array}$$

$$\begin{array}{r} 6 \\ 9\overline{)563} \\ 540 \\ \hline 23 \end{array}$$

$$\begin{array}{r} 62 \\ 9\overline{)563} \\ 540 \\ \hline 23 \\ 18 \end{array}$$

$$\begin{array}{r} 62 \\ 9\overline{)563} \\ 540 \\ \hline 23 \\ 18 \\ \hline 5 \end{array}$$

$$\begin{array}{r} 62\ \text{R}\ 5 \\ 9\overline{)563} \\ 540 \\ \hline 23 \\ 18 \\ \hline 5 \end{array}$$

Try These

Divide.

1. $3\overline{)198}$

2. $9\overline{)387}$

3. $3\overline{)654}$

4. $9\overline{)567}$

5. $9\overline{)298}$

6. $3\overline{)397}$

7. $9\overline{)654}$

8. $3\overline{)563}$

More Divisibility Rules and Remainders

How can we tell if a number is evenly divisible by 5 or 10?
A number is divisible by 5 if it ends in 5 or 0. A number is divisible
by 10 if it ends in 0. All numbers that are divisible by 10 are also divisible
by 5, but not all numbers divisible by 5 are divisible by 10.
Let's review the divisibility rules we have learned.

Evenly divisible by:	Rule
2	If the number is even
3	If the sum of the digits is divisible by 3
5	If the number ends in 5 or 0
9	If the sum of the digits is divisible by 9
10	If the number ends in 0

Study the examples.

$$5\overline{)575}$$

$$\begin{array}{r} 1 \\ 5\overline{)575} \\ 500 \end{array}$$

$$\begin{array}{r} 11 \\ 5\overline{)575} \\ \underline{500} \\ 75 \\ 50 \end{array}$$

$$\begin{array}{r} 115 \\ 5\overline{)575} \\ \underline{500} \\ 75 \\ \underline{50} \\ 25 \end{array}$$

$$\begin{array}{r} 115 \\ \times\quad 5 \\ \hline 575 \end{array}$$

$$10\overline{)250}$$

$$\begin{array}{r} 2 \\ 10\overline{)250} \\ 200 \end{array}$$

$$\begin{array}{r} 25 \\ 10\overline{)250} \\ \underline{200} \\ 50 \end{array}$$

$$\begin{array}{r} 25 \\ \times\ 10 \\ \hline 250 \end{array}$$

$$10\overline{)362}$$

$$\begin{array}{r} 3 \\ 10\overline{)362} \\ 300 \\ 62 \end{array}$$

$$\begin{array}{r} 36 \\ 10\overline{)362} \\ \underline{300} \\ 62 \\ 60 \end{array}$$

$$\begin{array}{r} 36\ R\ 2 \\ 10\overline{)362} \\ \underline{300} \\ 62 \\ \underline{60} \\ 2 \end{array}$$

$$5\overline{)421}$$

$$\begin{array}{r} 8 \\ 5\overline{)421} \\ 400 \end{array}$$

$$\begin{array}{r} 84 \\ 5\overline{)421} \\ \underline{400} \\ 21 \\ 20 \end{array}$$

$$\begin{array}{r} 84\ R\ 1 \\ 5\overline{)421} \\ \underline{400} \\ 21 \\ \underline{20} \\ 1 \end{array}$$

$$5\overline{)637}$$

$$\begin{array}{r} 1 \\ 5\overline{)637} \\ 500 \\ 137 \end{array}$$

$$\begin{array}{r} 12 \\ 5\overline{)637} \\ \underline{500} \\ 137 \\ 100 \\ 37 \end{array}$$

$$\begin{array}{r} 127\ R\ 2 \\ 5\overline{)637} \\ \underline{500} \\ 137 \\ \underline{100} \\ 37 \\ \underline{35} \\ 2 \end{array}$$

Try These

Divide.

1. $5\overline{)255}$ 2. $10\overline{)480}$ 3. $5\overline{)654}$ 4. $10\overline{)567}$

Divide.

1. $\dfrac{64}{8} =$ _____

2. $\dfrac{28}{28} =$ _____

3. $\dfrac{16}{2} =$ _____

4. $28 \div 4 =$ _____

5. $35 \div 1 =$ _____

6. $32 \div 8 =$ _____

7. $1\overline{)7}$

8. $9\overline{)81}$

9. $3\overline{)0}$

10. $6\overline{)36}$

11. $2\overline{)642}$

12. $3\overline{)543}$

13. $5\overline{)745}$

14. $9\overline{)882}$

15. $10\overline{)140}$

16. $5\overline{)625}$

17. $3\overline{)369}$

18. $2\overline{)543}$

19. $9\overline{)689}$

20. $3\overline{)215}$

21. $2\overline{)563}$

22. $10\overline{)429}$

23. $2\overline{)352}$

24. $3\overline{)126}$

25. $5\overline{)847}$

26. $9\overline{)982}$

Division

We will take more time and do quite a few more exercises to practice and develop our division skill.

Solve the problems and look for patterns.

1. $\begin{array}{r} 10 \\ \times\ \ 3 \\ \hline \end{array}$

2. $\begin{array}{r} 6 \\ \times\ \ 3 \\ \hline \end{array}$

3. $3\overline{)48}$

4. $\begin{array}{r} 16 \\ \times\ \ 3 \\ \hline \end{array}$

5. $\begin{array}{r} 20 \\ \times\ \ 4 \\ \hline \end{array}$

6. $\begin{array}{r} 3 \\ \times\ \ 4 \\ \hline \end{array}$

7. $4\overline{)92}$

8. $\begin{array}{r} 23 \\ \times\ \ 4 \\ \hline \end{array}$

9. $\begin{array}{r} 10 \\ \times\ \ 2 \\ \hline \end{array}$

10. $\begin{array}{r} 7 \\ \times\ \ 2 \\ \hline \end{array}$

11. $2\overline{)34}$

12. $\begin{array}{r} 17 \\ \times\ \ 2 \\ \hline \end{array}$

13. $\begin{array}{r} 10 \\ \times\ \ 6 \\ \hline \end{array}$

14. $\begin{array}{r} 3 \\ \times\ \ 6 \\ \hline \end{array}$

15. $6\overline{)78}$

16. $\begin{array}{r} 13 \\ \times\ \ 6 \\ \hline \end{array}$

17. $\begin{array}{r} 20 \\ \times\ \ 4 \\ \hline \end{array}$

18. $\begin{array}{r} 1 \\ \times\ \ 4 \\ \hline \end{array}$

19. $4\overline{)84}$

20. $\begin{array}{r} 21 \\ \times\ \ 4 \\ \hline \end{array}$

Exercise

Solve the problems and look for patterns.

1. 84 ÷ 3

2. 28 × 3

3. 80 ÷ 5

4. 16 × 5

5. 56 ÷ 4

6. 14 × 4

7. 45 ÷ 3

8. 15 × 3

9. 90 ÷ 2

10. 45 × 2

11. 88 ÷ 2

12. 2 × 44

13. 68 ÷ 4

14. 4 × 17

15. 85 ÷ 5

16. 5 × 17

17. 96 ÷ 6

18. 16 × 6

19. 58 ÷ 2

20. 29 × 2

21. 72 ÷ 3

22. 3 × 24

Division

A quotient will have a remainder when the last subtraction leaves a number that is less than the divisor, unless, of course, the remaining number after the last subtraction is zero.

$$3\overline{)49}$$
  $\underline{1}$
  49
  $\underline{30}$
  19

1. Divide
2. Multiply
3. Subtract
4. If the number is larger than the divisor, then repeat

$$3\overline{)49}$$ 16 R 1
  49
  $\underline{30}$
  19
  $\underline{18}$
  1

1. Divide
2. Multiply
3. Subtract
4. If the number is smaller than the divisor, then write the quotient with the remainder.

Exercise

Divide.

1. $4\overline{)53}$ 2. $5\overline{)99}$ 3. $8\overline{)98}$ 4. $3\overline{)59}$

5. $6\overline{)87}$ 6. $7\overline{)99}$ 7. $5\overline{)92}$ 8. $8\overline{)91}$

9. $3\overline{)47}$ 10. $6\overline{)83}$ 11. $2\overline{)75}$ 12. $4\overline{)89}$

Exercise

Divide.

1. 97 ÷ 6

2. 86 ÷ 4

3. 87 ÷ 5

4. 98 ÷ 9

5. 92 ÷ 3

6. 51 ÷ 4

7. 25 ÷ 2

8. 72 ÷ 5

9. 96 ÷ 7

10. 91 ÷ 2

11. 49 ÷ 3

12. 67 ÷ 4

13. 83 ÷ 5

14. 87 ÷ 4

15. 99 ÷ 2

16. 74 ÷ 6

17. 59 ÷ 2

18. 83 ÷ 3

19. 90 ÷ 4

20. 65 ÷ 6

21. 59 ÷ 3

22. 80 ÷ 6

Division Review

Let's review the steps. Moving from left to right, going through each place we:

1. Divide   2. Multiply   3. Subtract   4. Repeat as necessary

Study the examples.

$$
\begin{array}{r}
100 \\
4\overline{)744}
\end{array}
\qquad
\begin{array}{r}
100 \\
4\overline{)744}
\end{array}
$$

1. Divide

4 goes into 7, one time

$$
\begin{array}{r}
100 \\
4\overline{)744} \\
400
\end{array}
$$

2. Multiply

$4 \times 100 = 400$

$$
\begin{array}{r}
100 \\
4\overline{)744} \\
400 \\
\hline
344
\end{array}
$$

3. Subtract

$744 - 400 = 344$

$$
\begin{array}{r}
18 \\
4\overline{)744} \\
400 \\
\hline
344 \\
320
\end{array}
$$

$$
\begin{array}{r}
186 \\
4\overline{)744} \\
400 \\
\hline
344 \\
320 \\
\hline
24 \\
24
\end{array}
$$

4. Repeat as necessary

$$
\begin{array}{r}
186 \\
4\overline{)744} \\
400 \\
\hline
344 \\
300 \\
\hline
24 \\
24 \\
\hline
0
\end{array}
$$

$$
7\overline{)786}
\qquad
\begin{array}{r}
100 \\
7\overline{)786}
\end{array}
\qquad
\begin{array}{r}
100 \\
7\overline{)786} \\
700
\end{array}
\qquad
\begin{array}{r}
100 \\
7\overline{)786} \\
700 \\
\hline
86
\end{array}
$$

$$
\begin{array}{r}
110 \\
7\overline{)786} \\
700 \\
\hline
86 \\
70
\end{array}
\qquad
\begin{array}{r}
112 \\
7\overline{)786} \\
700 \\
\hline
86 \\
70 \\
\hline
16 \\
14
\end{array}
\qquad
\begin{array}{r}
112 \text{ R}2 \\
7\overline{)786} \\
700 \\
\hline
86 \\
70 \\
\hline
16 \\
14 \\
\hline
2
\end{array}
$$

Exercise

Divide.

1. $4\overline{)642}$ 2. $6\overline{)546}$ 3. $7\overline{)742}$ 4. $8\overline{)984}$

5. $8\overline{)140}$ 6. $4\overline{)625}$ 7. $7\overline{)369}$ 8. $6\overline{)543}$

9. $7\overline{)689}$ 10. $6\overline{)215}$ 11. $8\overline{)563}$ 12. $4\overline{)429}$

13. 6)352

14. 8)126

15. 4)847

16. 7)982

17. 6)694

18. 8)992

19. 4)879

20. 7)882

21. 6)842

22. 8)876

23. 4)472

24. 7)875

25. 6)794

26. 5)593

27. 2)987

28. 9)979

29. 3)949

30. 4)856

31. 5)949

32. 3)856

1. $3\overline{)25}$ 2. $7\overline{)23}$ 3. $9\overline{)57}$ 4. $8\overline{)84}$

5. $6\overline{)84}$ 6. $4\overline{)64}$ 7. $7\overline{)91}$ 8. $3\overline{)69}$

9. $4\overline{)49}$ 10. $8\overline{)91}$ 11. $3\overline{)37}$ 12. $5\overline{)86}$

13. $2\overline{)632}$ 14. $5\overline{)568}$ 15. $8\overline{)936}$ 16. $3\overline{)988}$

17. $8\overline{)608}$ 18. $5\overline{)543}$ 19. $6\overline{)358}$ 20. $9\overline{)472}$

21. There are 5280 feet in a mile and 3 feet in a yard.
How many yards are in a mile? _____

22. Each stack had 6 containers in it. There were
288 containers. How many stacks would that be? _____

Complete each number sentence.

1. $7 + 2 =$ ____   2. $9 + 9 =$ ____   3. $3 + 2 =$ ____   4. $8 + 9 =$ ____

5. $2 + 8 =$ ____   6. $3 + 5 =$ ____   7. $1 + 7 =$ ____   8. $7 + 5 =$ ____

9. $6 + 2 =$ ____   10. $8 + 7 =$ ____   11. $5 + 4 =$ ____   12. $9 + 3 =$ ____

13. $10 - 4 =$ ____   14. $5 - 0 =$ ____   15. $6 - 3 =$ ____   16. $7 - 6 =$ ____

17. $12 - 3 =$ ____   18. $11 - 4 =$ ____   19. $15 - 8 =$ ____   20. $14 - 9 =$ ____

21. $11 - 6 =$ ____   22. $9 - 8 =$ ____   23. $16 - 9 =$ ____   24. $10 - 1 =$ ____

25. $5 \times 5 =$ ____   26. $4 \times 3 =$ ____   27. $4 \times 7 =$ ____   28. $3 \times 6 =$ ____

29. $9 \times 4 =$ ____   30. $2 \times 2 =$ ____   31. $7 \times 9 =$ ____   32. $9 \times 9 =$ ____

33. $6 \times 9 =$ ____   34. $8 \times 6 =$ ____   35. $3 \times 9 =$ ____   36. $8 \times 3 =$ ____

37. $64 \div 8 =$ ____   38. $18 \div 2 =$ ____   39. $28 \div 4 =$ ____   40. $18 \div 3 =$ ____

41. $54 \div 6 =$ ____   42. $49 \div 7 =$ ____   43. $9 \div 3 =$ ____   44. $63 \div 7 =$ ____

45. $56 \div 8 =$ ____   46. $32 \div 4 =$ ____   47. $28 \div 7 =$ ____   48. $24 \div 8 =$ ____

Another Look at Division

A dividend with 3 digits divided by a divisor with 1 digit will have either a 2 or 3 digit quotient. Can you figure out why that is so? When we first encounter a division problem, we should think about it. We should see if we can figure out what the answer might be like. For example, look at this problem and see if you can come to any conclusions about it.

$$4\overline{)531}$$

We see that the dividend is 3 digits and the divisor is 1 digit. That tells us that the quotient will have either 2 or 3 digits. We also see that the dividend is odd and the divisor is even. This tells us that the quotient will have a remainder. We see that the first digit of the dividend is greater than the divisor, so we know the quotient will begin in the hundreds place, and so, will be three digits. Examine these problems and see if you can figure out any conclusions about them. Then look at the examples to test your conclusions.

$$3\overline{)807} \qquad 2\overline{)747} \qquad 3\overline{)105} \qquad 9\overline{)711}$$

Questions to ask yourself:

Is there a rule of divisibility to apply?
Will there be a remainder?
Is the first digit of the dividend larger than the divisor?
Will the quotient be 2 or 3 digits?

$$
\begin{array}{r}
269 \\
3\overline{)807} \\
600 \\
\hline
207 \\
180 \\
\hline
27 \\
27 \\
\hline
0
\end{array}
\qquad
\begin{array}{r}
373 \text{ R } 1 \\
2\overline{)747} \\
600 \\
\hline
147 \\
140 \\
\hline
7 \\
6 \\
\hline
1
\end{array}
\qquad
\begin{array}{r}
35 \\
3\overline{)105} \\
90 \\
\hline
15 \\
15 \\
\hline
0
\end{array}
\qquad
\begin{array}{r}
79 \\
9\overline{)711} \\
630 \\
\hline
81 \\
81 \\
\hline
0
\end{array}
$$

807 is evenly divisible by 3 and will have no remainder. The first digit of the dividend is larger than the divisor so the quotient will have 3 digits.

An odd number divided by an even will have a remainder. The divisor is 2 so the remainder will be 1. The first digit of the dividend is larger than the divisor so the quotient will have 3 digits.

Evenly divisible by 3. No remainder. First digit of dividend smaller than divisor. Quotient will have 2 digits.

Notice that the first product is 90 and we must be careful about place value. Product must be placed in the right position.

Evenly divisible by 9. No remainder. First digit of dividend smaller than divisor. Quotient will have 2 digits.

Always watch place value.

Exercise

Divide.

1. 2)352
2. 5)615
3. 3)981
4. 9)999

5. 6)871
6. 7)791
7. 8)376
8. 3)639

9. 4)456
10. 6)672
11. 9)827
12. 4)968

13. 371 ÷ 2
14. 494 ÷ 3
15. 453 ÷ 5
16. 841 ÷ 9

17. 641 ÷ 5
18. 472 ÷ 8
19. 591 ÷ 4
20. 832 ÷ 7

21. 652 ÷ 3
22. 971 ÷ 7
23. 127 ÷ 2
24. 721 ÷ 6

Place Value in Division

We know the basic steps of division are:

1. Divide
2. Multiply
3. Subtract
4. Repeat as necessary

We also know that we should examine the problem carefully and think about it before beginning. Look, think, and plan.

When we actually begin the division, we will need to keep the place values of the quotient in mind. When we do the multiplication step, we will need to remember the proper place values of the factors. For example:

$$5\overline{)435}$$

First, we look, think, and plan. We see that the dividend ends in 5 and the divisor is 5, so there will be no remainder. We also note that the divisor is too large for the first digit of the dividend, so the quotient will be 2 digits. The first digit of the quotient will be in the tens place. Estimating, we determine that the quotient will be eighty-something. We know quite a lot and we haven't even begun!

$$\begin{array}{r} 8 \\ 5\overline{)435} \\ 400 \end{array}$$

As we begin the division, pay attention to place value. 5 will go into 43, 8 times. We place the 8 in the **tens place** because that is where the 43 ends. Then we multiply. We multiply the quotient by the divisor, the 8 by the 5, remembering that it is actually 80 × 5. We write that product below the dividend, making sure that we line up the **places**. Finish the problem.

Study these examples:

$$\begin{array}{r} 3 \\ 3\overline{)912} \\ 900 \\ \hline 12 \end{array}$$

In this case, we see there will be a 3-digit quotient with no remainder. We divide. Place the quotient in the **hundreds place**. Then multiply the quotient by the divisor. Remember: the quotient is in **hundreds**. Place the quotient underneath the dividend, making sure it is lined up in the correct places. Then subtract.

$$\begin{array}{r} 304 \\ 3\overline{)912} \\ 900 \\ \hline 12 \\ 12 \\ \hline 0 \end{array}$$

Now we begin again with the next division. This time the quotient should go in the **ones place**. But what about the tens place in the quotient? It is blank. We fill in the space with 0 because there are no **tens** in the quotient. There are only **hundreds** and **ones**.

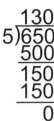

$5\overline{)650}$

$\begin{array}{r} 1 \\ 5\overline{)650} \\ 500 \\ \hline 150 \end{array}$

$\begin{array}{r} 130 \\ 5\overline{)650} \\ 500 \\ \hline 150 \\ 150 \\ \hline 0 \end{array}$

In this case also, we see there will be a 3-digit quotient with no remainder. We divide. Place the quotient in the **hundreds place**. Then multiply the quotient by the divisor. Remember the quotient is in **hundreds**. Place the quotient underneath the dividend, making sure it is lined up in the correct places. Then subtract.

Now we begin again with the next division. This time the quotient should go in the **tens place**. Again, we multiply, remembering that we are multiplying by **tens**. We subtract and have nothing left. We have nothing left to divide, but the ones place in the quotient is empty. We fill in the space with 0 because there are no **ones**. There are only **hundreds** and **tens**.

Exercise

Divide.

1. $4\overline{)212}$
2. $5\overline{)380}$
3. $8\overline{)632}$
4. $3\overline{)141}$

5. $6\overline{)497}$
6. $7\overline{)698}$
7. $5\overline{)429}$
8. $8\overline{)791}$

9. $3\overline{)217}$
10. $6\overline{)384}$
11. $2\overline{)193}$
12. $4\overline{)229}$

13. $371 \div 4$
14. $494 \div 5$
15. $453 \div 6$
16. $456 \div 9$

17. 422 ÷ 5   18. 395 ÷ 8   19. 781 ÷ 4   20. 962 ÷ 7

21. 273 ÷ 3   22. 367 ÷ 7   23. 127 ÷ 9   24. 423 ÷ 6

25. 114 ÷ 3   26. 950 ÷ 6   27. 835 ÷ 8   28. 119 ÷ 4

29. 4)683   30. 4)112   31. 8)859   32. 7)758

33. 2)441   34. 3)931   35. 3)116   36. 4)842

37. 735 ÷ 7   38. 963 ÷ 9   39. 630 ÷ 6   40. 461 ÷ 2

41. 614 ÷ 3   42. 975 ÷ 9   43. 534 ÷ 5   44. 826 ÷ 8

Exercise

Divide.

1. $4\overline{)852}$ 2. $3\overline{)651}$ 3. $8\overline{)896}$ 4. $7\overline{)784}$

5. $6\overline{)583}$ 6. $5\overline{)328}$ 7. $4\overline{)321}$ 8. $9\overline{)566}$

9. $3\overline{)115}$ 10. $6\overline{)610}$ 11. $2\overline{)817}$ 12. $9\overline{)951}$

13. $788 \div 4$ 14. $727 \div 5$ 15. $516 \div 6$ 16. $301 \div 7$

17. $429 \div 5$ 18. $142 \div 2$ 19. $939 \div 9$ 20. $422 \div 6$

21. $985 \div 9$ 22. $902 \div 3$ 23. $832 \div 8$ 24. $113 \div 4$

Division with Larger Numbers

Dividing a larger number still uses the same process. We still move from left to right and follow the steps.

1. Divide   2. Multiply   3. Subtract   4. Repeat as necessary

Study the examples.

```
        1              1              1              18           189          1894
4)7576      4)7576      4)7576      4)7576      4)7576       4)7576       4)7576
                        4000         4000         4000         4000         4000
                                     3576         3576         3576         3576
We start at the left with                        3200         3200         3200
  the thousands.        Multiply and                          376          376
                        subtract, then                        360          360
                        move on to    Repeat as necessary      16           16
                        the hundreds                                        16
```

```
        1              1              14           145          1455 R 4
6)8734      6)8734      6)8734      6)8734      6)8734       6)8734
                        6000         6000         6000         6000
                                     2734         2734         2734
                                     2400         2400         2400
                                                  334          334
                                                  300          300
                                                   34           34
                                                               30
                                                                4
```

Exercise

Divide.

1. 4)9560   2. 6)1344   3. 7)4361   4. 8)3600

5. 2884 ÷ 8   6. 6204 ÷ 4   7. 3225 ÷ 7   8. 2418 ÷ 6

132

9. 7)2982

10. 6)5043

11. 8)7249

12. 4)2242

13. 6)1332

14. 8)4336

15. 4)2562

16. 7)2501

17. 6)4638

18. 8)3915

19. 4)8182

20. 7)6904

21. 6)8734

22. 3)9219

23. 9)8625

24. 6)9842

25. 6)7579

26. 5)4630

A dividend with 4 digits divided by a divisor with 1 digit will have either a 3 or 4 digit quotient, depending on whether or not the divisor will go into the first digit of the dividend. This is a pattern that always occurs with 1 digit divisors.

We know the basic steps of division are:

1. Divide
2. Multiply
3. Subtract
4. Repeat as necessary

We also know that we should examine the problem carefully and think about it before beginning. Look, think, and plan.

Questions to ask yourself:

Is there a rule of divisibility to apply?
Will there be a remainder?
Is the first digit of the dividend larger than the divisor?
Can I estimate roughly what the quotient will be?

$$3\overline{)4731}$$

First, we look, think and plan. We can apply the divisibility rule for the divisor, so there will be no remainder. The divisor can be divided into the first digit of the dividend, so the quotient will be 4 digits. The first digit of the quotient will be in the thousands place. Estimating, we determine that the quotient will be somewhere more than 1000 and less than 2000. We start at the left and move right, following the steps and watching place value.

$$
\begin{array}{r}
15 \\
3\overline{)4731} \\
3000 \\
\hline
1731 \\
1500 \\
\hline
231 \\
\end{array}
$$

Study the example to the left. Finish the problem.

Does your answer fall within the range of your estimate?
Is there a remainder?

Exercise

Divide.

1. 8576 ÷ 4   2. 6170 ÷ 5   3. 9438 ÷ 6   4. 9918 ÷ 9

5. 6)7695

6. 7)8421

7. 5)7791

8. 8)9327

9. 2)8916

10. 9)1962

11. 3)1311

12. 9)4828

13. 6135 ÷ 3

14. 3512 ÷ 4

15. 5496 ÷ 7

16. 8721 ÷ 6

17. 3762 ÷ 9

18. 2973 ÷ 8

19. 7145 ÷ 5

20. 2792 ÷ 2

21. 4)6891

22. 3)7123

23. 7)9621

24. 6)8476

135

Dividing Money

Dividing money is like other division but involves proper placement of the dollar sign and decimal point. We still use the same process but before we begin, we should place the dollar sign and decimal point. Place the dollar sign and decimal point in the quotient area directly above the dollar sign and decimal point in the dividend. They should be lined up. Then we can begin the division. We still move from left to right and follow the steps.

1. Divide   2. Multiply   3. Subtract   4. Repeat as necessary

Study the examples.

```
                  $                $1  .            $14.            $14.9            $14.97
5)$74.85       5)$74.85        5)$74.85         5)$74.85         5)$74.85         5)$74.85
                                 50 00            50 00            50 00            50 00
                                 24 85            24 85            24 85            24 85
                                                  20 00            20 00            20 00
                                                                    4 85             4 85
                                                                    4 50             4 50
                                                                      35               35
                                                                                       35
```

Start by placing the dollar sign
and decimal point.

```
                  $                $ 9.             $ 9.9          $ 9.9           $ 9.98
9)$89.82       9)$89.82        9)$89.82         9)$89.82       9)$89.82         9)$89.82
                                 81 00            81 00          81 00            81 00
                                  8 82             8 82           8 82             8 82
                                                   8 10           8 10             8 10
                                                                    72               72
                                                                                     72
```

Study these examples.

```
  $1.06            $.12             $ 5.20            $ .09
9)$9.54          7)$.84          5)$26.00          8)$0.72
  9 00             70              25 00              72
   54              14              1 00
   54              14              1 00
```

Exercise

Divide.

1. 9)$\overline{\$65.16}$ 2. 4)$\overline{\$63.00}$ 3. 7)$\overline{\$2.31}$ 4. 8)$\overline{\$20.88}$

5. 5)$\overline{\$1.35}$ 6. 4)$\overline{\$20.84}$ 7. 7)$\overline{\$14.28}$ 8. 6)$\overline{\$22.20}$

9. 4)$\overline{\$2.44}$ 10. 8)$\overline{\$5.36}$ 11. 9)$\overline{\$11.43}$ 12. 5)$\overline{\$1.30}$

13. 6)$\overline{\$14.82}$ 14. 8)$\overline{\$24.16}$ 15. 7)$\overline{\$87.64}$ 16. 2)$\overline{\$23.96}$

17. 8)$\overline{\$98.80}$ 18. 5)$\overline{\$67.95}$ 19. 5)$\overline{\$26.00}$ 20. 7)$\overline{\$17.01}$

Exercise

Divide.

1. $9\overline{)\$49.77}$ 2. $7\overline{)\$21.63}$ 3. $2\overline{)\$4.94}$ 4. $2\overline{)\$8.58}$

5. $6\overline{)\$44.88}$ 6. $4\overline{)\$31.96}$ 7. $4\overline{)\$95.92}$ 8. $3\overline{)\$50.94}$

9. $9\overline{)\$73.53}$ 10. $5\overline{)\$41.65}$ 11. $3\overline{)\$9.18}$ 12. $6\overline{)\$2.88}$

13. $\$8.13 \div 3$ 14. $\$9.20 \div 4$ 15. $\$9.52 \div 7$ 16. $\$1.56 \div 6$

17. $\$7.65 \div 9$ 18. $\$4.24 \div 8$ 19. $\$6.25 \div 5$ 20. $\$10.38 \div 2$

138

21. $4\overline{)\$9.96}$ 22. $6\overline{)440}$ 23. $7\overline{)597}$ 24. $9\overline{)703}$

25. $5\overline{)448}$ 26. $8\overline{)764}$ 27. $3\overline{)136}$ 28. $7\overline{)185}$

29. $9\overline{)563}$ 30. $5\overline{)612}$ 31. $4\overline{)953}$ 32. $7\overline{)861}$

Simplify using the order of operations.

33. $6 \times 4 - 12 \div 2 =$ _____   34. $45 - 10 + 81 \div 9 =$ _____

35. $50 + 100 \div 2 \div 10 =$ _____   36. $40 \times 2 + 10 - 45 =$ _____

37. $25 \div 5 + 4 \times 3 - 3 =$ _____   38. $18 \times 2 \div 9 + 4 =$ _____

39. $6 + 5 \div 1 - 3 \times 3 =$ _____   40. $8 \times 6 + 24 \div 8 =$ _____

41. $23 - 21 \div 7 + 5 \times 2 =$ _____   42. $20 + 6 \div 6 - 7 =$ _____

Averages

To find the average of a set of numbers, we first add the numbers and then we divide the sum by the number of addends.

Find the average of 75, 63, 77, 80, and 90.

First, we add the numbers.

Then we divide the sum by the number of addends.

```
   75
   63
   77
   80
 + 90
  385
```

```
        77
    5)385
       350
        35
        35
```

Find the average.

1. 86, 85, 92, 82, 70

2. 93, 102, 115, 83, 42

3. 82, 73, 68, 72, 85

4. 72, 216, 96, 108

5. 75, 76, 94, 83, 87

6. 93, 126, 117

7. 82, 68, 85, 80, 85

8. 88, 0, 78, 90

Exercise

Find the average.

1. 45, 238, 70, 875

2. $3.05, $2.29, $1.30, $4.04

3. $2.15, $1.98, $1.00, $3.79

4. 72, 216, 96, 108

5. $4.25, $6.71, $3.24, $5.06, $4.94

6. 633, 495, 711

7. $8.44, $.31, $2.97, $3.13, $.80

8. 420, 504, 297

9. $1.84, $2.76, $4.08, $2.32

10. 517, 423, 648, 212, 555

Multiply.

1.
$$
\begin{array}{r}
328 \\
\times\ 36 \\
\hline
\end{array}
$$

2.
$$
\begin{array}{r}
479 \\
\times\ 24 \\
\hline
\end{array}
$$

3.
$$
\begin{array}{r}
965 \\
\times\ 98 \\
\hline
\end{array}
$$

4.
$$
\begin{array}{r}
621 \\
\times\ 27 \\
\hline
\end{array}
$$

5.
$$
\begin{array}{r}
\$\,2.39 \\
\times\ 29 \\
\hline
\end{array}
$$

6.
$$
\begin{array}{r}
\$\,9.52 \\
\times\ 15 \\
\hline
\end{array}
$$

7.
$$
\begin{array}{r}
\$\,4.21 \\
\times\ 47 \\
\hline
\end{array}
$$

8.
$$
\begin{array}{r}
\$\,7.96 \\
\times\ 83 \\
\hline
\end{array}
$$

Add or subtract.

9.
$$
\begin{array}{r}
278 \\
279 \\
+321 \\
\hline
\end{array}
$$

10.
$$
\begin{array}{r}
622 \\
498 \\
54 \\
+\ 77 \\
\hline
\end{array}
$$

11.
$$
\begin{array}{r}
2146 \\
+\ 3959 \\
\hline
\end{array}
$$

12.
$$
\begin{array}{r}
5291 \\
+\ 5479 \\
\hline
\end{array}
$$

13.
$$
\begin{array}{r}
4278 \\
-\ 3179 \\
\hline
\end{array}
$$

14.
$$
\begin{array}{r}
7961 \\
-\ 3254 \\
\hline
\end{array}
$$

15.
$$
\begin{array}{r}
3284 \\
+\ 2192 \\
\hline
\end{array}
$$

16.
$$
\begin{array}{r}
8523 \\
-\ 2796 \\
\hline
\end{array}
$$

Solve for n.

17. $5 \times n = 40$

18. $63 \div n = 7$

19. $n \times 4 = 36$

20. $54 \div n = 9$

21. $n \div 8 = 6$

22. $n \times 7 = 28$

23. $3 \times n = 12$

24. $n \div 3 = 6$

25. $27 \div n = 3$

Divide.

26. 2)586

27. 4)979

28. 3)785

29. 6)513

30. 8)327

31. 7)448

32. 5)139

33. 9)358

34. 1)930

35. 3)856

36. 8)758

37. 6)245

Solve using the order of operations.

38. 8 × 6 ÷ 4

39. 54 ÷ 6 × 3

40. 85 − 15 × 2

41. 10 ÷ 5 + 5 × 3

42. 24 + 4 ÷ 4 − 5

43. 12 − 8 ÷ 4 + 6

44. 6 × 3 ÷ 9 + 100 − 102

45. 64 ÷ 8 × 10 − 40 − 5

46. 68 + 10 ÷ 2 − 7 × 2

47. 25 × 3 − 50 ÷ 2 + 25

Dividing by Two Digits

Division with a two-digit divisor requires some initial estimation. With a one-digit divisor, we could rely on our division facts and didn't really need to guess. With a two-digit divisor, we don't have the facts so we have to estimate and then try our guess with multiplication.

For example: 22)71

One way to estimate is with rounding: 70 ÷ 20. We would then have a pretty good idea of what quotient to try, in this case, 3.

We then multiply and check to see if we were right.
22 × 3 = 66.

We then subtract and if the difference
is less than the divisor, we are done
and have the remainder.   71 − 66 = 5
5 is less than 22 so our answer is 3 R 5.

$$\begin{array}{r} 3\ R\ 5 \\ 22\overline{)71} \\ \underline{66} \\ 5 \end{array}$$

Study these examples:

$$\begin{array}{r} 2\ R\ 5 \\ 39\overline{)83} \\ \underline{78} \\ 5 \end{array}$$
$$\begin{array}{r} 3\ R\ 1 \\ 32\overline{)97} \\ \underline{96} \\ 1 \end{array}$$
$$\begin{array}{r} 4\ R\ 2 \\ 72\overline{)290} \\ \underline{288} \\ 2 \end{array}$$
$$\begin{array}{r} 6\ R\ 3 \\ 31\overline{)189} \\ \underline{186} \\ 3 \end{array}$$

Exercise

Divide.

1. 59)358

2. 77)448

3. 35)139

4. 43)344

5. 56)180

6. 39)250

7. 62)512

8. 85)743

9. $72\overline{)608}$　　10. $43\overline{)172}$　　11. $51\overline{)153}$　　12. $62\overline{)186}$

13. $32\overline{)162}$　　14. $22\overline{)176}$　　15. $62\overline{)189}$　　16. $22\overline{)155}$

17. $51\overline{)268}$　　18. $32\overline{)200}$　　19. $49\overline{)325}$　　20. $24\overline{)168}$

21. $55\overline{)476}$　　22. $21\overline{)148}$　　23. $81\overline{)489}$　　24. $18\overline{)142}$

25. $816 \div 86$　　26. $214 \div 28$　　27. $250 \div 62$

28. $312 \div 48$　　29. $128 \div 21$　　30. $616 \div 83$

31. $163 \div 37$　　32. $321 \div 47$　　33. $456 \div 63$

With two-digit divisors and three-digit or four-digit dividends, we may need to try a quotient more than once. This is especially true when the divisor is a teen. With a one-digit divisor, we could rely on our division facts and didn't really need to guess. With a two-digit divisor, we don't have the facts so we have to sometimes use trial and error until we find the right quotient.

Study the example.

$$34\overline{)198}$$

We always start by examining the problem. We look, think and plan. What can we tell about this problem? We see that our quotient will have one digit. The smallest two-digit quotient is 10 and 10 × 34 would give us 340, which would be too large, so we know it will be only one digit.

What else can we tell? We have to do some estimating. There are different ways to estimate. We could round 34 to 30 and try 6 as a quotient because 6 × 30 is 180. That would be close. We could notice that half of 340 is 170 and half of 10 is 5 so we could try 5. It all depends on how much you notice and how accurately you can guess. Finally, we just need to try one and see how it fits. Let's try 6. We need to do the multiplication: 6 × 34 = 204. Will that work? No, it is too large. 204 is more than 198. That means that 5 will work. We multiply and then subtract. The difference is 28 which is smaller than the dividend. The remainder, then, is 28.

$$\begin{array}{r} 5 \text{ R } 28 \\ 34\overline{)198} \\ \underline{170} \\ 28 \end{array}$$

Examine these examples, and decide which quotients you would try.

$$95\overline{)275} \qquad 37\overline{)295} \qquad 88\overline{)704} \qquad 26\overline{)182}$$

If we look at the 1st digit of the divisor and the 1st two digits of the dividend, we could try 3, but we can see that 90 × 3 would give us 270 and then 3 × 5 would put us over 275, so we should try 2.	If we round both the divisor and the dividend, we would try 7 (40 × 7 = 280), then test it by multiplying: 37 × 7 = 259 Then we subtract: 295-259=36 The difference is smaller than the divisor, so we guessed correctly. What if the difference had been larger?	If we round both the divisor and the dividend, and then test it by multiplying, we would have chosen 7. 90 × 7 = 630 88 × 7 = 616 That seems low so we would try 8. 90 × 8 = 720 88 × 8 = 704 Sometimes we just need to try different quotients.	26 rounds to 30 30 into 180, 6 times Test by multiplying, then subtracting 26×6=156 182–156=26 so we know 6 was too little and the real quotient is 7.

For these kinds of division problems, there are usually a number of ways to estimate the quotient. The first way is to take the first digit of the divisor and the first 2 digits of the dividend and see how many times the divisor will go into the dividend. A second way is to round the divisor and make an estimate based on that. A third way is to round both the divisor and the dividend and make the estimate that way. Sometimes there is something else about the problem that will give us a clue. Let take the problem: 158 ÷ 45, and try different methods of estimating.

① If we take the first digit of the divisor and the first two of the dividend we would have 15 ÷ 4 and our estimate would be 3.

② If we use the rounding approach for the divisor, we would have 158 ÷ 50 and our estimate would still be 3.

③ If we use the rounding approach for both the divisor and the dividend, we would have 160 ÷ 50 and still our estimate would be 3.

Study these examples.

```
63)378
```

```
      6
63)378
   378
     0
```

Examine the problem and then estimate a quotient. Upon examination, we can see that we will have a 1-digit quotient. Then we make an estimate. If we look at the first digit of the divisor and the first two digits of the dividend, we will choose 6 as a quotient to try. We multiply and subtract to test our estimate.   63 × 6 = 378

We have a perfect match and our first estimate was correct.

```
      7 R 8          9 R 11          7 R 9          8 R 41
31)225          89)812          32)233          68)585
   217             801             224             544
     8              11               9              41
```

What method of estimating would you choose on each of the above?

Try These

Divide.

1. 92)369   2. 21)149   3. 42)129   4. 42)252

Exercise

Divide.

1. 72)598

2. 28)186

3. 92)846

4. 58)561

5. 12)108

6. 44)308

7. 75)474

8. 51)489

9. 95)380

10. 53)348

11. 22)176

12. 53)265

13. 33)132

14. 43)258

15. 31)248

16. 32)160

17. 23)160

18. 68)308

19. 96)214

20. 27)268

21. 57)273

22. 52)104

23. 24)144

24. 41)330

25. 43)130

26. 84)340

27. 81)327

28. 22)135

More Quotient Estimation

We have seen that estimating is part of our "look, think, and plan" method of solving problems. We have looked at some ways to do an estimate. We know how to test our estimate by multiplying and subtracting. And finally, we know that sometimes we just have to use trial and error until we find the right quotient. Let's look at some more examples of estimating and testing.

Study these examples.

$$\begin{array}{r} 5 \\ 37\overline{)222} \\ 185 \\ \hline 37 \end{array}$$

If we try rounding the divisor and dividend. the quotient would be 5. Would that work?

$$\begin{array}{r} 5 \\ 40\overline{)220} \end{array}$$

If we try taking the first digit of the divisor and the first two digits of the dividend the quotient would be 7. Would that work?

$$\begin{array}{r} 7 \\ 3\overline{)22} \end{array}$$

$$\begin{array}{r} 7 \\ 37\overline{)222} \\ 259 \end{array}$$

We see that neither 5 nor 7 works, though they were both reasonable estimates.

$$\begin{array}{r} 6 \\ 37\overline{)222} \\ 222 \\ \hline 0 \end{array}$$

Study the examples. Think about what you would try and how you would test your estimates.

$$\begin{array}{r} 2 \text{ R } 83 \\ 95\overline{)273} \\ 190 \\ \hline 83 \end{array} \qquad \begin{array}{r} 7 \\ 26\overline{)182} \\ 182 \\ \hline 0 \end{array} \qquad \begin{array}{r} 6 \\ 28\overline{)168} \\ 168 \\ \hline 0 \end{array} \qquad \begin{array}{r} 7 \\ 58\overline{)406} \\ 406 \\ \hline 0 \end{array}$$

Try These

Examine and decide which quotients you would try, then check them by multiplying and subtracting. Then complete the problem.

1. $94\overline{)715}$ 2. $16\overline{)100}$ 3. $48\overline{)288}$ 4. $75\overline{)536}$

Divide.

1. $64\overline{)310}$

2. $86\overline{)657}$

3. $66\overline{)542}$

4. $94\overline{)638}$

5. $85\overline{)327}$

6. $63\overline{)245}$

7. $89\overline{)801}$

8. $19\overline{)114}$

9. $54\overline{)260}$

10. $14\overline{)112}$

11. $16\overline{)128}$

12. $17\overline{)139}$

13. $732 \div 88$

14. $544 \div 68$

15. $288 \div 48$

16. $450 \div 68$

17. $186 \div 24$

18. $192 \div 22$

19. $389 \div 53$

20. $322 \div 46$

21. $144 \div 36$

Facts Review

Add.

1. 8 + 9	2. 9 + 7	3. 3 + 8	4. 2 + 6	5. 9 + 6	6. 6 + 4

7. 8 + 5	8. 8 + 8	9. 5 + 9	10. 4 + 7	11. 5 + 3	12. 9 + 5

Subtract.

13. 6 − 5	14. 9 − 2	15. 12 − 9	16. 7 − 1	17. 10 − 5	18. 13 − 8

19. 16 − 8	20. 12 − 5	21. 13 − 9	22. 12 − 4	23. 13 − 6	24. 14 − 9

Multiply.

25. 6 × 8	26. 8 × 5	27. 5 × 9	28. 6 × 6	29. 7 × 7	30. 0 × 6

31. 5 × 3	32. 3 × 9	33. 12 ×12	34. 11 ×11	35. 10 ×10	36. 9 ×12

Divide.

37. 8)48	38. 9)81	39. 7)35	40. 3)6	41. 5)15	42. 2)18

43. 6)30	44. 7)42	45. 5)10	46. 9)63	47. 1)5	48. 5)0

151

Division Practice

1. 4)976

2. 2)524

3. 6)119

4. 7)931

5. 7)868

6. 62)248

7. 81)648

8. 6)918

9. 5)860

10. 35)124

11. 59)354

12. 2)922

13. 3)537

14. 9)981

15. 74)222

16. 4)872

17. 5)815

18. 4)356

19. 7)301

20. 6)576

21. 99)828

22. 87)569

23. 76)571

24. 78)624

Dividing by a teen number (13-19) can be a little tricky sometimes because the estimating can be difficult. Let's look at an example.

14)957   When we look this problem over, it may not be immediately obvious what quotient we should try first. We ask, "How many times will 14 go into 95? We can start by at least eliminating some possibilities by seeing how many times 10 and 20 go into 95. 10 goes into 95, 9 times. 20 goes into 95, 4 times. So we know that the quotient will be more than 4 and less than 9. That leaves 5, 6, 7, and 8. We might try to perform the multiplication tests mentally. Can you multiply 14 by 5, 6, 7, and 8 mentally?

```
 10     20
× 9    × 4
 90     80
```

Let's try.   14 × 5 =   14 × 6 =   14 × 7 =   14 × 8 =

We break it into two parts, the tens and the ones.
The tens are easy.   50, 60, 70, and 80

Then we add the product of the ones to each.   +20, +24, +28, +32

We can see that 7 (70+28) and 8 (80+32) are going to be too much.

Continuing in our heads, we see that 5 (50+20) will give us 70 and 6 (60+24) will give us 84. If you can do that kind of mental math, you will find that dividing by teens is easier than you thought.

Another thing that is sometimes helpful is doubling. If the divisor is 14, double like this: 14   28   56   112   This tells us that 8 is too large by 17 and 4 is way too small. Based on that, we would know that 6 was the right quotient to try.

Just for fun, try to find these products mentally. Multiply the tens, then add the product of the ones to that.

```
   19         18         17         16         15         14
  × 4        × 5        × 6        × 7        × 8        × 9
```

40 + 36   50 + 40   60 + 42   70 + 42   80 + 40   90 + 36

Study the examples.

```
   61 R 11      12 R 7         22          42 R 1       21 R 8
15)926        15)187       13)286       19)799       16)344
   900           150          260          760          320
    26            37           26           39           24
    15            30           26           38           16
    11             7            0            1            8
```

153

Find the products mentally.

1. 15
   × 9

2. 19
   × 4

3. 16
   × 2

4. 14
   × 3

5. 18
   × 3

6. 13
   × 4

7. 16
   × 5

8. 18
   × 4

9. 17
   × 7

10. 15
    × 4

Divide.

11. $13\overline{)641}$

12. $19\overline{)309}$

13. $14\overline{)456}$

14. $17\overline{)195}$

15. $133 \div 14$

16. $226 \div 12$

17. $482 \div 15$

18. $381 \div 18$

19. $15\overline{)180}$

20. $19\overline{)399}$

21. $14\overline{)490}$

22. $12\overline{)504}$

23. $605 \div 11$

24. $987 \div 18$

25. $812 \div 16$

26. $653 \div 11$

Other Quotients and Dividends

Dividing a larger number still uses the same process. We still move from left to right and follow the steps.

    1. Divide   2. Multiply   3. Subtract   4. Repeat as necessary

Larger division problems are actually just a series of smaller division problems done one at a time. This example shows the series of smaller division problems. Every time we do the subtraction step, we get a new partial dividend.

Study the example.

```
                      1,232,815
                 23)28,354,745
                    23,000,000
  partial dividend — 5,354,745
                     4,600,000
    partial dividend — 754,745
                      690,000
      partial dividend — 64,745
                       46,000
        partial dividend — 18,745
                         18,400
          partial dividend — 345
                           230
            partial dividend — 115
                             115
                               0
```

hundred thousands
```
            2
23)5,354,745
   4,600,000
```

thousands
```
        2
23)64,745
   46,000
```

tens
```
       1
23)000
   230
```

ten thousands
```
         3
23)754,754
   690,000
```

hundreds
```
        8
23)18,745
   18,400
```

ones
```
       5
23)000
   115
```

Study the examples.

```
      20 R 26          24 R 19          21 R 8           11 R 7
28)000            40)000           37)000           46)000
   560               800              740              460
    26               179               45               53
                     160               37               46
                      19                8                7
```

Try These

Divide.

1. 24)930   2. 35)856   3. 48)758   4. 83)913

Follow the same procedures with larger dividends.
Study the examples.

```
     227 R 3          213 R 1          264 R 17         62 R 34
29)6586          46)9799          37)9785          72)4498
   5800             9200             7400             4320
    786              599             2385              178
    580              460             2220              144
    206              139              165               34
    203              138              148
      3                1              165
                                      148
                                       17
```

Try These

Divide.

1. 41)9372   2. 54)8561   3. 75)2775   4. 22)9131

Place close attention to place value. Study the zeros in the quotient.
Study the examples.

```
      102            207 R 2           $ 3.07            4,003
57)5814          39)8075          23)$70.61         24)96,072
   5700             7800             69 00            96,000
    114              275              1.61               072
    114              273              1 61                72
      0                2                 0                 0
```

Try These

Divide.

1. 43)8735   2. 74)7904   3. 18)$37.44   4. 17)61,081

Exercise

Divide.

1. $29\overline{)468}$
2. $36\overline{)949}$
3. $43\overline{)916}$
4. $14\overline{)717}$

5. $17\overline{)189}$
6. $25\overline{)1250}$
7. $15\overline{)1050}$
8. $84\overline{)2559}$

9. $96\overline{)7128}$
10. $63\overline{)4914}$
11. $84\overline{)5284}$
12. $67\overline{)\$56.95}$

13. $24\overline{)7237}$
14. $39\overline{)6240}$
15. $92\overline{)9463}$
16. $49\overline{)9859}$

17. $67\overline{)4055}$
18. $63\overline{)6749}$
19. $73\overline{)7854}$
20. $52\overline{)5681}$

Divide.

1. 22)22,154

2. 21)2247

3. 19)5852

4. 32)9856

5. 46)9246

6. 48)4128

7. 73)5811

8. 44)2096

9. 21)6307

10. 26)$79.56

11. 35)2103

12. 57)5817

13. 38)2242

14. 62)6700

15. 13)9165

16. 28)8512

17. 51)5566

18. 56)$60.48

19. 85)$92.65

20. 43)61,081

Skills Maintenance

Multiply.

1. 4219 × 7

2. 47 × 56

3. $ 9.43 × 36

4. 294 × 86

Add or subtract.

5. 5987 + 3215

6. $ 3.98 + 7.49

7. 8576 − 2989

8. 457 − 378

Solve for n.

9. $7 \times n = 56$

10. $63 \div n = 9$

11. $n \times 4 = 48$

Divide.

12. 5)655

13. 3)$25.62

14. 9)7353

15. 17)631

16. 64)573

17. 42)3974

18. 25)$78.00

19. 35)25,235

Solve using the order of operations.

20. $6 \times 6 \div 9 + 1 - 5$

21. $64 \div 8 \times 12 - 12 - 6$

159

Problem Solving
READ – THINK – PLAN – EXECUTE

We have learned much of the mechanics of performing the four operations (addition, subtraction, multiplication, division) on the set of whole numbers. We also want to be able to use that knowledge to solve problems. Sometimes, solving word problems can seem complicated because there are many types of word problems. We have practiced the "look, think, plan" principles and we can apply the same principle to solving word problems. For word problems, we could say:
READ – THINK – PLAN – EXECUTE

READing the problem is an obvious first step. We must read the problem! We must, however, read the problem carefully, making sure we note accurately, all the information we are given as well as exactly what the problem is asking us to do. For example, suppose we were given this problem:

The farmer planted 240 acres in April, 310 acres in May, and another 240 acres in June. He has 300 head of cattle, 4 dogs, 3 cats, and 6 pigs, along with an assortment of different kinds of chickens. In July, how many letters will you have in your first name?

We see that this problem has a lot of information, but what the problem asks us for is the number of letters in our first name, so the other information doesn't matter. This is just an example to show that we must pay attention to what the problem asks of us.

The second step of the plan is to THINK. This is the step where we start asking ourselves questions and making sure we have all the information we need. This is also where we try to think of a reasonable estimate of what the answer might be. Let's look at the problem in the previous example and THINK about it. What if we were asked how many acres the farmer planted altogether in April, May, and June? What would be a reasonable answer? Would it be more than a thousand? Does the number of dogs and cats have anything to do with it? How about the chickens or the cattle? How would I find out the total number of acres he planted in those 3 months? Basically, during this step, we review the information and try to make a reasonable guess as to the answer. In this case, we would decide that the answer would be less than a thousand acres and figuring out the exact number will probably involve addition.

The farmer planted 240 acres in April, 310 acres in May, and another 240 acres in June. He has 300 head of cattle, 4 dogs, 3 cats, and 6 pigs, along with an assortment of different kinds of chickens. How many acres did the farmer plant altogether in April, May, and June?

The third step is to PLAN. This is where we get down to selecting the process that will obtain for us the answer that we are looking for. We select a strategy and we select one or more operations and then we make our plan. Let's look again at our problem.

Since we have read carefully and thought carefully, we can now make our plan fairly easily. Our plan should be to add up the number of acres planted in each of the 3 months: # of acres in April + # of acres in May + # of acres in June.

Then our final step is to EXECUTE, which means we do what the plan calls for us to do. In this case, our plan calls for us to add the 3 numbers.

We add the 3 numbers and then check to see if:
1. The answer is reasonable and consistent with our estimate?
2. Did we answer the question that was asked?

$$
\begin{array}{r}
240 \\
310 \\
+\ 240 \\
\hline
790
\end{array}
$$

Problem Solving

1. Alice, Brigitte, and Carol each had a dozen things to do. Deborah, Elizabeth, and Frances each had 15 things to do.

   How many more things to do did Elizabeth have than Brigitte? _____

2. Seventeen little piggies went to market and the rest stayed home. If there were 52 little piggies altogether, how many stayed home? _____

3. John and Sebastian were playing Monopoly. John had $395. When he landed on Sebastian's property, he paid Sebastian $175 rent.

   Then how much money did John have? _____

4. There were 39 fourth graders in room 142. There were another 47 in room 144.

   How many fourth graders were in the two rooms? _____

5. In the above problem, how many more fourth graders were in room 144 than in room 142? _____

6. The population of the larger town was 54,000.
   The population of the smaller town was 23,469.
   How many more people live in the larger town
   than in the smaller town?

   _____

7. The area of Virginia is 40,767 square miles and
   the area of Iceland is 39,768 square miles. How
   much total land area is covered by the two regions?

   _____

8. In the problem above, how much greater is the
   area of Virginia than the area of Iceland?

   _____

9. Charles drove 354 miles in 6 hours. How many
   miles per hour did he average?

   _____

10. Robert reported the following scores for the
    week: 77, 84, 86, 93, 100.
    What is his average score for the week?

    _____

11. The distance from Alpha Point to Bravo Point
    is 6,972 feet. How many yards is that?

    _____

12. If a can of peaches costs $1.19,
    how much would 24 cans of peaches cost?

    _____

13. If 27 squirrels divided 945 acorns evenly amongst
    themselves, how many acorns would each squirrel get?

    _____

14. In a special deal, the team bought 46 baseballs
    for a total cost of $93.38. At that rate, how
    much did each baseball cost?

    _____

15. The stadium had 13,824 seats. The seats were separated
    into 24 sections with an equal number of seats in each
    section. How many seats were in each section?

    _____

What is the value of the underlined digit?

1. 2,2<u>5</u>6 _____

2. 2<u>2</u>,593 _____

3. 2,3<u>7</u>5 _____

4. 2,2<u>2</u>2,256 _____

5. <u>2</u>,222,593 _____

Write the word name for each number.

6. 472,000 _____

7. 2,983,000 _____

8. 1,050,392 _____

Fill in the number for each period.

9. 728,359,376

_____ million _____ thousand _____

10. 941,706,690

_____ million _____ thousand _____

Write the words for each period.

11. 362,978,416

_____ million

_____ thousand

_____

163

Write each number in expanded notation.

12. 41,930,271

_____

13. 6,486,623

_____

Round each number to the indicated place.

14. Round 934,398,476
to the nearest **hundred thousand**   _____

15. Round 587,327,945 to the nearest **million**   _____

Write each of the following in standard form.

16. CD   _____   17. XLI   _____

18. MMCDXXX_____   19. DXL   _____

20. MCDXLIV_____   21. CMXLIV _____

Find the sum of each column.

22.
```
   5
   6
   3
 + 8
____
```

23.
```
   4
   7
   3
 + 6
____
```

24.
```
   8
   2
   1
 + 9
____
```

25.
```
  234
  497
  611
 +273
_____
```

26.
```
  458
  379
  156
 +297
_____
```

Write a number sentence for each word sentence.

27. The sum of eight and five is thirteen. _____

28. The sum of nine and six is fifteen. _____

29. Twelve is the sum of four and eight. _____

Find the missing number

30. $8 + 7 = n$ 31. $0 + n = 7$ 32. $n + 7 = 13$

   $n =$ _____ $n =$ _____ $n =$ _____

33. $16 - 7 = n$ 34. $7 - n = 5$ 35. $n - 6 = 6$

   $n =$ _____ $n =$ _____ $n =$ _____

Find the missing numbers in each sequence.

36. 4, 8, 12, 16, _____, 24, 28, ... 37. 48, 42, 36, _____, 24, 18, ...

38. 3, 6, 9, 12, _____, 18, 21, ... 39. 10, 15, 20, _____, 30, 35, ..

Multiply.

40. $10 \times 7 =$ _____ 41. $100 \times 4 =$ _____ 42. $1000 \times 2 =$ _____

43. $20 \times 9 =$ _____ 44. $600 \times 8 =$ _____ 45. $2000 \times 3 =$ _____

46. $300 \times 6 =$ _____ 47. $70 \times 11 =$ _____ 48. $5000 \times 5 =$ _____

Fill in the blanks with the missing terms.

1. _____ + _____ = sum

2. _____ × _____ = product

3. dividend ÷ divisor = _____

Finish the equations to show the Commutative Property.

4. a + b = _____   5. a × b = _____

6. State the Commutative Property for addition
   and multiplication in your own words.

   _____

   _____

Finish the equations to show the Associative Property.

7. (a + b) + c = _____

8. (a × b) × c = _____

9. State the Associative Property for addition
   and multiplication in your own words.

   _____

   _____

Add or subtract.

10.
$$\begin{array}{r} 2793 \\ + 4125 \\ \hline \end{array}$$

11.
$$\begin{array}{r} \$3.49 \\ + \$2.79 \\ \hline \end{array}$$

12.
$$\begin{array}{r} 5463 \\ - 2575 \\ \hline \end{array}$$

13.
$$\begin{array}{r} 493 \\ - 198 \\ \hline \end{array}$$

Finish the equations to show the Distributive Property of Multiplication.

14. a × (b + c) = _____

15. 4 × (3 + 6) = _____

16. State the Identity Property of Addition and Subtraction in your own words.

_____

_____

17. State the Identity Property of Multiplication in your own words.

_____

_____

Multiply.

18.
$$\begin{array}{r} 7963 \\ \times\ \ \ \ 3 \\ \hline \end{array}$$

19.
$$\begin{array}{r} 27 \\ \times\ 45 \\ \hline \end{array}$$

20.
$$\begin{array}{r} \$\,5.99 \\ \times\ \ 20 \\ \hline \end{array}$$

21.
$$\begin{array}{r} 344 \\ \times\ \ 15 \\ \hline \end{array}$$

22. How many cents are there in 6 dimes? _____

23. How many days are in five weeks? _____

24. There were 14 warriors on the left and 23 warriors on the right. How many warriors were there altogether?

_____

25. James read 42 pages in the morning and 37 pages in the afternoon. How many pages did he read altogether?

_____

Write the divisibility rule for each of the numbers.

26. Divisible by 2 if: _____

27. Divisible by 3 if: _____

28. Divisible by 5 if: _____

29. Divisible by 9 if: _____

30. Divisible by 10 if: _____

31. Is it possible to divide a number by zero? _____

32. What do you get for a quotient when you divide a number by itself? _____

33. What answer would you get if you divided zero by one hundred? _____

34. What answer do you get if you multiply by zero? _____

Write two related division sentences for each multiplication sentence.

35. 5 × 4 = 20   _____   _____

36. 7 × 6 = 42   _____   _____

37. How many yards are in 2640 feet?   _____

Find the averages.

38. 45, 32, 64, 51, 23   39. 93, 72, 65, 86

168

Solve using the order of operations.

40. $6 \times 12 \div 9 + 8 - 4$

41. $24 \div 6 \times 8 - 10 - 1$

Solve for n.

42. $5 \times n = 45$

43. $48 \div n = 12$

44. $n \times 7 = 63$

45. There are 24 hours in a day. How many days are there in 288 hours? _____

Divide.

46. $2\overline{)348}$

47. $3\overline{)\$25.77}$

48. $9\overline{)6543}$

49. $24\overline{)768}$

50. $13\overline{)525}$

51. $61\overline{)4526}$

52. $34\overline{)\$26.86}$

53. $54\overline{)98,742}$

54. Able had 47 marbles. Baker had 36 marbles, and Charlie had 53 marbles. If they all lost all their marbles at the same time, how many marbles would they lose? _____

55. If the archer started with a quiver of 63 arrows and he shot 46 of them at various targets, how many arrows would he have left in this quiver?

56. The farmer planted 16 rows of corn in the field. In each row, there were 27 plants. Altogether, how many plants were in the cornfield?

169

Division Practice

Divide.

1. 22)910   2. 20)633   3. 50)677   4. 70)814

5. 19)411   6. 22)278   7. 62)699   8. 19)176

9. 38)760   10. 63)5321   11. 12)925   12. 16)289

13. 29)2983   14. 69)8280   15. 47)9655   16. 32)704

17. There were 2,304 potatoes in the pile. Each
    potato sack will hold 36 potatoes. How many
    sacks will we need to sack all the potatoes in the pile?   _____

18. If I distribute 884 shares equally among 26 students,
    how many shares will each student receive?   _____

READ – THINK – PLAN – EXECUTE

Problem Solving

1. Maryann received some money as a birthday present. She received $23 but spent $6. How much did she have left?

   _____

2. Sally paid $5 for a book about the Rosary and $3 for a scapular. How much did Sally spend?

   _____

3. Jacinta visited the Daughters of St. Paul book and film center. She bought a small statue of St. Joseph for her father, costing $11, a St. Joseph birthday card for $3, and some holy cards to use as bookmarks for $4. How much did Jacinta pay the sisters?

   _____

4. Frank's aunt went to Fatima last year. When she returned, she brought Frank some post cards. There were 79 in all, but he gave 27 away to his homeschooling friends. How many did Frank have left?

   _____

5. Timothy bought a rosary for his mother for $3 and one for his father for $5. Timothy gave the clerk a $10 bill. How much change did he receive?

   _____

6. By railroad, the trip between a certain two cities covers 2,873 miles. By airplane, the trip covers 2,536 miles. Which way is shorter?

   _____

7. Last year, Sister Maria's chickens laid 878 eggs
   and Sister Lucia's chickens laid 793 eggs.
   Which sister's chickens laid more eggs?

   _____

8. TAN Publishers is open 5 days a week for 6 hours a day.
   How many hours is TAN open each week?

   _____

9. When Jesus went to the wedding feast at Cana,
   there were six jugs of wine. Each jug held 9 gallons.
   How many gallons did all of the jugs hold?

   _____

10. Marie was saving nickels. She finally collected 12 nickels.
    How much money did she have?

   _____

11. Father bought sets of holy cards for the students in the
    Confirmation class. There were 12 holy cards in each set.
    If there were 9 students in the class, how many holy cards
    did the class receive?

   _____

12. One student decided to get the same 12-card sets for
    the 8 people in his family. How many cards did he buy?

   _____

Fractions

Fractions name part of something, for example, one-fourth $\frac{1}{4}$ of a figure or $\frac{1}{4}$ of a group.

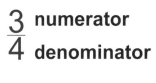

Since fractions are a part rather than a whole, they are not whole numbers. They are part of the set of *rational* numbers. Rational numbers are numbers that can be represented as a *ratio* of two integers.

You need not concern yourself with any of those terms right now.
We are simply going to be studying fractions.

A fraction is written with two numbers. The bottom number is called the **denominator**. It signifies how many equal parts are in the whole. The top number is the **numerator**. The numerator tells how *many* parts are being counted.

$\frac{3}{4}$ **numerator**
denominator

Do you remember the three ways to express division?

$$8 \div 4 = 2 \qquad 4\overline{)8} \; ^2 \qquad \frac{8}{4} = 2$$

Naturally, then, any of the rules and properties that apply to division, also apply to fractions. Let's look.

$n \div n = 1$	Any number divided by itself is one.	When the numerator and the denominator are the same, the number is one.	$\frac{n}{n} = 1$
$n \div 1 = n$	Any number divided by one is that number.	When the denominator is one, the number is the numerator.	$\frac{n}{1} = n$
$0 \div n = 0$	Zero divided by any number is still zero.	If the numerator is zero, the number is zero.	$\frac{0}{n} = 0$
n ÷ 0 = ?	Dividing by 0 is not allowed.	The denominator cannot be zero.	

Divide.

1. $\dfrac{8}{8} =$ _____

2. $\dfrac{8}{1} =$ _____

3. $\dfrac{0}{8} =$ _____

4. $\dfrac{0}{3} =$ _____

5. $\dfrac{3}{3} =$ _____

6. $\dfrac{3}{1} =$ _____

7. $\dfrac{12}{1} =$ _____

8. $\dfrac{0}{12} =$ _____

9. $\dfrac{12}{12} =$ _____

We have seen that when the numerator and the denominator are the same, the number is one.

$$1 = \tfrac{2}{2} = \tfrac{3}{3} = \tfrac{4}{4} = \tfrac{5}{5} = \tfrac{6}{6} = \tfrac{7}{7} = \tfrac{8}{8} = \tfrac{9}{9} = \tfrac{10}{10} = \tfrac{12}{12} = \tfrac{16}{16}$$

We also know that *multiplying or dividing a number by 1 does not change the number.* We can use these properties to change a particular fraction into another fraction that is equivalent. That means it is equal, but just appears in a different form. To obtain an equivalent fraction, we simply multiply or divide the original fraction by a fractional form of one. There are an infinite number of possibilities.

Study these examples where we multiply or divide the fraction by another fraction that is equal to one.

Multiply or divide each fraction by a form of 1 to obtain an equivalent fraction.

$$\dfrac{2 \times 2}{3 \times 2} = \dfrac{4}{6} \qquad \dfrac{7 \times 3}{8 \times 3} = \dfrac{21}{24} \qquad \dfrac{8 \div 4}{24 \div 4} = \dfrac{2}{6} \qquad \dfrac{30 \div 5}{40 \div 5} = \dfrac{6}{8}$$

Multiply or divide each fraction by a form of 1 to obtain an equivalent fraction.

1. $\dfrac{1 \times \rule{1cm}{0.4pt}}{3 \times \rule{1cm}{0.4pt}} =$ _____

2. $\dfrac{6 \div \rule{1cm}{0.4pt}}{12 \div \rule{1cm}{0.4pt}} =$ _____

3. $\dfrac{1}{4} \, \rule{1cm}{0.4pt} =$ _____

4. $\dfrac{2}{5} \, \rule{1cm}{0.4pt} =$ _____

5. $\dfrac{3}{4} \, \rule{1cm}{0.4pt} =$ _____

6. $\dfrac{5}{6} \, \rule{1cm}{0.4pt} =$ _____

7. $\dfrac{9}{10} \, \rule{1cm}{0.4pt} =$ _____

8. $\dfrac{6}{21} \, \rule{1cm}{0.4pt} =$ _____

9. $\dfrac{5}{50} \, \rule{1cm}{0.4pt} =$ _____

One of the ways equivalent fractions can help us is in reducing a fraction to its simplest form. *A fraction is in its simplest form when the only whole number that will divide the numerator and the denominator is 1.* Let's look at an example.

Change the fraction to its simplest form. The way that we do that is to divide both the numerator and the denominator by the same number.

$$\frac{12 \div 6}{18 \div 6} = \frac{2}{3}$$

Remember that $\frac{6}{6} = 1$ and dividing a number by 1 does not change the number. We have not changed $\frac{12}{18}$, we have simply renamed it.

Is $\frac{2}{3}$ in its simplest form? Yes, because the only whole number that will divide both the numerator and the denominator is 1.

In the above example, we could have divided by $\frac{3}{3}$ or by $\frac{2}{2}$. In that case, we would have obtained equivalent fractions of $\frac{4}{6}$ or $\frac{6}{9}$. Neither one of those fractions is in simplest form. We would have had to divide them again by a form of 1 to reduce them to simplest form.

$$\frac{4 \div 2}{6 \div 2} = \frac{2}{3} \qquad \frac{6 \div 3}{9 \div 3} = \frac{2}{3}$$

Study the examples.

Change each fraction to its simplest form.

$$\frac{4 \div 2}{6 \div 2} = \frac{2}{3} \qquad \frac{14 \div 2}{16 \div 2} = \frac{7}{8} \qquad \frac{3 \div 3}{24 \div 3} = \frac{1}{8} \qquad \frac{15 \div 5}{20 \div 5} = \frac{3}{4}$$

Try These

Change each fraction to its simplest form.

1. $\dfrac{14 \div \rule{1cm}{0.4pt}}{21 \div \rule{1cm}{0.4pt}} = \rule{1.5cm}{0.4pt}$ 　2. $\dfrac{6 \div \rule{1cm}{0.4pt}}{10 \div \rule{1cm}{0.4pt}} = \rule{1.5cm}{0.4pt}$ 　3. $\dfrac{10 \div \rule{1cm}{0.4pt}}{12 \div \rule{1cm}{0.4pt}} = \rule{1.5cm}{0.4pt}$

4. $\dfrac{8 \div \rule{1cm}{0.4pt}}{16 \div \rule{1cm}{0.4pt}} = \rule{1.5cm}{0.4pt}$ 　5. $\dfrac{12 \div \rule{1cm}{0.4pt}}{16 \div \rule{1cm}{0.4pt}} = \rule{1.5cm}{0.4pt}$ 　6. $\dfrac{6 \div \rule{1cm}{0.4pt}}{8 \div \rule{1cm}{0.4pt}} = \rule{1.5cm}{0.4pt}$

7. $\dfrac{10 \div \rule{1cm}{0.4pt}}{16 \div \rule{1cm}{0.4pt}} = \rule{1.5cm}{0.4pt}$ 　8. $\dfrac{12 \rule{1cm}{0.4pt}}{32 \rule{1cm}{0.4pt}} = \rule{1.5cm}{0.4pt}$ 　9. $\dfrac{8 \rule{1cm}{0.4pt}}{10 \rule{1cm}{0.4pt}} = \rule{1.5cm}{0.4pt}$

10. $\dfrac{4 \rule{1cm}{0.4pt}}{16 \rule{1cm}{0.4pt}} = \rule{1.5cm}{0.4pt}$ 　11. $\dfrac{12 \rule{1cm}{0.4pt}}{15 \rule{1cm}{0.4pt}} = \rule{1.5cm}{0.4pt}$ 　12. $\dfrac{18 \rule{1cm}{0.4pt}}{24 \rule{1cm}{0.4pt}} = \rule{1.5cm}{0.4pt}$

Factors are what we multiply together to get a product. *Common* factors would be the factors that 2 or more products have in *common*. The factors of 6, for example, are 1, 2, 3, 6. The factors of 12 are 1, 2, 3, 4, 6,12. The factors that 6 and 12 have in *common* are 1,2,3, 6. The greatest of the factors that 6 and 12 have in common is 6. Six is the **greatest common factor** of 6 and 12. When we reduce a fraction to its simplest form, we divide both the numerator and the denominator by the greatest common factor of both.

Factors of 8: 1, 2, 4, 8
Factors of 10: 1, 2, 5, 10

Greatest common factor (GCF): 2

List the factors of the numerator and the denominator, then write the greatest *common* factor (GCF), then divide the numerator and the denominator by the GCF in order to reduce the fraction to its simplest form.

Example:

$$\frac{16}{24} \quad \frac{1,2,4,8,16}{1,2,3,4,6,8,12,24} \quad GCF = 8 \quad \frac{16 \div 8}{24 \div 8} = \frac{2}{3}$$

Try These

List the factors of the numerator and the denominator, then write the greatest common factor (GCF), then divide the numerator and the denominator by the GCF in order to reduce the fraction to its simplest form.

1. $\frac{6}{12}$ _____ GCF = _____ $\frac{6}{12} \div \frac{}{} =$ _____

2. $\frac{3}{18}$ _____ GCF = _____ $\frac{3}{18} \div \frac{}{} =$ _____

3. $\frac{16}{24}$ _____ GCF = _____ $\frac{16}{24} \div \frac{}{} =$ _____

List all the factors of each.

1. 9 _____

2. 14 _____

3. 12 _____

4. 24 _____

5. 27 _____

6. 36 _____

Find the GCF for each pair of numbers.

7. 8 and 10 _____

8. 8 and 9 _____

9. 12 and 15 _____

10. 10 and 20 _____

11. 6 and 18 _____

12. 12 and 16 _____

Reduce each fraction to its simplest form.

13. $\dfrac{4}{16}$ _____

14. $\dfrac{12}{15}$ _____

15. $\dfrac{4}{24}$ _____

16. $\dfrac{4}{8}$ _____

17. $\dfrac{10}{25}$ _____

18. $\dfrac{12}{28}$ _____

19. $\dfrac{20}{36}$ _____

20. $\dfrac{24}{32}$ _____

21. $\dfrac{21}{35}$ _____

Facts Review

Add.

1. $\begin{array}{r} 1 \\ +9 \\ \hline \end{array}$
2. $\begin{array}{r} 8 \\ +6 \\ \hline \end{array}$
3. $\begin{array}{r} 5 \\ +4 \\ \hline \end{array}$
4. $\begin{array}{r} 2 \\ +9 \\ \hline \end{array}$
5. $\begin{array}{r} 7 \\ +2 \\ \hline \end{array}$
6. $\begin{array}{r} 4 \\ +7 \\ \hline \end{array}$

7. $\begin{array}{r} 1 \\ +1 \\ \hline \end{array}$
8. $\begin{array}{r} 1 \\ +8 \\ \hline \end{array}$
9. $\begin{array}{r} 4 \\ +1 \\ \hline \end{array}$
10. $\begin{array}{r} 7 \\ +6 \\ \hline \end{array}$
11. $\begin{array}{r} 0 \\ +9 \\ \hline \end{array}$
12. $\begin{array}{r} 7 \\ +3 \\ \hline \end{array}$

Subtract.

13. $\begin{array}{r} 9 \\ -8 \\ \hline \end{array}$
14. $\begin{array}{r} 5 \\ -2 \\ \hline \end{array}$
15. $\begin{array}{r} 10 \\ -3 \\ \hline \end{array}$
16. $\begin{array}{r} 8 \\ -3 \\ \hline \end{array}$
17. $\begin{array}{r} 11 \\ -7 \\ \hline \end{array}$
18. $\begin{array}{r} 15 \\ -9 \\ \hline \end{array}$

19. $\begin{array}{r} 13 \\ -6 \\ \hline \end{array}$
20. $\begin{array}{r} 12 \\ -8 \\ \hline \end{array}$
21. $\begin{array}{r} 14 \\ -9 \\ \hline \end{array}$
22. $\begin{array}{r} 11 \\ -9 \\ \hline \end{array}$
23. $\begin{array}{r} 12 \\ -6 \\ \hline \end{array}$
24. $\begin{array}{r} 14 \\ -7 \\ \hline \end{array}$

Multiply.

25. $\begin{array}{r} 5 \\ \times 1 \\ \hline \end{array}$
26. $\begin{array}{r} 6 \\ \times 4 \\ \hline \end{array}$
27. $\begin{array}{r} 8 \\ \times 4 \\ \hline \end{array}$
28. $\begin{array}{r} 0 \\ \times 4 \\ \hline \end{array}$
29. $\begin{array}{r} 9 \\ \times 6 \\ \hline \end{array}$
30. $\begin{array}{r} 3 \\ \times 8 \\ \hline \end{array}$

31. $\begin{array}{r} 7 \\ \times 9 \\ \hline \end{array}$
32. $\begin{array}{r} 4 \\ \times 8 \\ \hline \end{array}$
33. $\begin{array}{r} 9 \\ \times 9 \\ \hline \end{array}$
34. $\begin{array}{r} 4 \\ \times 5 \\ \hline \end{array}$
35. $\begin{array}{r} 5 \\ \times 8 \\ \hline \end{array}$
36. $\begin{array}{r} 7 \\ \times 5 \\ \hline \end{array}$

Divide.

37. $2\overline{)6}$
38. $5\overline{)35}$
39. $2\overline{)8}$
40. $8\overline{)0}$
41. $2\overline{)2}$
42. $7\overline{)63}$

43. $5\overline{)30}$
44. $5\overline{)45}$
45. $8\overline{)18}$
46. $3\overline{)12}$
47. $6\overline{)54}$
48. $7\overline{)14}$

Prime Numbers

A prime number is a whole number that has *exactly* two factors, 1 and the number itself. A composite number has more than two factors. There are 25 prime numbers between 1 and 100. There is a fairly straightforward way to identify the prime numbers from 1 to 100. The first four prime numbers are 2, 3, 5, and 7. The first four prime numbers are circled in the chart below. Follow the instructions to identify the rest of the prime numbers through 100.

1	2	3	4	5	6	7	8	9	10
11	12	13	14	15	16	17	18	19	20
21	22	23	24	25	26	27	28	29	30
31	32	33	34	35	36	37	38	39	40
41	42	43	44	45	46	47	48	49	50
51	52	53	54	55	56	57	58	59	60
61	62	63	64	65	66	67	68	69	70
71	72	73	74	75	76	77	78	79	80
81	82	83	84	85	86	87	88	89	90
91	92	93	94	95	96	97	98	99	100

Cross out all the multiples of 2. (the even numbers)

Cross out all the multiples of 3 or, if you prefer, all the numbers evenly divisible by 3.

Cross out all the multiples of 5. (numbers ending in 0 or 5)

Cross out all the multiples of 7. You may find it easier to first make a list of the multiples of 7 and then go through the chart, crossing out.

Circle what you have left on the chart and these will be the 25 prime numbers between 1 and 100.

Check your answers with the list below.

Prime Numbers Between 1 and 100

2, 3, 5, 7, 11, 13, 17, 19, 23, 29, 31, 37, 41, 43, 47, 53, 59, 61, 67, 71, 73, 79, 83, 89, 97

Every composite number can be expressed as the product of prime factors.

This prime factorization of a number can be useful in simplifying fractions.

You can use a factor tree to help you find all the prime factors of a composite number. We start with a composite number and then branch by branch we write the factors of the number. When a branch comes to a prime factor, that branch ends. If the branch is another composite number, we write the factors for that number and so on and so forth until every branch ends in a prime factor.

Examine the factor trees below.

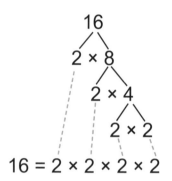

$16 = 2 \times 2 \times 2 \times 2$

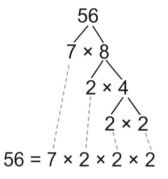

$56 = 7 \times 2 \times 2 \times 2$

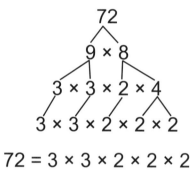

$72 = 3 \times 3 \times 2 \times 2 \times 2$

Let's try one.

Write the prime factorization for 60.

Think of a pair of factors for 60, such as 2 × 30, or 4 × 15, or 6 × 10.

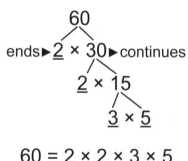

$60 = 2 \times 2 \times 3 \times 5$

The 2 is a prime factor, so that branch will end, and we continue with the composite factor branch by thinking of two more factors: 2 × 15

The 2 is again a prime factor, and that branch ends, and we think of 2 more factors for the composite factor: 3 × 5

Both 3 and 5 are prime so all our branches have ended in prime numbers. We just write them down in order from least to greatest and our factorization is complete.

Other possibilities:

$$\begin{array}{c} 60 \\ 4 \times 15 \\ 2 \times 2 \quad 3 \times 5 \end{array}$$

$$\begin{array}{c} 60 \\ 6 \times 10 \\ 2 \times 3 \quad 2 \times 5 \end{array}$$

$$\begin{array}{c} 60 \\ 3 \times 20 \\ 4 \times 5 \\ 2 \times 2 \end{array}$$

$$\begin{array}{c} 60 \\ 5 \times 12 \\ 3 \times 4 \\ 2 \times 2 \end{array}$$

Another method for determining the prime factorization of a number is called division by primes. As the name implies, this method involves dividing the composite number by only prime numbers. Unlike the factor tree, division by primes requires that each factor by which we divide must be a prime number.

For example, if we are trying to find the prime factorization of 60, we could not start by dividing by 4 or by 6 or by 10 or by 12, because they are not prime numbers. We would have to start with a prime number. It is best to start with the lowest possible prime number. The three lowest prime numbers are 2, 3, and 5. We will start with those.

We write the 60 and then put a partial box (like a division sign or the corner of a rectangle) around the 60.

$$\overline{)60} \quad \text{or} \quad \underline{|60\ }$$

Then we try dividing by the lowest prime number, which is 2.

We can either stack up or step down.

$$\frac{30}{2\overline{)60}} \quad \text{or} \quad \frac{2|60\ }{30}$$

The quotient is 30.
We have a quotient of 30 and we again divide by 2.

$$\frac{15}{2\overline{)30}} \qquad \frac{2|60\ }{\frac{2|30\ }{15}}$$
$$2\overline{)60}$$

Now we have a quotient of 15.

We continue to divide each quotient by prime numbers until we arrive at a quotient that is also a prime number.

15 is not a prime number, so we must divide by a prime number. We divide 15 by another prime number, which is 3.

Now we have a quotient of 5.
It is a prime number and we are done.
We have the prime factorization.
Write it down.

$$\frac{5}{3\overline{)15}} \qquad \frac{2|60\ }{\frac{2|30\ }{\frac{3|15\ }{5}}}$$
$$2\overline{)30}$$
$$2\overline{)60}$$

$$60 = 2 \times 2 \times 3 \times 5$$

Below are some examples of the division-by-primes method of determining the prime factorization. Study the examples.

Division by primes (step down)

$$\frac{2|16\ }{\frac{2|8\ }{\frac{2|4\ }{2}}} \qquad \frac{2|56\ }{\frac{2|28\ }{\frac{2|14\ }{7}}} \qquad \frac{2|72\ }{\frac{2|36\ }{\frac{2|18\ }{\frac{3|9\ }{3}}}}$$

$$16 = 2 \times 2 \times 2 \times 2 \qquad 56 = 2 \times 2 \times 2 \times 7 \qquad 72 = 2 \times 2 \times 2 \times 3 \times 3$$

181

Division by primes (stack up)

$$
\begin{array}{r}
2 \\
\hline
2\,)\,4 \\
2\,)\,8 \\
2\,)\,16 \\
\end{array}
\qquad
\begin{array}{r}
7 \\
\hline
2\,)\,14 \\
2\,)\,28 \\
2\,)\,56 \\
\end{array}
\qquad
\begin{array}{r}
3 \\
\hline
3\,)\,9 \\
2\,)\,18 \\
2\,)\,36 \\
2\,)\,72 \\
\end{array}
$$

16 = 2 × 2 × 2 × 2   56 = 2 × 2 × 2 × 7   72 = 2 × 2 × 2 × 3 × 3

Try These

Write the prime factorization for each. Use either method.

1. 24 _____

2. 27 _____

3. 36 _____

4. 54 _____

5. 40 _____

6. 32 _____

7. 20 _____

8. 48 _____

9. 12 _____

We can use prime factorization to help us reduce fractions to their simplest form. We remember a few things we have learned:

Recall the Identity Property of Multiplication (One) on page 64.

Multiplying a number by 1 does not change the number.

Also, on page 110:

Any number divided by itself is one.

And on page 173:

When the numerator and the denominator are the same, the number is one.

These principles, along with prime factorization, help us to reduce fractions to their simplest form. It is sometimes referred to as "canceling" or "canceling out."

Here are the steps for this way of reducing fractions to their simplest form.

1. Find the prime factorization for the numerator and the denominator

2. Rewrite the fraction as the prime factorization.

3. Eliminate the fractions that are equal to one.

4. What remains is the simplified form of the original fraction.

Let's go through an example.

Reduce the fraction to simplest form using prime factorization. $\dfrac{16}{48}$

The first step is to find the prime factorization of the numerator and the denominator.

$16 = 2 \times 2 \times 2 \times 2$

$48 = 2 \times 2 \times 2 \times 2 \times 3$

Then rewrite the fraction as the prime factorization.

$$\dfrac{16}{48} = \dfrac{2 \times 2 \times 2 \times 2}{2 \times 2 \times 2 \times 2 \times 3}$$

Eliminate the fractions that are equal to one.

$$\dfrac{2 \times 2 \times 2 \times 2}{2 \times 2 \times 2 \times 2 \times 3} = \dfrac{1 \times 1 \times 1 \times 1}{1 \times 1 \times 1 \times 1 \times 3} = \dfrac{1}{3}$$

What remains is the simplified form of the original fraction. $= \dfrac{1}{3}$

Look at another example.

$$\dfrac{12}{18} = \dfrac{2 \times 2 \times 3}{2 \times 3 \times 3} = \dfrac{2 \times 2 \times 3}{2 \times 3 \times 3} = \dfrac{1 \times 2 \times 1}{1 \times 3 \times 1} = \dfrac{2}{3} = \dfrac{2}{3}$$

Study the examples.

Reduce the fractions to simplest form using prime factorization.

$$\dfrac{4}{8} = \dfrac{2 \times 2}{2 \times 2 \times 2} = \dfrac{1}{2} = \dfrac{1}{2} \qquad\qquad \dfrac{3}{18} = \dfrac{3}{2 \times 3 \times 3} = \dfrac{1}{6}$$

Exercise
_____

Reduce the fractions to simplest form using prime factorization.

1. $\dfrac{16}{24} =$ _____   2. $\dfrac{9}{99} =$ _____   3. $\dfrac{18}{72} =$ _____

4. $\dfrac{27}{36} =$ _____   5. $\dfrac{26}{52} =$ _____   6. $\dfrac{16}{48} =$ _____

Change each fraction to its simplest form. You may use any means.

7. $\frac{40}{100} =$ _____

8. $\frac{9}{18} =$ _____

9. $\frac{24}{48} =$ _____

10. $\frac{14}{21} =$ _____

11. $\frac{8}{64} =$ _____

12. $\frac{6}{21} =$ _____

13. $\frac{12}{30} =$ _____

14. $\frac{15}{18} =$ _____

15. $\frac{16}{24} =$ _____

16. $\frac{15}{35} =$ _____

17. $\frac{42}{49} =$ _____

18. $\frac{24}{30} =$ _____

Write the prime factorization for each. Use either method.

19. 81 _____

20. 64 _____

21. 52 _____

22. 51 _____

23. 33 _____

24. 99 _____

Find the GCF for each pair of numbers.

25. 8 and 12 _____

26. 18 and 36 _____

27. 12 and 48 _____

28. 14 and 63 _____

READ – THINK – PLAN – EXECUTE

Problem Solving

1. Four hundred and twenty-four people need seats at the reception. Eight people can be seated at each table. How many tables are needed?

   _____

2. Susan sold 75 tickets at $2.35 each for the baseball game. How much did she collect for the tickets?

   _____

3. My father drove 3276 miles in six months traveling to various pro-life conferences. How many miles did he average each month?

   _____

4. Peter went out and caught 56 fish in his net. When he returned to shore, he distributed his catch equally among seven boys for their families. How many fish did each boy receive?

   _____

5. Sister read on the outside of the box of books that the total weight of the box was 56 pounds. If the box contained 14 identical books, how much did each book weigh?

   _____

6. Mary had 96 scapulars she wanted to package in 6 small boxes. How many scapulars should she put in each box?

   _____

7. Mr. Douglas drives 437 miles each week. How many miles does he drive in seven weeks?

   _____

Exercise

Reduce the fractions to simplest form.

1. $\dfrac{16}{20} =$ _____   2. $\dfrac{12}{16} =$ _____   3. $\dfrac{8}{32} =$ _____

4. $\dfrac{3}{12} =$ _____   5. $\dfrac{20}{24} =$ _____   6. $\dfrac{6}{18} =$ _____

7. $\dfrac{6}{9} =$ _____   8. $\dfrac{5}{15} =$ _____   9. $\dfrac{4}{12} =$ _____

10. $\dfrac{8}{16} =$ _____   11. $\dfrac{5}{10} =$ _____   12. $\dfrac{8}{12} =$ _____

13. $\dfrac{3}{15} =$ _____   14. $\dfrac{6}{8} =$ _____   15. $\dfrac{20}{25} =$ _____

16. $\dfrac{2}{6} =$ _____   17. $\dfrac{4}{20} =$ _____   18. $\dfrac{3}{9} =$ _____

19. $\dfrac{10}{20} =$ _____   20. $\dfrac{2}{4} =$ _____   21. $\dfrac{3}{6} =$ _____

Multiply.

1. 4306
   × 9

2. 86
   × 27

3. $ 8.96
   × 75

4. 507
   × 37

Add or subtract.

5. 3129
   + 5986

6. $9.99
   + 4.49

7. 6247
   − 2389

8. 600
   − 289

Solve for n.

9. 6 × n = 72

10. 54 ÷ n = 9

11. n × 3 = 36

Divide.

12. 7)895

13. 7)$34.93

14. 4)1824

15. 22)489

16. 11)375

17. 37)1349

18. 19)$38.19

19. 62)25,358

Solve using the order of operations.

20. 64 ÷ 8 × 2 + 50 + 137

21. 30 + 20 − 25 ÷ 5 × 5

Finding Equivalent Fractions

To find an equivalent fraction, we multiply the numerator and the denominator by the same number.

$$\frac{3}{4} \times \frac{5}{5} = \frac{15}{20}$$

To obtain a *particular* equivalent fraction, we must select a *particular* form of one.

$$\frac{3}{4} = \frac{?}{12} \qquad\qquad \frac{3}{4} \times \frac{3}{3} = \frac{9}{12}$$

We select the fraction $\frac{3}{3}$ so that when we multiply, we will get the denominator of 12. Then multiply the numerators and we have the completed equivalent fraction that we were searching for.

Study the examples.

$\frac{1}{3} = \frac{?}{9}$	$\frac{2}{4} = \frac{4}{?}$	$\frac{2}{5} = \frac{?}{20}$	$\frac{3}{7} = \frac{15}{?}$
$\frac{1}{3} \times \frac{3}{3} = \frac{3}{9}$	$\frac{2}{4} \times \frac{2}{2} = \frac{4}{8}$	$\frac{2}{5} \times \frac{4}{4} = \frac{8}{20}$	$\frac{3}{7} \times \frac{5}{5} = \frac{15}{35}$
$\frac{1}{3} = \frac{3}{9}$	$\frac{2}{4} = \frac{4}{8}$	$\frac{2}{5} = \frac{8}{20}$	$\frac{3}{7} = \frac{15}{35}$

Try These

Find the missing parts.

1. $\frac{4}{6} = \frac{?}{12}$ _____

2. $\frac{3}{4} = \frac{?}{8}$ _____

3. $\frac{1}{5} = \frac{?}{25}$ _____

4. $\frac{2}{6} = \frac{?}{18}$ _____

5. $\frac{3}{7} = \frac{?}{14}$ _____

6. $\frac{3}{10} = \frac{?}{20}$ _____

7. $\frac{2}{3} = \frac{?}{9}$ _____

8. $\frac{2}{6} = \frac{?}{12}$ _____

9. $\frac{4}{8} = \frac{?}{24}$ _____

Exercise

Find the missing parts.

1. $\dfrac{3}{4} = \dfrac{?}{12}$ _____

2. $\dfrac{4}{7} = \dfrac{?}{14}$ _____

3. $\dfrac{1}{4} = \dfrac{?}{8}$ _____

4. $\dfrac{2}{3} = \dfrac{?}{12}$ _____

5. $\dfrac{3}{4} = \dfrac{?}{16}$ _____

6. $\dfrac{5}{24} = \dfrac{?}{72}$ _____

7. $\dfrac{1}{6} = \dfrac{?}{24}$ _____

8. $\dfrac{4}{5} = \dfrac{?}{30}$ _____

9. $\dfrac{1}{9} = \dfrac{?}{45}$ _____

Reduce the fractions to simplest form.

10. $\dfrac{8}{12} =$ _____

11. $\dfrac{7}{21} =$ _____

12. $\dfrac{8}{20} =$ _____

Write each as a whole number.

13. $\dfrac{8}{1} =$ _____

14. $\dfrac{0}{8} =$ _____

15. $\dfrac{8}{8} =$ _____

Find the GCF for each pair of numbers.

16. 4 and 12 _____

17. 6 and 8 _____

Write the prime factorization for each.

18. 123 _____

19. 68 _____

20. 80 _____

Comparing Fractions

To compare fractions with the same denominator, we simply compare the numerators. If the denominators are the same then the fraction with the larger numerator will be the greater fraction.

Compare: $\frac{3}{5}$ __?__ $\frac{4}{5}$ The denominators are the same, so we compare the numerators. $3 < 4$ so: $\frac{3}{5}$ __<__ $\frac{4}{5}$

If we are comparing two fractions whose denominators are not the same, we must first rename the fractions as equivalent fractions with denominators that are the same.

Compare: $\frac{2}{3}$ __?__ $\frac{6}{9}$

$$\frac{2}{3} \times \frac{3}{3} = \frac{6}{9}$$

$$\frac{6}{9} = \frac{6}{9}$$

$6 = 6$ $\frac{6}{9} = \frac{6}{9}$

$$\frac{2}{3} \underline{\;=\;} \frac{6}{9}$$

The denominators are not the same, so we must first rename as equivalent fractions with the same denominators. Then we can compare the numerators.

Study the examples.

Compare.

$\frac{2}{3}$ ___ $\frac{3}{5}$	$\frac{1}{3}$ ___ $\frac{3}{12}$	$\frac{5}{6}$ ___ $\frac{4}{5}$	$\frac{3}{8}$ ___ $\frac{5}{6}$
$\frac{2}{3} \times \frac{5}{5} = \frac{10}{15}$	$\frac{1}{3} \times \frac{4}{4} = \frac{4}{12}$	$\frac{5}{6} \times \frac{5}{5} = \frac{25}{30}$	$\frac{3}{8} \times \frac{3}{3} = \frac{9}{24}$
$\frac{3}{5} \times \frac{3}{3} = \frac{9}{15}$	$\frac{3}{12} = \frac{3}{12}$	$\frac{4}{5} \times \frac{6}{6} = \frac{24}{30}$	$\frac{5}{6} \times \frac{4}{4} = \frac{20}{24}$
$10 > 9$ $\frac{10}{15} > \frac{9}{15}$	$4 > 3$ $\frac{4}{12} > \frac{3}{12}$	$25 > 24$ $\frac{25}{30} > \frac{24}{30}$	$9 < 24$ $\frac{9}{24} < \frac{20}{24}$
$\frac{2}{3} \underline{\;>\;} \frac{3}{5}$	$\frac{1}{3} \underline{\;>\;} \frac{3}{12}$	$\frac{5}{6} \underline{\;>\;} \frac{4}{5}$	$\frac{3}{8} \underline{\;<\;} \frac{5}{6}$

Exercise

Compare. Write < or >. (Note: Many of these can be done mentally.)

1. $\dfrac{5}{8}$ ____ $\dfrac{3}{4}$

2. $\dfrac{3}{4}$ ____ $\dfrac{4}{5}$

3. $\dfrac{2}{3}$ ____ $\dfrac{3}{4}$

4. $\dfrac{3}{5}$ ____ $\dfrac{5}{6}$

5. $\dfrac{7}{9}$ ____ $\dfrac{2}{3}$

6. $\dfrac{2}{3}$ ____ $\dfrac{3}{12}$

7. $\dfrac{3}{4}$ ____ $\dfrac{5}{6}$

8. $\dfrac{5}{8}$ ____ $\dfrac{2}{3}$

9. $\dfrac{7}{8}$ ____ $\dfrac{8}{10}$

10. $\dfrac{3}{5}$ ____ $\dfrac{2}{8}$

11. $\dfrac{3}{5}$ ____ $\dfrac{2}{3}$

12. $\dfrac{4}{5}$ ____ $\dfrac{3}{5}$

13. $\dfrac{2}{3}$ ____ $\dfrac{5}{7}$

14. $\dfrac{2}{5}$ ____ $\dfrac{3}{7}$

15. $\dfrac{2}{13}$ ____ $\dfrac{1}{5}$

16. $\dfrac{2}{7}$ ____ $\dfrac{1}{5}$

17. $\dfrac{2}{11}$ ____ $\dfrac{1}{5}$

18. $\dfrac{1}{3}$ ____ $\dfrac{3}{7}$

Find the missing part.

19. $\dfrac{5}{9} = \dfrac{?}{27}$ _____

20. $\dfrac{6}{8} = \dfrac{18}{?}$ _____

21. $\dfrac{4}{5} = \dfrac{?}{20}$ _____

Reduce the fractions to simplest form.

22. $\dfrac{9}{12} =$ _____

23. $\dfrac{4}{24} =$ _____

24. $\dfrac{2}{16} =$ _____

Write each as a whole number.

25. $\dfrac{5}{5}$ = _____

26. $\dfrac{5}{1}$ = _____

27. $\dfrac{0}{5}$ = _____

Find the GCF for each pair of numbers.

28. 8 and 12 _____

29. 7 and 21 _____

Write the prime factorization for each.

30. 36 _____

31. 45 _____

32. 55 _____

Find the averages.

33. 74, 79, 81, 82, 84

34. 31, 28, 31

Write each number in expanded notation.

35. 90,303

_____

36. 75,260,080

_____

Write each of the following in standard form.

37. MDCLXVI _____

38. CCXXIV _____

Problem Solving

1. Father Mark is doing missionary work in Nigeria.
    He uses his motorcycle to travel from one village to another.
    He has been traveling 135 miles a week for the past 9 weeks.
    How many miles has he traveled?

    _____

2. David's father works 40 hours each week.
    How many hours does he work in 50 weeks?

    _____

3. David made $320 a week last year.
    In 50 weeks, how much did he earn?

    _____

4. For 27 weeks, Mary earned $56 each week at
    her part-time job. How much did Mary earn altogether?

    _____

5. Martha paid $5.55 to bowl 3 games.
    How much is each game?

    _____

6. If a car can travel 432 miles on 12 gallons of gas,
    how far does it go for each gallon?

    _____

7. If a pilgrim can walk 117 miles in 9 days,
    what is her average miles per day?

    _____

8. If a car travels 434 miles in 7 hours,
    what is its average miles per hour?

    _____

Unit Fractions

A unit fraction is a fraction with a numerator of one. To find one part of a number, we multiply and then divide.

Find $\frac{1}{12}$ of 180. We first write 180 as a fraction. $\frac{180}{1}$

Then we multiply. $\frac{1}{12} \times \frac{180}{1} = \frac{180}{12}$

Then we divide. $\frac{180}{12} = 12\overline{)180} = 12\overline{)180}$

$$\frac{180}{12} = 12\overline{)180} = \begin{array}{r} 15 \\ 12\overline{)180} \\ \underline{120} \\ 60 \\ \underline{60} \\ 0 \end{array}$$

$\frac{1}{12}$ of 180 = 15

When multiplying by a unit fraction, you may take a shortcut and just immediately divide the number by the denominator, if you wish. Many of the problems of this type can be solved mentally, if you know your facts.

Study the examples.

Find each part.

$\frac{1}{15}$ of 750	$\frac{1}{7}$ of 84 $\quad$ 7×12=84	$\frac{1}{6}$ of 96	$\frac{1}{3}$ of 672
$\frac{1}{15} \times \frac{750}{1} = \frac{750}{15}$	$\frac{1}{7} \times \frac{84}{1} = \frac{84}{7}$	$\frac{1}{6} \times \frac{96}{1} = \frac{96}{6}$	$\frac{1}{3} \times \frac{672}{1} = \frac{672}{3}$
$\frac{750}{15} = 15\overline{)750}$	$\frac{84}{7} = 7\overline{)84}$	$\frac{96}{6} = 6\overline{)96}$	$\frac{672}{3} = 3\overline{)672}$
$\begin{array}{r} 50 \\ 15\overline{)750} \\ \underline{750} \\ 0 \end{array}$	$\begin{array}{r} 12 \\ 7\overline{)84} \\ \underline{70} \\ 14 \\ \underline{14} \\ 0 \end{array}$	$\begin{array}{r} 16 \\ 6\overline{)96} \\ \underline{60} \\ 36 \\ \underline{36} \\ 0 \end{array}$	$\begin{array}{r} 224 \\ 3\overline{)672} \\ \underline{600} \\ 72 \\ \underline{60} \\ 12 \\ \underline{12} \\ 0 \end{array}$
$\frac{1}{15}$ of 750 = 50	$\frac{1}{7}$ of 84 = 12	$\frac{1}{6}$ of 96 = 16	$\frac{1}{3}$ of 672 = 224

Exercise

Find each part. (Note: Use the facts to solve mentally when possible.)

1. $\frac{1}{2}$ of 56

2. $\frac{1}{3}$ of 48

3. $\frac{1}{16}$ of 608

4. $\frac{1}{6}$ of 156

5. $\frac{1}{8}$ of 16

6. $\frac{1}{5}$ of 15

7. $\frac{1}{6}$ of 24

8. $\frac{1}{3}$ of 87

9. $\frac{1}{4}$ of 96

10. $\frac{1}{5}$ of 65

11. $\frac{1}{7}$ of 42

12. $\frac{1}{4}$ of 36

13. $\frac{1}{9}$ of 36

14. $\frac{1}{12}$ of 216

15. $\frac{1}{12}$ of 72

16. $\frac{1}{5}$ of 30

17. $\frac{1}{10}$ of 90

18. $\frac{1}{3}$ of 924

19. $\frac{1}{8}$ of 24

20. $\frac{1}{4}$ of 20

21. $\frac{1}{5}$ of 50

Compare. Write <, = , or >.

22. $\frac{2}{11}$ _____ $\frac{1}{7}$

23. $\frac{1}{3}$ _____ $\frac{2}{5}$

24. $\frac{1}{5}$ _____ $\frac{3}{11}$

Find the missing parts.

25. $\frac{5}{12} = \frac{?}{72}$ _____

26. $\frac{3}{10} = \frac{6}{?}$ _____

27. $\frac{2}{3} = \frac{?}{18}$ _____

Reduce the fractions to simplest form.

28. $\frac{2}{6} =$ _____

29. $\frac{6}{18} =$ _____

30. $\frac{2}{12} =$ _____

31. $\frac{15}{25} =$ _____

32. $\frac{8}{12} =$ _____

33. $\frac{4}{16} =$ _____

34. $\frac{16}{24} =$ _____

35. $\frac{14}{16} =$ _____

36. $\frac{4}{8} =$ _____

Write each as a whole number.

37. $\frac{11}{1} =$ _____

38. $\frac{3}{1} =$ _____

39. $\frac{4}{4} =$ _____

Find the GCF for each pair of numbers.

40. 5 and 10 _____

41. 3 and 9 _____

Write the prime factorization for each.

42. 77 _____

43. 26 _____

44. 51 _____

Finding a Fraction of a Number

To find a fraction of a number, we follow the same procedure as we did to find one part of a number. To find a fraction of a number, we change the number to fractional form and then we multiply and then divide.

Find $\frac{3}{5}$ of 365. We first write 365 as a fraction.

$\frac{365}{1}$ Then we multiply. $\frac{3}{5} \times \frac{365}{1} = \frac{1095}{5}$

Then we divide. $\frac{1095}{5}$ $=$ $5\overline{)1095}$

$$\begin{array}{r} 219 \\ 5\overline{)1095} \\ \underline{1000} \\ 95 \\ \underline{50} \\ 45 \\ \underline{45} \\ 0 \end{array}$$

$\frac{3}{5}$ of 365 = 219

Study the examples. Many of the problems of this type can be solved mentally, if you know your facts.

Find each part.

$\frac{4}{15}$ of 750	$\frac{3}{7}$ of 84	$\frac{5}{6}$ of 96	$\frac{2}{3}$ of 672

$\frac{4}{15} \times \frac{750}{1} = \frac{3000}{15}$ $\frac{3}{7} \times \frac{84}{1} = \frac{252}{7}$ $\frac{5}{6} \times \frac{96}{1} = \frac{480}{6}$ $\frac{2}{3} \times \frac{672}{1} = \frac{1344}{3}$

$\frac{3000}{15} = 15\overline{)3000}$ $\frac{252}{7} = 7\overline{)252}$ $\frac{480}{6} = 6\overline{)480}$ $\frac{1344}{3} = 3\overline{)1344}$

$$\begin{array}{r} 200 \\ 15\overline{)3000} \\ \underline{3000} \\ 0 \end{array} \quad \begin{array}{r} 36 \\ 7\overline{)252} \\ \underline{210} \\ 42 \\ \underline{42} \\ 0 \end{array} \quad \begin{array}{r} 80 \\ 6\overline{)480} \\ \underline{480} \\ 0 \end{array} \quad \begin{array}{r} 448 \\ 3\overline{)1344} \\ \underline{1200} \\ 144 \\ \underline{120} \\ 24 \\ \underline{24} \\ 0 \end{array}$$

$\frac{4}{15}$ of 750 = 200 $\frac{3}{7}$ of 84 = 36 $\frac{5}{6}$ of 96 = 80 $\frac{2}{3}$ of 672 = 448

Exercise

Find each part.   (Note: Use the facts to solve mentally when possible.)

1. $\frac{2}{3}$ of 150

2. $\frac{3}{4}$ of 84

3. $\frac{5}{6}$ of 126

4. $\frac{2}{3}$ of 5280

5. $\frac{2}{5}$ of 65

6. $\frac{4}{11}$ of 121

7. $\frac{5}{9}$ of 90

8. $\frac{2}{3}$ of 42

9. $\frac{3}{5}$ of 140

10. $\frac{2}{3}$ of 57

11. $\frac{5}{8}$ of 64

12. $\frac{2}{3}$ of 51

13. $\frac{5}{6}$ of 54

14. $\frac{4}{5}$ of 585

15. $\frac{4}{5}$ of 25

16. $\frac{7}{12}$ of 144

17. $\frac{3}{4}$ of 80

18. $\frac{5}{7}$ of 49

19. $\frac{1}{2}$ of 96

20. $\frac{1}{3}$ of 5280

21. $\frac{1}{3}$ of 51

22. One fifth of the 35 students in the class scored above ninety percent.
How many students scored above ninety percent? _____

23. How many students did not score above ninety percent? _____

24. The ushers counted 564 people at the noon Mass. One third of them were adults. How many were children? _____

Compare. Write <, =, or >.

25. $\dfrac{1}{3}$ ___ $\dfrac{2}{7}$

26. $\dfrac{2}{11}$ ___ $\dfrac{3}{13}$

27. $\dfrac{2}{5}$ ___ $\dfrac{3}{11}$

Find the missing parts.

28. $\dfrac{3}{8} = \dfrac{?}{16}$ _____

29. $\dfrac{5}{9} = \dfrac{?}{54}$ _____

30. $\dfrac{3}{16} = \dfrac{?}{96}$ _____

Reduce the fractions to simplest form.

31. $\dfrac{5}{10} =$ _____

32. $\dfrac{4}{10} =$ _____

33. $\dfrac{2}{16} =$ _____

34. $\dfrac{6}{14} =$ _____

35. $\dfrac{4}{6} =$ _____

36. $\dfrac{2}{20} =$ _____

Find the GCF for each pair of numbers.

37. 20 and 36 _____

38. 6 and 14 _____

Write the prime factorization for each.

39. 66 _____

40. 130 _____

41. 105 _____

Mixed Numbers and Improper Fractions

A mixed number is a number with two parts. One part is a whole number and the other part is a fraction.

An improper fraction is a fraction that is greater than or equal to 1. Its numerator is greater than or equal to its denominator.

$$3\frac{2}{3}$$

mixed number

$$\frac{11}{3}$$

improper fraction

To convert a mixed number to an improper fraction we use three steps:

1. Multiply the denominator of the fraction part by the whole number.

2. Add the numerator to the product from step 1.

3. Write the sum from step 2 over the denominator of the fraction.

Study the examples.

Convert the mixed numbers to improper fractions.

$$3\frac{2}{3} = \frac{3 \times 3 + 2}{3} = \frac{11}{3}$$

$$6\frac{3}{7} = \frac{7 \times 6 + 3}{7} = \frac{45}{7}$$

$$8\frac{4}{5} = \frac{5 \times 8 + 4}{5} = \frac{44}{5}$$

Try These

Convert the mixed numbers to improper fractions.

1. $4\frac{6}{7} =$ _____

2. $6\frac{2}{9} =$ _____

3. $2\frac{1}{2} =$ _____

4. $4\frac{2}{3} =$ _____

5. $2\frac{5}{8} =$ _____

6. $4\frac{1}{9} =$ _____

7. $5\frac{1}{6} =$ _____

8. $3\frac{1}{2} =$ _____

9. $7\frac{1}{5} =$ _____

To convert an improper fraction to a mixed number, we also use three steps:

1. Divide the numerator by the denominator.
2. Write the quotient as the whole number part.
3. Write the remainder over the divisor as the fractional part.

Study the examples.

Convert the improper fractions to mixed numbers in simplest form.

$$\frac{11}{3}$$

$$3\overline{)11}$$
$$\underline{9}$$
$$\;\;2$$ (quotient 3)

$$3\frac{2}{3}$$

$$\frac{45}{7}$$

$$7\overline{)45}$$
$$\underline{42}$$
$$\;\;3$$ (quotient 6)

$$6\frac{3}{7}$$

$$\frac{44}{5}$$

$$5\overline{)44}$$
$$\underline{40}$$
$$\;\;4$$ (quotient 8)

$$8\frac{4}{5}$$

Try These

Convert the improper fractions to mixed numbers in simplest form.

1. $\frac{11}{5}$ = _____

2. $\frac{8}{3}$ = _____

3. $\frac{18}{4}$ = _____

4. $\frac{25}{6}$ = _____

5. $\frac{19}{9}$ = _____

6. $\frac{37}{8}$ = _____

7. $\frac{15}{6}$ = _____

8. $\frac{56}{9}$ = _____

9. $\frac{34}{7}$ = _____

Convert the mixed numbers to improper fractions.

1. $2\frac{1}{3} =$ _____

2. $5\frac{1}{3} =$ _____

3. $8\frac{6}{15} =$ _____

4. $7\frac{3}{10} =$ _____

5. $3\frac{3}{8} =$ _____

6. $5\frac{1}{2} =$ _____

7. $3\frac{1}{5} =$ _____

8. $6\frac{5}{12} =$ _____

9. $5\frac{3}{7} =$ _____

10. $2\frac{2}{7} =$ _____

11. $2\frac{9}{10} =$ _____

12. $4\frac{3}{4} =$ _____

Convert the improper fractions to mixed numbers in simplest form.

13. $\frac{5}{2} =$ _____

14. $\frac{7}{5} =$ _____

15. $\frac{9}{4} =$ _____

16. $\frac{16}{3} =$ _____

17. $\frac{11}{7} =$ _____

18. $\frac{10}{8} =$ _____

19. $\frac{11}{9} =$ _____

20. $\frac{16}{6} =$ _____

21. $\frac{20}{8} =$ _____

22. $\frac{50}{4} =$ _____

23. $\frac{40}{3} =$ _____

24. $\frac{44}{8} =$ _____

25. Gerald worked in the produce at the local grocery store. The manager asked him to tie up the carrots in bunches. There were 1584 carrots to be tied up into bunches of 8. How many bunches would Gerald end up with when finished?

_____

26. Mary earns $30 a week. She gives $\frac{1}{10}$ of her earnings to the church each week in the collection basket. How much does she put in the basket?

_____

27. Thomas has a paper route with 23 customers. Each customer owes $8.60 each week for paper delivery. How much money do all of his customers owe him each week?

_____

28. The baseball player was being paid $630 a week. How much does he make in 4 weeks?

_____

29. How much does he make in 52 weeks?

_____

30. Tickets to the Christian Music Festival cost $12.50 each. The managers were able to sell 67 tickets. How much did the managers collect?

_____

Facts Review

Add.

1.	2.	3.	4.	5.	6.
0 + 5	5 + 8	7 + 8	4 + 2	8 + 2	7 + 4

7.	8.	9.	10.	11.	12.
2 + 7	8 + 8	5 + 3	9 + 4	4 + 8	3 + 9

Subtract.

13.	14.	15.	16.	17.	18.
9 − 7	9 − 6	11 − 2	10 − 1	9 − 6	7 − 7

19.	20.	21.	22.	23.	24.
9 − 5	13 − 4	8 − 0	15 − 7	9 − 1	7 − 0

Multiply.

25.	26.	27.	28.	29.	30.
2 × 9	4 × 4	5 × 6	7 × 2	5 × 2	4 × 9

31.	32.	33.	34.	35.	36.
2 × 4	0 × 2	7 × 4	9 × 2	3 × 0	0 × 0

Divide.

37.	38.	39.	40.	41.	42.
7)28	8)40	5)25	7)49	5)5	8)64

43.	44.	45.	46.	47.	48.
4)20	6)6	4)0	6)36	2)18	3)3

Adding and Subtracting Fractions

Adding and subtracting fractions is very simple and straightforward, if the fractions have the same denominator. If the fractions have the same denominator, we simply add or subtract the numerators and then simplify.

Add:

$$\begin{array}{r} \frac{2}{3} \\[4pt] +\ \frac{1}{3} \\ \hline \frac{3}{3} = 1 \end{array}$$

We add the numerators.

$$2 + 1 = 3$$

Then simplify as necessary.

$$\frac{3}{3} = 1$$

Subtract:

$$\begin{array}{r} \frac{5}{6} \\[4pt] -\ \frac{1}{6} \\ \hline \frac{4}{6} = \frac{2}{3} \end{array}$$

We subtract the numerators.

$$5 - 1 = 4$$

Then simplify as necessary.

$$\frac{4}{6} = \frac{2}{3}$$

Study the examples.

Add or subtract:

$$\begin{array}{r} \frac{2}{3} \\[4pt] +\ \frac{2}{3} \\ \hline \frac{4}{3} = 1\frac{1}{3} \end{array}$$
$$\begin{array}{r} \frac{3}{4} \\[4pt] -\ \frac{1}{4} \\ \hline \frac{2}{4} = \frac{1}{2} \end{array}$$
$$\begin{array}{r} \frac{3}{5} \\[4pt] +\ \frac{2}{5} \\ \hline \frac{5}{5} = 1 \end{array}$$
$$\begin{array}{r} \frac{3}{5} \\[4pt] -\ \frac{2}{5} \\ \hline \frac{1}{5} \end{array}$$

Try These

Add or subtract.

1.
$$\begin{array}{r} \frac{5}{8} \\[4pt] +\ \frac{3}{8} \\ \hline \end{array}$$

2.
$$\begin{array}{r} \frac{7}{12} \\[4pt] -\ \frac{5}{12} \\ \hline \end{array}$$

3.
$$\begin{array}{r} \frac{7}{12} \\[4pt] +\ \frac{5}{12} \\ \hline \end{array}$$

4.
$$\begin{array}{r} \frac{5}{9} \\[4pt] -\ \frac{2}{9} \\ \hline \end{array}$$

Exercise

Add or subtract.

1. $\dfrac{1}{3}$
   $+\ \dfrac{1}{3}$

2. $\dfrac{2}{3}$
   $+\ \dfrac{2}{3}$

3. $\dfrac{2}{7}$
   $+\ \dfrac{4}{7}$

4. $\dfrac{4}{5}$
   $+\ \dfrac{3}{5}$

5. $\dfrac{4}{5}$
   $-\ \dfrac{2}{5}$

6. $\dfrac{2}{3}$
   $-\ \dfrac{1}{3}$

7. $\dfrac{7}{9}$
   $-\ \dfrac{4}{9}$

8. $\dfrac{5}{7}$
   $-\ \dfrac{2}{7}$

9. $\dfrac{5}{8}$
   $+\ \dfrac{2}{8}$

10. $\dfrac{5}{8}$
    $-\ \dfrac{3}{8}$

11. $\dfrac{7}{8}$
    $+\ \dfrac{7}{8}$

12. $\dfrac{3}{5}$
    $-\ \dfrac{1}{5}$

13. $\dfrac{7}{8}$
    $-\ \dfrac{3}{8}$

14. $\dfrac{3}{4}$
    $+\ \dfrac{3}{4}$

15. $\dfrac{6}{7}$
    $-\ \dfrac{4}{7}$

16. $\dfrac{8}{9}$
    $+\ \dfrac{5}{9}$

17. $\dfrac{1}{4}$
    $+\ \dfrac{2}{4}$

18. $\dfrac{7}{8}$
    $-\ \dfrac{1}{8}$

19. $\dfrac{2}{5}$
    $+\ \dfrac{2}{5}$

20. $\dfrac{5}{6}$
    $-\ \dfrac{1}{6}$

21. $\dfrac{1}{3}$
    $+\ \dfrac{1}{3}$

22. $\dfrac{8}{9}$
    $-\ \dfrac{1}{9}$

23. $\dfrac{4}{9}$
    $+\ \dfrac{1}{9}$

24. $\dfrac{7}{12}$
    $-\ \dfrac{5}{12}$

Convert the mixed numbers to improper fractions.

25. $3\frac{2}{3} =$ _____

26. $5\frac{7}{8} =$ _____

27. $11\frac{4}{5} =$ _____

28. $9\frac{9}{10} =$ _____

29. $7\frac{3}{4} =$ _____

30. $4\frac{1}{2} =$ _____

Convert the improper fractions to mixed numbers in simplest form.

31. $\frac{5}{3} =$ _____

32. $\frac{8}{5} =$ _____

33. $\frac{15}{4} =$ _____

34. $\frac{16}{2} =$ _____

35. $\frac{11}{6} =$ _____

36. $\frac{21}{8} =$ _____

Find each part. (Note: Use the facts to solve mentally when possible.)

37. $\frac{2}{3}$ of 90

38. $\frac{3}{4}$ of 48

39. $\frac{1}{6}$ of 126

40. $\frac{2}{3}$ of 51

41. $\frac{3}{5}$ of 65

42. $\frac{7}{11}$ of 121

Reduce the fractions to simplest form.

43. $\frac{5}{15} =$ _____

44. $\frac{5}{10} =$ _____

45. $\frac{12}{16} =$ _____

46. $\frac{6}{28} =$ _____

47. $\frac{9}{12} =$ _____

48. $\frac{4}{20} =$ _____

Adding Mixed Numbers

To add mixed numbers, we add the fractional parts and then we add the whole number parts. If the sum of the fractional parts is equal to or greater than 1 we add it to the whole number parts.

Add:

$$4\frac{3}{5}$$
$$+\ 5\frac{4}{5}$$
$$\overline{9\frac{7}{5}} = 10\frac{2}{5}$$

We add the numerators of the fractional parts.

$$3 + 4 = 7 \qquad \frac{7}{5}$$

We simplify the sum of the fractional parts as necessary.

$$\frac{7}{5} = 1\frac{2}{5}$$

We add the whole number parts, including any whole numbers from the simplified sum of the fractional parts.

$$4 + 5 + 1 = 10$$

Study the examples.

Add.

$$\begin{array}{c} 3\frac{2}{3} \\ +\ 4\frac{2}{3} \\ \hline 7\frac{4}{3} = 8\frac{1}{3} \end{array} \qquad \begin{array}{c} 6\frac{3}{4} \\ +\ 2\frac{1}{4} \\ \hline 8\frac{4}{4} = 9 \end{array} \qquad \begin{array}{c} 5\frac{3}{5} \\ +\ 1\frac{2}{5} \\ \hline 6\frac{5}{5} = 7 \end{array} \qquad \begin{array}{c} 2\frac{3}{8} \\ +\ 4\frac{7}{8} \\ \hline 6\frac{10}{8} = 7\frac{1}{4} \end{array}$$

Try These

Add.

1. $$\begin{array}{c} 3\frac{2}{3} \\ +\ 4\frac{2}{3} \\ \hline \end{array}$$

2. $$\begin{array}{c} 6\frac{3}{8} \\ +\ 7\frac{1}{8} \\ \hline \end{array}$$

3. $$\begin{array}{c} 8\frac{7}{8} \\ +\ 4\frac{5}{8} \\ \hline \end{array}$$

4. $$\begin{array}{c} 5\frac{3}{10} \\ +\ 2\frac{7}{10} \\ \hline \end{array}$$

To add mixed numbers with 3 or more addends, we follow the same procedures.

1. Add the fractional parts.

2. If the sum of the fractional parts is an improper fraction, then we change it to a mixed number and simplify.

3. Then we add the whole number parts, including the whole number from the sum of the fractional parts.

Make sure your answer is in simplest form.

Study these examples.

$$
\begin{array}{r}
3\frac{1}{2} \\
3\frac{1}{2} \\
+\ 4\frac{1}{2} \\
\hline
10\frac{3}{2} = 11\frac{1}{2}
\end{array}
\qquad
\begin{array}{r}
4\frac{1}{3} \\
2\frac{2}{3} \\
+\ 1 \\
\hline
7\frac{3}{3} = 8
\end{array}
\qquad
\begin{array}{r}
2\frac{1}{4} \\
1\frac{3}{4} \\
+\ 4\frac{3}{4} \\
\hline
7\frac{7}{4} = 8\frac{3}{4}
\end{array}
\qquad
\begin{array}{r}
3\frac{2}{5} \\
3\frac{4}{5} \\
+\ 4\frac{3}{5} \\
\hline
10\frac{9}{5} = 11\frac{4}{5}
\end{array}
$$

Try These

Add.

1. $\begin{array}{r} 6\frac{1}{2} \\ 7\frac{1}{2} \\ +\ 8\frac{1}{2} \\ \hline \end{array}$

2. $\begin{array}{r} 9\frac{1}{3} \\ 2\frac{2}{3} \\ +\ 5\frac{1}{3} \\ \hline \end{array}$

3. $\begin{array}{r} 2\frac{1}{4} \\ 7\frac{3}{4} \\ +\ 6\frac{1}{4} \\ \hline \end{array}$

4. $\begin{array}{r} 7\frac{2}{5} \\ 6\frac{4}{5} \\ +\ 8\frac{1}{5} \\ \hline \end{array}$

Exercise

Add.

1. $7\frac{5}{6}$
   $4\frac{1}{6}$
   $+ 6\frac{5}{6}$

2. $8\frac{3}{10}$
   $7\frac{9}{10}$
   $+ 5\frac{7}{10}$

3. $4\frac{5}{7}$
   $5\frac{3}{7}$
   $+ 6\frac{4}{7}$

4. $9\frac{1}{5}$
   $8\frac{4}{5}$
   $+ 2\frac{3}{5}$

5. $26\frac{9}{11}$
   $17\frac{7}{11}$
   $+ 18\frac{6}{11}$

6. $39\frac{2}{3}$
   $24\frac{2}{3}$
   $+ 51\frac{2}{3}$

7. $22\frac{4}{9}$
   $27\frac{4}{9}$
   $+ 16\frac{1}{9}$

8. $18\frac{3}{5}$
   $13\frac{1}{5}$
   $+ 10\frac{1}{5}$

9. $7\frac{2}{7}$
   $+ 8\frac{5}{7}$

10. $6\frac{3}{4}$
    $+ 9\frac{1}{4}$

11. $10\frac{7}{8}$
    $+ 10\frac{3}{8}$

12. $4\frac{7}{12}$
    $+ 8\frac{5}{12}$

Add or subtract. Simplify when necessary.

13. $\frac{5}{8}$
    $+ \frac{1}{8}$

14. $\frac{7}{8}$
    $- \frac{3}{8}$

15. $\frac{5}{9}$
    $- \frac{2}{9}$

16. $\frac{4}{5}$
    $+ \frac{1}{5}$

17. $\frac{3}{4}$
    $- \frac{3}{4}$

18. $\frac{3}{4}$
    $+ \frac{1}{4}$

19. $\frac{6}{7}$
    $- \frac{3}{7}$

20. $\frac{8}{9}$
    $+ \frac{7}{9}$

Convert the mixed numbers to improper fractions.

21. $6\frac{3}{4} =$ _____

22. $4\frac{5}{6} =$ _____

23. $9\frac{3}{7} =$ _____

Convert the improper fractions to mixed numbers in simplest form.

24. $\frac{12}{9} =$ _____

25. $\frac{15}{5} =$ _____

26. $\frac{18}{4} =$ _____

Find each part.   (Note: Use the facts to solve mentally when possible.)

27. $\frac{1}{3}$ of 99

28. $\frac{3}{4}$ of 64

29. $\frac{5}{6}$ of 144

Reduce the fractions to simplest form.

30. $\frac{12}{48} =$ _____

31. $\frac{48}{64} =$ _____

32. $\frac{12}{24} =$ _____

33. Sally wanted to buy material for the altar. She bought $3\frac{2}{3}$ yards of white satin, 1 yard of white lace, and $3\frac{1}{3}$ yards of cream satin. How many yards did she buy?

_____

34. Miss Strayer bought 2¾ yards of percale for Cathy's dress and 3¾ yards of percale for Susan's dress. How many yards of percale did she buy?

_____

35. Father bought meat for the family. He bought 5¼ pounds of chicken and 1¾ pounds of steak. How many pounds of meat did he buy in all?

_____

Subtracting Mixed Numbers

To subtract mixed numbers, we first subtract the fractional parts and then we subtract the whole number parts. If the minuend of the fractional part is less than that of the subtrahend, then we need to regroup from the whole number part.

Example:

$$8\frac{5}{7} \qquad 8\frac{5}{7}$$
$$-6\frac{2}{7} \qquad -6\frac{2}{7}$$
$$\overline{} \qquad \overline{2\frac{3}{7}}$$

First we subtract the fractional part. Then we subtract the whole number part.

Example:

$$9\frac{1}{4}$$
$$-6\frac{3}{4}$$

$\frac{1}{4}$ is less than $\frac{3}{4}$ so we must rename $9\frac{1}{4}$ to $8\frac{5}{4}$ before we can begin the subtraction.

$$9\frac{1}{4} = 8 + 1 + \frac{1}{4}$$
$$= 8 + \frac{4}{4} + \frac{1}{4}$$
$$= 8\frac{5}{4}$$

$$8\frac{5}{4}$$
$$-6\frac{3}{4}$$
$$\overline{}$$

Now we can subtract the fractional part. Then we subtract the whole number part. Simplify as necessary.

$$8\frac{5}{4}$$
$$-6\frac{3}{4}$$
$$\overline{2\frac{2}{4} = 2\frac{1}{2}}$$

Study these examples.

$$7\frac{3}{10} \qquad 6\frac{13}{10} \qquad\qquad 4 \qquad 3\frac{4}{4} \qquad\qquad 27\frac{3}{8} \qquad 26\frac{11}{8}$$
$$-2\frac{7}{10} \qquad -2\frac{7}{10} \qquad\qquad -1\frac{3}{4} \qquad -1\frac{3}{4} \qquad\qquad -15\frac{5}{8} \qquad -15\frac{5}{8}$$
$$\qquad\qquad \overline{4\frac{6}{10} = 4\frac{3}{5}} \qquad\qquad\qquad \overline{2\frac{1}{4}} \qquad\qquad\qquad\qquad \overline{11\frac{6}{8} = 11\frac{3}{4}}$$

Try These

Subtract.

1.
$$6\frac{2}{9}$$
$$-4\frac{5}{9}$$
$$\overline{}$$

2.
$$5$$
$$-2\frac{3}{5}$$
$$\overline{}$$

3.
$$21\frac{3}{8}$$
$$-14\frac{7}{8}$$
$$\overline{}$$

4.
$$3\frac{4}{7}$$
$$-1\frac{6}{7}$$
$$\overline{}$$

Exercise

Add.

1. $5\frac{7}{8}$
   $2\frac{3}{8}$
   $+\ 3\frac{6}{8}$

2. $8\frac{1}{4}$
   $1\frac{3}{4}$
   $+\ 5\frac{3}{4}$

3. $6\frac{1}{6}$
   $8\frac{5}{6}$
   $+\ 7\frac{5}{6}$

4. $3\frac{3}{7}$
   $1\frac{6}{7}$
   $+\ 2\frac{5}{7}$

5. $1\frac{2}{3}$
   $+\ 5\frac{1}{3}$

6. $5\frac{9}{10}$
   $+\ 2\frac{9}{10}$

7. $5\frac{4}{5}$
   $+\ 9\frac{3}{5}$

8. $7\frac{7}{8}$
   $+\ 4\frac{3}{8}$

Subtract.

9. $7\frac{2}{9}$
   $-\ 2\frac{8}{9}$

10. 9
    $-\ 3\frac{4}{5}$

11. $21\frac{3}{8}$
    $-\ 14\frac{7}{8}$

12. $3\frac{4}{7}$
    $-\ 1\frac{6}{7}$

13. $5\frac{1}{5}$
    $-\ 2\frac{4}{5}$

14. $4\frac{1}{7}$
    $-\ 2\frac{6}{7}$

15. $6\frac{1}{8}$
    $-\ 2\frac{3}{8}$

16. $5\frac{3}{12}$
    $-\ 2\frac{11}{12}$

17. $5\frac{1}{3}$
    $-\ 1\frac{2}{3}$

18. $1\frac{4}{15}$
    $-\ \frac{7}{15}$

19. $9\frac{1}{4}$
    $-\ 2\frac{3}{4}$

20. $7\frac{7}{10}$
    $-\ 3\frac{9}{10}$

21. When the homeschoolers went to pick strawberries, Kathy picked $2\frac{1}{4}$ quarts, Nancy picked $1\frac{3}{4}$ quarts, and Amy picked $4\frac{3}{4}$ quarts.
How many quarts did they pick altogether?

_____

22. The boys also picked strawberries. Tom picked $4\frac{1}{4}$ quarts, Jerry picked $2\frac{3}{4}$ quarts, and Paul picked $1\frac{1}{4}$ quarts. How many quarts did they pick altogether?

_____

23. The boys went to the orchards in Winchester and picked $3\frac{2}{3}$ baskets of apples on Saturday and $5\frac{2}{3}$ baskets of apples on Sunday. How many more baskets did they pick on Sunday than Saturday?

_____

24. How many baskets did they pick altogether on Saturday and Sunday?

_____

25. Father bought meat for the family. He bought 5¼ pounds of chicken and 1¾ pounds of steak.
How much more chicken did he buy than steak?

_____

Find each part. (Note: Use the facts to solve mentally when possible.)

26. $\frac{2}{3}$ of 180

27. $\frac{3}{4}$ of 88

28. $\frac{5}{6}$ of 132

29. $\frac{2}{3}$ of 2640

30. $\frac{2}{5}$ of 75

31. $\frac{4}{11}$ of 110

Compare. Write <, =, or >.

32. $\frac{2}{3}$ ____ $\frac{5}{7}$

33. $\frac{3}{11}$ ____ $\frac{3}{13}$

34. $\frac{2}{5}$ ____ $\frac{4}{11}$

Find the missing parts.

35. $\frac{1}{8} = \frac{?}{16}$ _____

36. $\frac{4}{9} = \frac{?}{54}$ _____

37. $\frac{5}{16} = \frac{?}{96}$ _____

Reduce the fractions to simplest form.

38. $\frac{6}{10} =$ _____

39. $\frac{4}{12} =$ _____

40. $\frac{4}{16} =$ _____

Find the GCF for each pair of numbers.

41. 12 and 16 _____

42. 9 and 21 _____

Write the prime factorization for each.

43. 52 _____

44. 120 _____

45. 110 _____

Problem Solving

READ – THINK – PLAN – EXECUTE

Problem Solving

1. Mary went shopping with her mother when they were visiting the Basilica of the Shrine of the Immaculate Conception. She bought three postcards showing the Marian altars. The postcard depicting the Lourdes Grotto cost $2, the postcard depicting a Byzantine icon cost $3, and the postcard depicting Our Lady of Guadalupe cost $5. How much did Mary spend?

   _____

2. Last summer, Uncle Will had 93 cows on his farm.
   He sold 24 to Mr. Miller down the road.
   How many cows did Uncle Will have left?

   _____

3. Henry wanted to learn to play tennis, but he needed a racket.
   The racket he picked out cost $79. He had only $56 in his wallet.
   How much more money did he need?

   _____

4. Mr. Clark bought several tulip bulbs for the garden
   at the Seton Home Study School headquarters.
   The first summer, they produced only 12 flowers.
   The second summer, there were 87 beautiful red flowers.
   How many more flowers were there in the second summer?

   _____

5. Nancy weighs 72¼ pounds and Helene weighs 69¾ pounds. How much do they both weigh together?

   _____

6. How much more does Nancy weigh than Helene?

   _____

7. What is the difference between $17\frac{7}{8}$ and $23\frac{3}{8}$?

   _____

Multiply.

1. 305
    × 18

2. 702
    × 67

3. 450
    × 23

4. 325
    × 15

5. $ 6.86
    × 14

6. $ 5.75
    × 60

7. $ 4.21
    × 47

8. $ 1.13
    × 34

Add or subtract.

9. 334
    389
    +298

10. 703
    472
    38
    + 65

11. 1945
    + 1298

12. 9809
    + 3479

13. 4509
    − 3352

14. 7800
    − 3564

15. 3790
    + 2631

16. 8523
    − 4155

Solve for n.

17. $5 \times n = 60$

18. $63 \div n = 9$

19. $n \times 4 = 48$

20. $54 \div n = 6$

21. $n \div 8 = 8$

22. $n \times 7 = 35$

23. $4 \times n = 12$

24. $n \div 3 = 7$

25. $27 \div n = 9$

Divide.

26. $14\overline{)686}$ 27. $95\overline{)3230}$ 28. $19\overline{)1045}$ 29. $27\overline{)6102}$

30. $13\overline{)1131}$ 31. $68\overline{)2584}$ 32. $19\overline{)684}$ 33. $22\overline{)968}$

34. $8\overline{)496}$ 35. $6\overline{)972}$ 36. $9\overline{)288}$ 37. $7\overline{)688}$

Solve using the order of operations.

38. $18 - 5 + 6$ 39. $9 + 6 - 7$ 40. $20 + 20 - 16$

41. $8 - 4 \div 4 + 4$ 42. $35 - 5 + 10 \div 2$ 43. $6 \times 6 + 10 \div 5 - 1$

44. $30 \div 6 \times 9 + 9 - 1$ 45. $18 + 6 \div 2 - 11 + 5$

46. $20 \div 4 + 54 \div 6 + 4$ 47. $7 \times 30 - 10 + 150 \div 3$

Find the GCF for each set of numbers.

48. 36 and 42 _____   49. 9, 20, and 40 _____

Write the prime factorization for each.

50. 24 _____   51. 51 _____   52. 93 _____

53. Write the prime numbers that are less than 50.
(Hint: There are 15 prime numbers less than 50.) _____

_____

Compare. Write < or >.

54. $\dfrac{3}{4}$ ____ $\dfrac{5}{8}$ 55. $\dfrac{9}{10}$ ____ $\dfrac{4}{5}$ 56. $\dfrac{7}{8}$ ____ $\dfrac{1}{4}$

Find the missing parts.

57. $\dfrac{3}{4} = \dfrac{?}{12}$ _____   58. $\dfrac{1}{2} = \dfrac{?}{10}$ _____   59. $1 = \dfrac{?}{96}$ _____

Find each part.   (Note: Use the facts to solve mentally when possible.)

60. $\dfrac{1}{2}$ of 14   61. $\dfrac{2}{3}$ of 18   62. $\dfrac{3}{4}$ of 24

Convert the mixed numbers to improper fractions.

63. $15\dfrac{2}{5} =$ _____   64. $10\dfrac{5}{9} =$ _____   65. $7\dfrac{3}{7} =$ _____

Convert the improper fractions to mixed numbers in simplest form.

66. $\dfrac{11}{2} =$ _____

67. $\dfrac{17}{7} =$ _____

68. $\dfrac{18}{9} =$ _____

Add or subtract. Simplify when necessary.

69.
$$\dfrac{5}{8}$$
$$+ \dfrac{3}{8}$$

70.
$$\dfrac{5}{6}$$
$$- \dfrac{1}{6}$$

71.
$$\dfrac{5}{9}$$
$$- \dfrac{2}{9}$$

72.
$$\dfrac{5}{6}$$
$$+ \dfrac{5}{6}$$

73.
$$3\dfrac{7}{12}$$
$$4\dfrac{11}{12}$$
$$+ 3\dfrac{5}{12}$$

74.
$$11\dfrac{1}{5}$$
$$13\dfrac{3}{5}$$
$$+ 19\dfrac{4}{5}$$

75.
$$5\dfrac{1}{8}$$
$$3\dfrac{3}{8}$$
$$+ 7\dfrac{7}{8}$$

76.
$$5\dfrac{1}{9}$$
$$2\dfrac{2}{9}$$
$$+ 9\dfrac{5}{9}$$

77.
$$6\dfrac{2}{3}$$
$$+ 3\dfrac{1}{3}$$

78.
$$9\dfrac{7}{10}$$
$$+ 5\dfrac{8}{10}$$

79.
$$21\dfrac{6}{7}$$
$$+ 11\dfrac{4}{7}$$

80.
$$14\dfrac{3}{4}$$
$$+ 12\dfrac{3}{4}$$

81.
$$17\dfrac{7}{12}$$
$$- 14\dfrac{11}{12}$$

82.
$$8$$
$$- 3\dfrac{3}{5}$$

83.
$$13\dfrac{1}{5}$$
$$- 10\dfrac{3}{5}$$

84.
$$9\dfrac{7}{10}$$
$$- 5\dfrac{8}{10}$$

Multiplying Fractions and Mixed Numbers

Multiplying fractions is simple but we have to remember a few things from previous lessons about simplifying fractions, GCF, and prime factorization.

$n \div n = 1$ Any number divided by itself is one.

When the numerator and the denominator are the same, the number is one. $\frac{n}{n} = 1$

Fractions equal to 1

$$1 = \frac{2}{2} = \frac{3}{3} = \frac{4}{4} = \frac{5}{5} = \frac{6}{6} = \frac{7}{7} = \frac{8}{8} = \frac{9}{9} = \frac{10}{10} = \frac{12}{12} = \frac{16}{16}$$

We also know that *multiplying or dividing a number by 1 does not change the number*. We can use this property to simplify a fraction.

Identity Property of Multiplication (One)

Multiplying a number by 1 does not change the number.

The product of any number and 1 is that number.

$$n \times 1 = n$$

Every composite number can be expressed as the product of prime factors.

The prime factorization of a number can be useful in simplifying fractions.

Prime Factorization

We start with the composite number, select a prime factor as a divisor, bring down the partial quotient, and then select another prime as a divisor until the partial quotient is also a prime number.

```
2 |8          2 |16          2 |24
  2 |4          2 |8           2 |12
     2            2 |4           2 |6
                    2             3
```

$8 = 2 \times 2 \times 2$ $16 = 2 \times 2 \times 2 \times 2$ $24 = 2 \times 2 \times 2 \times 3$

Common factors are factors that 2 or more products have in common. The greatest common factor (GCF) is the largest factor that the products have in common.

When we reduce a fraction to its simplest form, we divide both the numerator and the denominator by the greatest common factor of both.

Study these examples

Write the prime factorization of the numerator and the denominator of each fraction. Then match up numerators and denominators that are the same. Then write the simplified fraction.

$$\frac{16}{24} = \frac{2\times2\times2\times2}{2\times2\times2\times3} = \frac{2}{2} \times \frac{2}{2} \times \frac{2}{2} \times \frac{2}{3} = 1\times1\times1\times\frac{2}{3} = \frac{2}{3}$$

$$\frac{9}{36} = \frac{3\times3}{2\times2\times3\times3} = \frac{1}{2} \times \frac{1}{2} \times \frac{3}{3} \times \frac{3}{3} = \frac{1}{2} \times \frac{1}{2} \times 1 \times 1 = \frac{1}{4}$$

$$\frac{12}{72} = \frac{2\times2\times3}{2\times2\times2\times3\times3} = \frac{2\times2\ \ \times3}{2\times2\times2\times3\times3} = 1 \times 1 \times \frac{1}{2} \times 1 \times \frac{1}{3} = \frac{1}{2} \times \frac{1}{3} = \frac{1}{6}$$

For the sake of convenience, after we have obtained the prime factorization of the numerator and the denominator we may cross out matching factors of the numerator and denominator and the remaining fraction will be in simplified form.

$$\frac{16}{24} = \frac{2 \times 2 \times 2 \times 2}{2 \times 2 \times 2 \times 3} = \frac{2}{3}$$
$$\frac{9}{36} = \frac{3 \times 3}{2 \times 2 \times 3 \times 3} = \frac{1}{4}$$

$$\frac{12}{72} = \frac{2 \times 2 \times 3}{2 \times 2 \times 2 \times 3 \times 3} = \frac{1}{6}$$

List the factors of the numerator and the denominator, then identify the greatest common factor (GCF), and divide the numerator and the denominator by the GCF in order to reduce the fraction to its simplest form.

$\dfrac{16}{24}$ 1,2,4,8,16
1,2,3,4,6,8,12,24 $\dfrac{16}{24} \div \dfrac{8}{8} = \dfrac{2}{3}$

$\dfrac{9}{36}$ 1,3,9
1,2,3,4,6,8,9,12,18 $\dfrac{9}{36} \div \dfrac{9}{9} = \dfrac{1}{4}$

$\dfrac{12}{72}$ 1,2,3,4,6,12
1,2,3,4,6,8,9,12, ... $\dfrac{12}{72} \div \dfrac{12}{12} = \dfrac{1}{6}$

When one list of factors goes past the largest factor of the other list of factors, then it is not necessary to continue to list the factors of that number. This is because the greatest common factor (GCF) cannot be larger than the largest factor of either one of the numbers.

Multiplying Fractions and Mixed Numbers

Finally, we come to the multiplying of fractions and whole or mixed numbers.

To multiply two fractions we simply multiply their numerators together and multiply their denominators together. Then we reduce the product to simplest terms. Study these examples.

$$\dfrac{1}{4} \times \dfrac{2}{3} = \dfrac{2}{12} = \dfrac{1}{6} \qquad \dfrac{3}{4} \times \dfrac{5}{8} = \dfrac{15}{32} \qquad \dfrac{9}{15} \times \dfrac{5}{3} = \dfrac{45}{45} = 1$$

To multiply fractions and whole or mixed numbers, we have to rename the whole or mixed numbers as improper fractions. Then we can multiply the numerators together and the denominators together. Then we reduce the product to simplest terms. Study these examples.

$$7\dfrac{1}{4} \times \dfrac{2}{3} = \dfrac{29}{4} \times \dfrac{2}{3} = \dfrac{58}{12} = 4\dfrac{10}{12} = 4\dfrac{5}{6} \qquad \dfrac{3}{4} \times 6\dfrac{5}{8} = \dfrac{3}{4} \times \dfrac{53}{8} = \dfrac{159}{32} = 4\dfrac{31}{32}$$

$$8 \times 3\dfrac{1}{2} = \dfrac{8}{1} \times \dfrac{7}{2} = \dfrac{56}{2} = 28 \qquad 5\dfrac{3}{7} \times 2\dfrac{1}{5} = \dfrac{38}{7} \times \dfrac{11}{5} = \dfrac{418}{35} = 11\dfrac{33}{35}$$

Multiply.

1. $\dfrac{2}{3} \times \dfrac{3}{7} =$ _____

2. $\dfrac{3}{11} \times \dfrac{1}{3} =$ _____

3. $\dfrac{1}{5} \times \dfrac{3}{4} =$ _____

4. $\dfrac{3}{4} \times \dfrac{1}{3} =$ _____

5. $\dfrac{3}{8} \times \dfrac{1}{2} =$ _____

6. $\dfrac{7}{3} \times \dfrac{2}{5} =$ _____

7. $\dfrac{9}{10} \times \dfrac{5}{7} =$ _____

8. $\dfrac{1}{2} \times \dfrac{5}{8} =$ _____

9. $\dfrac{2}{3} \times \dfrac{9}{10} =$ _____

10. $\dfrac{7}{12} \times 18 =$ _____

11. $40 \times \dfrac{5}{6} =$ _____

12. $1\dfrac{1}{8} \times 1\dfrac{1}{3} =$ _____

13. $8\dfrac{2}{3} \times 3 =$ _____

14. $12 \times 3\dfrac{3}{4} =$ _____

15. $2\frac{1}{5} \times 3\frac{1}{2} =$ _____

16. $3\frac{1}{3} \times 1\frac{7}{10} =$ _____

17. $3 \times 1\frac{2}{9} =$ _____

18. $4\frac{1}{4} \times 6 =$ _____

19. $2\frac{1}{8} \times 1\frac{1}{9} =$ _____

20. $1\frac{1}{3} \times 2\frac{3}{8} =$ _____

21. $\frac{2}{3} \times 1\frac{4}{5} =$ _____

22. $\frac{3}{4} \times 20 =$ _____

23. $7\frac{1}{2} \times \frac{4}{5} =$ _____

24. $9 \times \frac{5}{6} =$ _____

25. $2\frac{2}{5} \times 5\frac{5}{6} =$ _____

26. $\frac{5}{9} \times \frac{7}{9} =$ _____

27. $8 \times \frac{3}{5} =$ _____

28. $2\frac{2}{5} \times 4 =$ _____

Skills Maintenance

Multiply.

1.
$$\begin{array}{r} 1234 \\ \times\ \ \ \ 8 \\ \hline \end{array}$$

2.
$$\begin{array}{r} 77 \\ \times\ \ 32 \\ \hline \end{array}$$

3.
$$\begin{array}{r} \$\,6.58 \\ \times\ \ \ 37 \\ \hline \end{array}$$

4.
$$\begin{array}{r} 476 \\ \times\ \ 67 \\ \hline \end{array}$$

Add or subtract.

5.
$$\begin{array}{r} 3798 \\ +\ 6129 \\ \hline \end{array}$$

6.
$$\begin{array}{r} \$\,3.21 \\ +\$\,2.97 \\ \hline \end{array}$$

7.
$$\begin{array}{r} 8723 \\ -\ 2948 \\ \hline \end{array}$$

8.
$$\begin{array}{r} 768 \\ -\ 299 \\ \hline \end{array}$$

Solve for n.

9. $8 \times n = 88$

10. $44 \div n = 4$

11. $n \times 4 = 72$

Divide.

12. $3\overline{)299}$

13. $7\overline{)\$16.45}$

14. $8\overline{)9600}$

15. $19\overline{)349}$

16. $14\overline{)798}$

17. $37\overline{)8392}$

18. $25\overline{)\$15.50}$

19. $42\overline{)41,775}$

Solve using the order of operations.

20. $8 \times 3 \div 4 + 6 - 2$

21. $76 \div 4 \times 5 - 3 + 7$

Facts Review

Add.

1.   1
    + 6

2.   6
    + 3

3.   6
    + 9

4.   4
    + 6

5.   8
    + 7

6.   3
    + 4

7.   6
    + 5

8.   9
    + 8

9.   2
    + 5

10.   0
    + 0

11.   7
    + 5

12.   8
    + 0

Subtract.

13.   14
    − 8

14.   9
    − 3

15.   14
    − 5

16.   8
    − 5

17.   13
    − 5

18.   1
    − 1

19.   8
    − 4

20.   8
    − 1

21.   9
    − 9

22.   4
    − 2

23.   2
    − 1

24.   8
    − 7

Multiply.

25.   3
    × 5

26.   8
    × 3

27.   9
    × 4

28.   6
    × 5

29.   0
    × 1

30.   5
    × 7

31.   8
    × 7

32.   2
    × 3

33.   5
    × 0

34.   8
    × 8

35.   0
    × 8

36.   1
    × 3

Divide.

37. 1)8

38. 5)20

39. 4)24

40. 9)72

41. 8)56

42. 3)27

43. 3)0

44. 6)42

45. 3)24

46. 7)21

47. 4)4

48. 2)0

227

Problem Solving
READ – THINK – PLAN – EXECUTE

1. The sisters at the convent wanted to buy a piano for the homeschoolers who visit there every other Friday afternoon. The piano was donated, but was going to cost $250 for the movers to transport it. Three people donated $75 each. How much more money did the sisters need to pay the movers?

   _____

2. St. Junipero Serra lived from 1713 to 1784. How old was St. Junipero Serra when he died?

   _____

3. On Monday, Mr. King drove his family to the Shrine of Our Lady of Consolation in Carey, Ohio, and back. On Wednesday he drove to the shrine of the Weeping Madonna of Mariapoch in Burton, Ohio and back. The round trip to Carey is 60 miles and the round trip to Burton is 75 miles. How many miles did he drive?

   _____

4. In 1990, Dr. Clark visited New Orleans and the Shrine of Our Lady of Prompt Succor. It was here that the people of New Orleans thanked our Blessed Mother for sparing their town from an invasion by the English. The shrine was built in 1810. How old was the shrine when Dr. Clark visited it?

   _____

5. A shrine in Garfield Heights, just outside the city of Cleveland, honors the beautiful picture of Our Lady of Czestochowa. It was built in 1939. How old was the shrine in 2008?

   _____

6. Last summer, Paul worked at the parish bookstore. He earned $390. However, he bought many books while he was working, spending $210 on stories of saints, especially ones about St. Paul. How much money did Paul have left at the end of the summer?

   _____

7. What is this year? Round to the nearest thousand.

   _____

When the product of two fractions is 1, the fractions are **reciprocals**. The reciprocal of a fraction is its **multiplicative inverse**. To find the reciprocal of a fraction, we simply **invert** it (flip it) so that the denominator becomes the numerator and the numerator becomes the denominator.

$$\circlearrowleft\frac{2}{3}\circlearrowright \longrightarrow \frac{3}{2} \qquad \frac{2}{3} \times \frac{3}{2} = \frac{6}{6} = 1 \qquad \circlearrowleft\frac{3}{4}\circlearrowright \longrightarrow \frac{4}{3} \qquad \frac{3}{4} \times \frac{4}{3} = \frac{12}{12} = 1$$

To find the reciprocal of a mixed number, we must first change it to an improper fraction, and then invert the improper fraction.

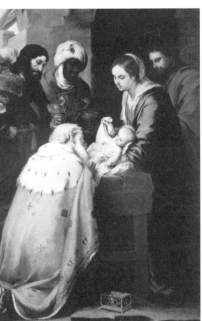

$$5\frac{2}{3} = \frac{17}{3} \qquad \circlearrowleft\frac{17}{3}\circlearrowright \longrightarrow \frac{3}{17} \qquad \frac{3}{17} \times \frac{17}{3} = \frac{51}{51} = 1$$

$$6\frac{3}{4} = \frac{27}{4} \qquad \circlearrowleft\frac{27}{4}\circlearrowright \longrightarrow \frac{4}{27} \qquad \frac{27}{4} \times \frac{4}{27} = \frac{108}{108} = 1$$

The reciprocal of a whole number is simply a fraction with the whole number as the denominator and 1 as the numerator.

$$7 = \frac{7}{1} \longrightarrow \frac{1}{7} \qquad \frac{7}{1} \times \frac{1}{7} = \frac{7}{7} = 1 \qquad 10 = \frac{10}{1} \longrightarrow \frac{1}{10} \qquad \frac{10}{1} \times \frac{1}{10} = \frac{10}{10} = 1$$

Think about these statements:

Zero has no reciprocal. The reciprocal of 1 is 1. The reciprocal of all other whole numbers and mixed numbers is less than one.

The reciprocal of fractions less than one is greater than one.

A number multiplied by a number less than one will become smaller.

A number multiplied by a number greater than one will become larger.

Exercise

Multiply.

1. $\dfrac{5}{12} \times \dfrac{12}{5} =$ _____

2. $\dfrac{9}{99} \times \dfrac{99}{9} =$ _____

3. $\dfrac{18}{72} \times \dfrac{72}{18} =$ _____

4. $4\dfrac{5}{6} \times \dfrac{6}{29} =$ _____

5. $2\dfrac{1}{11} \times \dfrac{11}{23} =$ _____

6. $12 \times \dfrac{1}{12} =$ _____

Find the reciprocal of each. Multiply to check.

7. $\dfrac{3}{10}$ _____

8. $\dfrac{1}{4}$ _____

9. $\dfrac{5}{8}$ _____

10. $1\dfrac{3}{4}$ _____

11. $2\dfrac{1}{2}$ _____

12. 9 _____

13. $\dfrac{1}{8}$ _____

14. $\dfrac{2}{3}$ _____

15. $\dfrac{3}{8}$ _____

16. $2\dfrac{1}{3}$ _____

17. $1\dfrac{5}{8}$ _____

18. 17 _____

19. $\dfrac{7}{8}$ _____

20. $\dfrac{5}{6}$ _____

21. $\dfrac{1}{2}$ _____

22. $1\dfrac{4}{5}$ _____

23. $2\dfrac{2}{3}$ _____

24. 11 _____

Division Practice

1. 3)268

2. 5)328

3. 7)948

4. 11)293

5. 13)144

6. 4)155

7. 12)108

8. 5)392

9. 2)307

10. 17)832

11. 19)947

12. 23)723

13. 39)8020

14. 26)3750

15. 9)5437

16. 42)8417

17. 15)750

18. 17)5168

19. 25)2515

20. 13)1427

21. James ran 222 yards. Then he ran 780 more yards. How many feet did he run in all? _____

22. Three partners made $42 profit at their lemonade stand. If they divided the profits equally, how much did each receive? _____

In order to divide with fractions and mixed numbers, we invert the divisor and multiply. Whenever either the dividend or the divisor is a fraction or a mixed number, we find the reciprocal of the divisor and multiply.

For example, if we want to divide $\frac{3}{4}$ by $\frac{2}{3}$,

we would multiply by the reciprocal of $\frac{2}{3}$,

which is $\frac{3}{2}$.

$$\frac{3}{4} \div \frac{2}{3} = \frac{3}{4} \times \frac{3}{2} = \frac{9}{8} = 1\frac{1}{8}$$

$$\frac{3}{4} \div \frac{2}{3} = 1\frac{1}{8}$$

When dividing fractions or mixed numbers we:

1. First rename any whole or mixed numbers as improper fractions.
2. Find the reciprocal of the divisor.
3. Multiply the dividend by the reciprocal of the divisor. (Invert and multiply.)
4. Simplify as necessary.

Study these examples.

$$\frac{2}{3} \div \frac{5}{6} = \frac{2}{3} \times \frac{6}{5} = \frac{12}{15}$$

$$\frac{12}{15} = \frac{2 \times 2 \times 3}{3 \times 5} = \frac{4}{5}$$

$$\frac{3}{11} \div \frac{6}{7} = \frac{3}{11} \times \frac{7}{6} = \frac{21}{66}$$

$$\frac{21}{66} = \frac{3 \times 7}{2 \times 3 \times 11} = \frac{7}{22}$$

When dividing with mixed numbers or whole numbers,
first rename the whole or mixed numbers as improper fractions.

$$5\frac{1}{4} \div 2\frac{3}{8} = \frac{21}{4} \div \frac{19}{8} = \frac{21}{4} \times \frac{8}{19} = \frac{168}{76} = 2\frac{16}{76} = 2\frac{4}{19}$$

$$8 \div 3\frac{3}{4} = \frac{8}{1} \div \frac{15}{4} = \frac{8}{1} \times \frac{4}{15} = \frac{32}{15} = 2\frac{2}{15}$$

$$8 \div \frac{3}{4} = \frac{8}{1} \div \frac{3}{4} = \frac{8}{1} \times \frac{4}{3} = \frac{32}{3} = 10\frac{2}{3}$$

$$3\frac{3}{4} \div 8 = \frac{15}{4} \div \frac{8}{1} = \frac{15}{4} \times \frac{1}{8} = \frac{15}{32}$$

Study the examples again and then think about these statements:

If the divisor is less than one, its reciprocal is greater than one.

If the divisor is greater than one, its reciprocal is less than one.

A number divided by a divisor less than one will become greater.

A number divided by a divisor greater than one will become smaller.

Try These

Divide.
1. First rename any whole or mixed numbers as improper fractions.
2. Find the reciprocal of the divisor.
3. Multiply the dividend by the reciprocal of the divisor. (Invert and multiply.)
4. Simplify as necessary.

1. $\frac{4}{7} \div \frac{5}{14} =$ _____

2. $3 \div 4\frac{1}{5} =$ _____

3. $2\frac{1}{5} \div 1\frac{1}{3} =$ _____

4. $8 \div \frac{2}{3} =$ _____

5. $\frac{5}{6} \div 30 =$ _____

6. $6\frac{5}{8} \div 4 =$ _____

233

Divide.

1. $\dfrac{4}{5} \div \dfrac{3}{10} =$ _____

2. $\dfrac{2}{3} \div \dfrac{1}{4} =$ _____

3. $\dfrac{3}{7} \div \dfrac{5}{8} =$ _____

4. $\dfrac{1}{4} \div \dfrac{1}{8} =$ _____

5. $\dfrac{3}{4} \div \dfrac{2}{3} =$ _____

6. $\dfrac{5}{8} \div \dfrac{3}{8} =$ _____

7. $\dfrac{1}{3} \div \dfrac{7}{8} =$ _____

8. $\dfrac{3}{5} \div \dfrac{5}{6} =$ _____

9. $\dfrac{3}{4} \div \dfrac{1}{2} =$ _____

10. $\dfrac{5}{8} \div 10 =$ _____

11. $3 \div \dfrac{7}{10} =$ _____

12. $1\dfrac{5}{9} \div 1\dfrac{3}{4} =$ _____

13. $8\dfrac{3}{4} \div 7 =$ _____

14. $7 \div 1\dfrac{3}{4} =$ _____

15. $3\frac{1}{5} \div 2\frac{1}{2} =$ _____

16. $1\frac{1}{2} \div 1\frac{5}{8} =$ _____

17. $1\frac{1}{4} \div 1\frac{1}{5} =$ _____

18. $3\frac{8}{9} \div 2\frac{1}{3} =$ _____

19. $5\frac{5}{6} \div 1\frac{1}{4} =$ _____

20. $1\frac{1}{2} \div 1\frac{1}{8} =$ _____

21. $7 \div 2\frac{1}{3} =$ _____

22. $7\frac{1}{5} \div 6 =$ _____

23. $\frac{3}{4} \div 4 =$ _____

24. $8 \div \frac{4}{5} =$ _____

25. $5\frac{1}{2} \div 9 =$ _____

26. $9 \div 1\frac{4}{5} =$ _____

27. $10 \div \frac{1}{2} =$ _____

28. $\frac{2}{3} \div 12 =$ _____

Practice Multiplying Fractions

Multiply.

1. $\dfrac{7}{8} \times \dfrac{4}{5} =$ _____

2. $\dfrac{8}{9} \times \dfrac{3}{4} =$ _____

3. $\dfrac{1}{8} \times \dfrac{3}{8} =$ _____

4. $\dfrac{3}{10} \times \dfrac{2}{3} =$ _____

5. $\dfrac{4}{5} \times \dfrac{5}{8} =$ _____

6. $\dfrac{1}{3} \times \dfrac{2}{5} =$ _____

7. $\dfrac{6}{7} \times \dfrac{7}{2} =$ _____

8. $\dfrac{8}{9} \times 6\dfrac{3}{4} =$ _____

9. $\dfrac{3}{3} \times \dfrac{9}{10} =$ _____

10. $\dfrac{2}{9} \times 7 =$ _____

11. $8 \times \dfrac{3}{16} =$ _____

12. $1\dfrac{5}{6} \times 3\dfrac{1}{3} =$ _____

13. $3\dfrac{1}{7} \times 35 =$ _____

14. $15 \times 5\dfrac{1}{3} =$ _____

15. $2\frac{3}{4} \times 1\frac{5}{11} =$ _____

16. $6\frac{1}{4} \times \frac{2}{5} =$ _____

17. $2\frac{1}{2} \times 3\frac{1}{3} =$ _____

18. $2\frac{1}{2} \times 2\frac{3}{4} =$ _____

19. $3\frac{2}{3} \times 2\frac{1}{4} =$ _____

20. $1\frac{1}{4} \times 3\frac{3}{5} =$ _____

21. $4\frac{2}{3} \times 7\frac{1}{2} =$ _____

22. $2\frac{1}{6} \times 1\frac{1}{8} =$ _____

23. $1\frac{3}{5} \times 1\frac{1}{3} =$ _____

24. $2\frac{4}{5} \times 1\frac{3}{7} =$ _____

25. $6\frac{1}{4} \times 2\frac{2}{5} =$ _____

26. $1\frac{3}{4} \times 3\frac{1}{5} =$ _____

27. $7\frac{3}{5} \times 2\frac{8}{9} =$ _____

28. $2\frac{1}{10} \times 3\frac{3}{7} =$ _____

Problem Solving
READ – THINK – PLAN – EXECUTE

1. What number do you multiply $5\frac{3}{4}$ by to obtain a product of 1?

   _____

2. The homeschoolers had a picnic last June. Everyone brought lots of food since there were 34 children at the picnic. Mrs. Doyle brought 2 packages of hot dogs, Mrs. Smith brought 7 packages and Mrs. Evans brought 4 packages. If each package contained 8 hot dogs, how many hot dogs were brought to the picnic?

   _____

3. Miss Gray made candy for the homeschoolers' picnic. She made 126 pieces of molasses candy, 138 pieces of caramel candy, and 203 pieces of peppermint candy. How many pieces did Miss Gray make for the picnic?

   _____

4. Many mothers did not want their children to eat so much candy. Miss Gray took much of the candy home to use for birthday presents later. She ended up taking 205 pieces home. How many pieces were eaten at the picnic?

   _____

5. Last week, our family presented a play for our homeschoolers' group. We sold tickets for $1 each. Before the play, we sold 83 tickets. The night of the play, we sold 55 tickets. How many tickets did we sell in all?

   _____

6. Since we had to make costumes for our play, it cost us $167 in materials. How much money did we "lose" on the play?

   _____

7. We presented our play again the next month, and sold 103 tickets at $1 each. How many more tickets were sold for the first presentation of the play? Did we finally make our costume money back with the second presentation?

   _____

Fractions as Percents

Fractions can easily be expressed as **percents** (%) because *percent* means "per one hundred."

$$\frac{37}{100} = 37\% \qquad \frac{22}{100} = 22\% \qquad \frac{8}{100} = 8\%$$

$$76\% = \frac{76}{100} \qquad 41\% = \frac{41}{100} \qquad 2\% = \frac{2}{100}$$

Fractions that do not have 100 as a denominator can be renamed as an equivalent fraction with a denominator of 100 and then easily expressed as a percent.

$$\frac{1}{2} = \frac{1}{2} \times \frac{50}{50} = \frac{50}{100} \qquad \frac{3}{4} = \frac{3}{4} \times \frac{25}{25} = \frac{75}{100} \qquad \frac{7}{10} = \frac{7}{10} \times \frac{10}{10} = \frac{70}{100}$$

Try These

Write each fraction as a percent with the percent sign (%).

1. $\frac{17}{100} =$ _____

2. $\frac{33}{100} =$ _____

3. $\frac{1}{100} =$ _____

Write each percent as a fraction with a denominator of 100.

4. $35\% =$ _____

5. $60\% =$ _____

6. $45\% =$ _____

Rename each fraction as an equivalent fraction with a denominator of 100.

7. $\frac{4}{25} =$ _____

8. $\frac{3}{5} =$ _____

9. $\frac{7}{20} =$ _____

10. $\frac{3}{10} =$ _____

Exercise

Write each fraction as a percent with the percent sign (%).

1. $\frac{21}{100}$ = _____

2. $\frac{3}{100}$ = _____

3. $\frac{99}{100}$ = _____

Write each percent as a fraction with a denominator of 100.

4. 14% = _____

5. 81% = _____

6. 12% = _____

Rename each fraction as an equivalent fraction with a denominator of 100.

7. $\frac{1}{4}$ = _____

8. $\frac{9}{10}$ = _____

9. $\frac{3}{20}$ = _____

10. $\frac{4}{5}$ = _____

11. $\frac{1}{5}$ = _____

12. $\frac{7}{25}$ = _____

Reduce each fraction to its simplest form.

13. $\frac{50}{100}$ = _____

14. $\frac{36}{100}$ = _____

15. $\frac{60}{100}$ = _____

16. $\frac{20}{100}$ = _____

17. $\frac{35}{100}$ = _____

18. $\frac{5}{100}$ = _____

Practice Dividing Fractions

Divide.

1. $\dfrac{5}{6} \div \dfrac{5}{9} =$ _____

2. $\dfrac{1}{8} \div \dfrac{1}{4} =$ _____

3. $\dfrac{1}{2} \div \dfrac{5}{8} =$ _____

4. $\dfrac{2}{9} \div \dfrac{5}{12} =$ _____

5. $\dfrac{6}{7} \div \dfrac{3}{5} =$ _____

6. $\dfrac{3}{8} \div \dfrac{3}{4} =$ _____

7. $\dfrac{4}{5} \div \dfrac{1}{3} =$ _____

8. $\dfrac{7}{10} \div \dfrac{2}{3} =$ _____

9. $\dfrac{7}{9} \div \dfrac{14}{15} =$ _____

10. $6\dfrac{2}{3} \div 5 =$ _____

11. $6 \div \dfrac{3}{4} =$ _____

12. $7\dfrac{3}{4} \div 2\dfrac{2}{3} =$ _____

13. $10\dfrac{1}{3} \div \dfrac{5}{8} =$ _____

14. $3 \div 3\dfrac{3}{10} =$ _____

15. $6\frac{4}{5} \div 1\frac{3}{10} =$ _____

16. $6\frac{2}{3} \div 1\frac{1}{9} =$ _____

17. $3\frac{1}{2} \div 2\frac{3}{4} =$ _____

18. $3\frac{1}{2} \div 5\frac{1}{4} =$ _____

19. $3\frac{1}{9} \div 3\frac{1}{2} =$ _____

20. $3\frac{3}{4} \div 7\frac{1}{2} =$ _____

21. $9 \div 5\frac{1}{4} =$ _____

22. $8\frac{1}{6} \div 7 =$ _____

23. $2\frac{4}{5} \div 7 =$ _____

24. $2\frac{5}{8} \div \frac{1}{2} =$ _____

25. $5\frac{5}{6} \div 14 =$ _____

26. $12 \div 2\frac{2}{3} =$ _____

27. $21 \div \frac{1}{2} =$ _____

28. $1\frac{5}{6} \div 11 =$ _____

Problem Solving
READ – THINK – PLAN – EXECUTE

1. When Jane and Laura were playing the quiz game, Jane got 7,616 points while Laura got 2,295 points. How many more points did Jane have than Laura?

   _____

2. The record for pennies collected for the missions is 22,719. The homeschoolers have now collected 17,504. How many more pennies do they need to collect to match the record?

   _____

3. Dana, the Catholic singer on EWTN, visited our town. The first night, 5,438 people attended the concert; the next night, 6,457 attended the concert. How many more people attended the second night?

   _____

4. Grandfather gave the Ignatius Press exhibitor a $20 bill, but the book cost only $16.50. How much change did grandfather receive?

   _____

5. The Knights of Columbus had a tootsie-roll candy sale to raise money to help the children in the hospital. They made $3,977 but it cost them $2000 to purchase the candy in the first place. How much profit did the Knights make for the children?

   _____

6. When my sister looked in her piggy bank, she had $96.38. She bought some presents for Christmas, totaling $56.73. How much money did my sister have left?

   _____

7. My dad had $654.18 in his bank account. After he wrote a check for our utilities for $247.48, how much was left in the account?

   _____

Common Multiples

The multiples of a number are the products (multiplication) that have the number as one of the factors.

For example, the multiples of 6 are: 0, 6, 12, 18, 24, 30, 36, 42, 48, . . .

Because:

$\underline{6} \times 0 = 0$	$\underline{6} \times 1 = 6$	$\underline{6} \times 2 = 12$
$\underline{6} \times 3 = 18$	$\underline{6} \times 4 = 24$	$\underline{6} \times 5 = 30$
$\underline{6} \times 6 = 36$	$\underline{6} \times 7 = 42$	$\underline{6} \times 8 = 48$

the multiples of 8 are: 0, 8, 16, 24, 32, 40, 48, 56, . . .

Because:

$\underline{8} \times 0 = 0$	$\underline{8} \times 1 = 8$	$\underline{8} \times 2 = 16$
$\underline{8} \times 3 = 24$	$\underline{8} \times 4 = 32$	$\underline{8} \times 5 = 40$
$\underline{8} \times 6 = 48$	$\underline{8} \times 7 = 56$	

For our purposes, we will eliminate 0 as a multiple because it will not be useful to us. We will also eliminate any multiples that are less than the largest of the two numbers. Also, we will eliminate any multiples (products) that are larger than the product of the two numbers. We will be left with:

revised list of multiples of 6:   0̶, 6̶, 12, 18, 24, 30, 36, 42, 48

revised list of multiples of 8:   0̶, 8, 16, 24, 32, 40, 48, 5̶6̶

Now we will look for multiples of the two numbers that are common to both.

multiples of 6:   0̶, 6̶, 12, 18, ⟨24⟩ 30, 36, 42, ⟨48⟩

multiples of 8:   0̶, 8, 16, ⟨24⟩ 32, 40, ⟨48⟩ 5̶6̶

The common multiples for 6 and 8 are 24 and 48. The smallest of these is 24 and it is called the least (smallest) common multiple (LCM).

Try These

List the multiples of each pair of numbers. Do not include 0 or a multiple less than the larger number. Do not include multiples that are larger than the product of the two numbers. Then circle the common multiples.

1. 2 and 5   _____

2. 8 and 2   _____

3. 2 and 3   _____

4. 4 and 5   _____

We use common multiples in order to rename fractions when we add or subtract fractions with different denominators.

We list the multiples of each denominator:

$\frac{3}{4}$ and $\frac{5}{6}$ 8, 12, 16, 20, 24

and

6, 12, 18, 24

Then we pick a multiple that is common to both denominators and multiply each of the fractions, so that we obtain equivalent fractions with the same denominator for each.

$\boxed{\frac{3}{4} \text{ and } \frac{5}{6}}$ $\frac{3}{4} \times \frac{3}{3} = \frac{9}{12}$ $\frac{5}{6} \times \frac{2}{2} = \frac{10}{12}$ $\boxed{\frac{9}{12} \text{ and } \frac{10}{12}}$

Study these examples.

Find the LCM for each pair of denominators, then rename the fractions to equivalent fractions with a common denominator.

$\frac{1}{4}$ and $\frac{3}{8}$ $\frac{8}{8}$ $\frac{1}{4} \times \frac{2}{2} = \frac{2}{8}$ $\frac{3}{8} \times \frac{1}{1} = \frac{3}{8}$ $\frac{2}{8}$ and $\frac{3}{8}$

$\frac{2}{5}$ and $\frac{2}{7}$ $\frac{35}{35}$ $\frac{2}{5} \times \frac{7}{7} = \frac{14}{35}$ $\frac{2}{7} \times \frac{5}{5} = \frac{10}{35}$ $\frac{14}{35}$ and $\frac{10}{35}$

Try These

Find the LCM for each pair of denominators, then rename the fractions to equivalent fractions with a common denominator.

1. $\frac{1}{3}$ and $\frac{3}{10}$ _____

2. $\frac{2}{5}$ and $\frac{1}{7}$ _____

Exercise

List the multiples of each pair of numbers. Do not include 0 or a multiple less than the larger number. Do not include multiples that are larger than the product of the two numbers. Then circle the common multiples.

1. 8 and 10 _____

2. 4 and 6 _____

3. 9 and 12 _____

4. 3 and 5 _____

5. 8 and 12 _____

6. 6 and 9 _____

Find the LCM for each pair of denominators, then rename the fractions to equivalent fractions with a common denominator.

7. $\frac{1}{3}$ and $\frac{5}{12}$ _____

8. $\frac{4}{9}$ and $\frac{2}{3}$ _____

9. $\frac{1}{2}$ and $\frac{5}{8}$ _____

10. $\frac{4}{9}$ and $\frac{4}{7}$ _____

11. $\frac{4}{5}$ and $\frac{3}{4}$ _____

12. $\frac{3}{10}$ and $\frac{2}{3}$ _____

Multiply. Reduce to simplest terms.

13. $\dfrac{6}{7} \times \dfrac{5}{12} =$ _____

14. $\dfrac{3}{4} \times \dfrac{4}{11} =$ _____

15. $\dfrac{5}{8} \times \dfrac{4}{7} =$ _____

16. $4 \times \dfrac{6}{7} =$ _____

17. $5\dfrac{1}{6} \times 3\dfrac{5}{6} =$ _____

18. $10\dfrac{1}{3} \times \dfrac{5}{8} =$ _____

Divide. Reduce to simplest terms.

19. $\dfrac{3}{10} \div \dfrac{2}{5} =$ _____

20. $\dfrac{8}{9} \div \dfrac{1}{2} =$ _____

21. $\dfrac{2}{7} \div \dfrac{10}{14} =$ _____

22. $12 \div \dfrac{3}{4} =$ _____

23. $4\dfrac{1}{6} \div 7\dfrac{1}{2} =$ _____

24. $8\dfrac{1}{4} \div 1\dfrac{1}{8} =$ _____

25. Mary had a roll of ribbon that she cut into 12 pieces, each $7\dfrac{2}{3}$ inches long. If she used all the ribbon exactly, how many inches of ribbon were there on the roll before she cut off the pieces?

_____

Problem Solving
READ – THINK – PLAN – EXECUTE

1. Julia picked 53 quarts of strawberries for the farm to raise money for the poor children in town. Her brother Philip picked 102 quarts.
How many quarts did the brother and sister pick?

_____

2. Mrs. Wood bought a St. Jude statue for $40 at a sale. It had originally been for sale at $53.
How much money did Mrs. Wood save?

_____

3. Peter had saved $1180 in his savings account. He took $850 out of the bank to help pay for his trip to Fatima with Father Fox.
How much money did he have left in the bank?

_____

4. Peter's father paid an additional $2379 for the Fatima trip. How much did the trip cost altogether?

_____

5. On Wednesday, TAN Publishers sold 15 copies of the Douay-Rheims Bible and on Thursday they sold 24. How many more Bibles were sold on Thursday than on Wednesday?

_____

6. If each Bible that TAN sold on Wednesday and Thursday cost $11.99, how much was spent on the Bibles that were sold on the two days?

_____

7. Arnold practiced the Ave Maria on the piano for 15 minutes this morning and 10 minutes at noon. He is supposed to practice for 45 minutes each day.
How many more minutes does Arnold have to practice?

_____

Adding Unlike Denominators

We have already learned about adding fractions; now we will look at adding fractions that have different denominators. In order to add fractions, they must all first be renamed so that they have the same denominators. We do this by finding a common multiple for the denominators of the fractions, and then multiply the fractions by a form of 1 that will allow us to rename the fractions with a common denominator. Then we add and simplify the answer if necessary. Simplify includes changing fractions to whole or mixed numbers if necessary. For example:

Add: $\frac{2}{3} + \frac{3}{5}$ Check to see if the denominators are the same.

If not, then find a common denominator for the fractions and rename them using the common multiples.

$\frac{2}{3}$ and $\frac{3}{5}$ $\begin{array}{l}3 \quad \underline{6.\ 9,\ 12,\ \textcircled{15}} \\ 5 \quad \underline{5,\ 10,\ \textcircled{15}}\end{array}$ $\frac{2}{3} \times \frac{5}{5} = \frac{10}{15}$ $\frac{3}{5} \times \frac{3}{3} = \frac{9}{15}$ $\frac{10}{15}$ and $\frac{9}{15}$

Now the fractions are in a form that we can add.

Then simplify the answer. $\frac{19}{15} = 1\frac{4}{15}$

$$\begin{array}{r} \frac{10}{15} \\ + \frac{9}{15} \\ \hline \frac{19}{15} \end{array}$$

Let's review the steps for adding fractions with unlike denominators.

1. List the multiples of each of the denominators. Find common multiples.
2. Use a common multiple for the new denominator for each fraction.
3. Use the necessary form of 1 to rename each fraction to one with the new common denominator.
4. Add the new renamed fractions with the common denominators.
5. Simplify as necessary.

Study the examples on the next page.

Add.

$$\begin{array}{ll}
\dfrac{3}{8} \times \dfrac{3}{3} = & \dfrac{9}{24} \\[2mm]
+ \dfrac{1}{6} \times \dfrac{4}{4} = & \dfrac{4}{24} \\[2mm]
\hline
\underline{12,18,24} & \dfrac{13}{24} \\
\underline{8,16,24} &
\end{array}$$

$$\begin{array}{ll}
\dfrac{4}{5} \times \dfrac{4}{4} = & \dfrac{16}{20} \\[2mm]
+ \dfrac{1}{4} \times \dfrac{5}{5} = & \dfrac{5}{20} \\[2mm]
\hline
\underline{5,10,15,20} & \dfrac{21}{20} = 1\dfrac{1}{20} \\
\underline{8,12,16,20} &
\end{array}$$

$$\begin{array}{ll}
\dfrac{4}{5} \times \dfrac{3}{3} = & \dfrac{12}{15} \\[2mm]
+ \dfrac{2}{3} \times \dfrac{5}{5} = & \dfrac{10}{15} \\[2mm]
\hline
\underline{5,10,15} & \dfrac{22}{15} = 1\dfrac{7}{15} \\
\underline{6,9,12,15} &
\end{array}$$

Exercise

Add.

1. $\dfrac{3}{5}$
    $+\dfrac{5}{10}$

2. $\dfrac{1}{6}$
    $+\dfrac{3}{12}$

3. $\dfrac{3}{4}$
    $+\dfrac{4}{5}$

4. $\dfrac{3}{8}$
    $+\dfrac{1}{3}$

5. $\dfrac{2}{3}$
    $+\dfrac{5}{9}$

6. $\dfrac{5}{6}$
    $+\dfrac{9}{10}$

7. $\dfrac{3}{4}$
    $+\dfrac{1}{7}$

8. $\dfrac{3}{5}$
    $+\dfrac{7}{10}$

9. $\dfrac{4}{5}$
    $+\dfrac{2}{10}$
    _____

10. $\dfrac{5}{8}$
    $+\dfrac{3}{4}$
    _____

11. $\dfrac{5}{6}$
    $+\dfrac{2}{3}$
    _____

12. $\dfrac{9}{10}$
    $+\dfrac{1}{2}$
    _____

13. $\dfrac{1}{3}$
    $+\dfrac{7}{15}$
    _____

14. $\dfrac{3}{8}$
    $+\dfrac{1}{2}$
    _____

15. $\dfrac{9}{16}$
    $+\dfrac{7}{8}$
    _____

16. $\dfrac{2}{8}$
    $+\dfrac{1}{4}$
    _____

17. Mary needs $\frac{1}{2}$ yard of material to finish her dress.

    Alice needs $\frac{5}{8}$ yard to finish hers.

    How much material do they need in all?

    _____

Multiply. Reduce to simplest terms.

18. $\dfrac{2}{9} \times \dfrac{1}{6} =$ _____

19. $\dfrac{6}{7} \times \dfrac{3}{25} =$ _____

Divide. Reduce to simplest terms.

20. $\dfrac{2}{7} \div \dfrac{10}{14} =$ _____

21. $10\dfrac{1}{3} \div \dfrac{5}{8} =$ _____

Facts Review

Add.

1. $\begin{array}{r} 5 \\ +\ 5 \\ \hline \end{array}$
2. $\begin{array}{r} 7 \\ +\ 7 \\ \hline \end{array}$
3. $\begin{array}{r} 4 \\ +\ 5 \\ \hline \end{array}$
4. $\begin{array}{r} 9 \\ +\ 3 \\ \hline \end{array}$
5. $\begin{array}{r} 2 \\ +\ 8 \\ \hline \end{array}$
6. $\begin{array}{r} 5 \\ +\ 6 \\ \hline \end{array}$

7. $\begin{array}{r} 1 \\ +\ 5 \\ \hline \end{array}$
8. $\begin{array}{r} 0 \\ +\ 0 \\ \hline \end{array}$
9. $\begin{array}{r} 6 \\ +\ 8 \\ \hline \end{array}$
10. $\begin{array}{r} 6 \\ +\ 2 \\ \hline \end{array}$
11. $\begin{array}{r} 2 \\ +\ 2 \\ \hline \end{array}$
12. $\begin{array}{r} 3 \\ +\ 7 \\ \hline \end{array}$

Subtract.

13. $\begin{array}{r} 11 \\ -\ 3 \\ \hline \end{array}$
14. $\begin{array}{r} 12 \\ -\ 7 \\ \hline \end{array}$
15. $\begin{array}{r} 11 \\ -\ 6 \\ \hline \end{array}$
16. $\begin{array}{r} 9 \\ -\ 0 \\ \hline \end{array}$
17. $\begin{array}{r} 18 \\ -\ 9 \\ \hline \end{array}$
18. $\begin{array}{r} 10 \\ -\ 4 \\ \hline \end{array}$

19. $\begin{array}{r} 13 \\ -\ 7 \\ \hline \end{array}$
20. $\begin{array}{r} 10 \\ -\ 2 \\ \hline \end{array}$
21. $\begin{array}{r} 15 \\ -\ 8 \\ \hline \end{array}$
22. $\begin{array}{r} 16 \\ -\ 9 \\ \hline \end{array}$
23. $\begin{array}{r} 12 \\ -\ 3 \\ \hline \end{array}$
24. $\begin{array}{r} 10 \\ -\ 6 \\ \hline \end{array}$

Multiply.

25. $\begin{array}{r} 5 \\ \times\ 5 \\ \hline \end{array}$
26. $\begin{array}{r} 6 \\ \times\ 3 \\ \hline \end{array}$
27. $\begin{array}{r} 9 \\ \times\ 1 \\ \hline \end{array}$
28. $\begin{array}{r} 2 \\ \times\ 5 \\ \hline \end{array}$
29. $\begin{array}{r} 5 \\ \times\ 4 \\ \hline \end{array}$
30. $\begin{array}{r} 2 \\ \times\ 2 \\ \hline \end{array}$

31. $\begin{array}{r} 1 \\ \times\ 7 \\ \hline \end{array}$
32. $\begin{array}{r} 3 \\ \times\ 6 \\ \hline \end{array}$
33. $\begin{array}{r} 7 \\ \times\ 6 \\ \hline \end{array}$
34. $\begin{array}{r} 4 \\ \times\ 3 \\ \hline \end{array}$
35. $\begin{array}{r} 9 \\ \times\ 7 \\ \hline \end{array}$
36. $\begin{array}{r} 2 \\ \times\ 1 \\ \hline \end{array}$

Divide.

37. $1\overline{)9}$
38. $9\overline{)0}$
39. $8\overline{)32}$
40. $6\overline{)48}$
41. $4\overline{)28}$
42. $7\overline{)56}$

43. $2\overline{)12}$
44. $8\overline{)72}$
45. $9\overline{)18}$
46. $4\overline{)8}$
47. $6\overline{)24}$
48. $9\overline{)9}$

Practice Multiplying Fractions

Multiply.

1. $4 \times \dfrac{2}{3} =$ _____

2. $\dfrac{4}{5} \times \dfrac{4}{5} =$ _____

3. $2\dfrac{1}{4} \times 8 =$ _____

4. $\dfrac{2}{7} \times \dfrac{1}{6} =$ _____

5. $\dfrac{1}{4} \times \dfrac{4}{5} =$ _____

6. $\dfrac{3}{4} \times \dfrac{7}{8} =$ _____

7. $\dfrac{5}{6} \times \dfrac{2}{3} =$ _____

8. $\dfrac{5}{21} \times \dfrac{7}{7} =$ _____

9. $\dfrac{3}{7} \times \dfrac{2}{5} =$ _____

10. $\dfrac{5}{8} \times 10 =$ _____

11. $3 \times \dfrac{5}{6} =$ _____

12. $1\dfrac{1}{8} \times 3\dfrac{1}{3} =$ _____

13. $3\dfrac{1}{5} \times 4 =$ _____

14. $6 \times 1\dfrac{5}{6} =$ _____

Problem Solving
READ – THINK – PLAN – EXECUTE

1. Tickets to the Christian Music Festival cost $12.50 each.
   The managers were able to sell 67 tickets.
   How much money did the managers collect?

   _____

2. The National Shrine of the Infant Jesus of Prague is
   located in Prague, Oklahoma. Seventy-five busloads
   of people visited the shrine on the feast of the Infant
   of Prague in September. Each bus carried 55 people.
   How many people came to the shrine by bus?

   _____

3. Eleanor buys her lunch at the cafeteria when she works
   for Sister at the shrine. Her lunch costs $7.25.
   How much did she spend after working there for 50 days?

   _____

4. Laura had 277 popcorn balls to sell at the Children's Theater.
   She decided to sell them for twenty-five cents each. How much
   money did Laura have after selling all the popcorn balls?

   _____

5. At the Shrine of Our Lady of La Leche in St. Augustine, Florida,
   there was a special ceremony on December 26. Two hundred and
   fifty people per parish participated. There are 35 parishes in the
   St. Augustine area. How many people from the parishes of the
   area of St. Augustine were involved in the ceremonies?

   _____

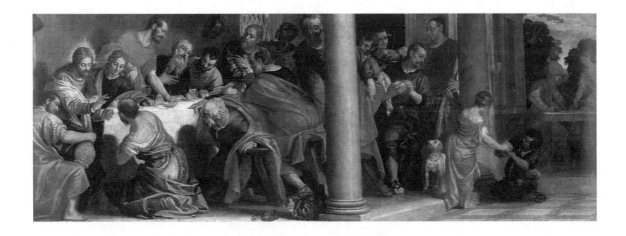

Adding Mixed Numbers

When adding mixed numbers, we simply add the fractional parts and simplify. Then we add the whole number parts. Then we add the sum of the whole number parts to the sum of the fractional parts.

Add $\quad 3\frac{1}{2} + 8\frac{7}{8}$ $\qquad$ First we add the fractions.

We find a common multiple and rename the fractions with a common denominator.

$$\frac{1}{2} \times \frac{4}{4} = \frac{4}{8}$$

$$+ \frac{7}{8} \qquad = \frac{7}{8}$$

Then we add and simplify.

$$2, 4, 8 \qquad \frac{11}{8} = 1\frac{3}{8}$$

$$8$$

We finish by adding the whole number parts to the sum of the fractional parts.

$$3 + 8 + 1\frac{3}{8} = 12\frac{3}{8} \qquad\qquad 3\frac{1}{2} + 8\frac{7}{8} = 12\frac{3}{8}$$

Study these examples.

$$3\frac{2}{3} + 6\frac{3}{5} \qquad \frac{2}{3} + \frac{3}{5} = \left(\frac{2}{3} \times \frac{5}{5}\right) + \left(\frac{3}{5} \times \frac{3}{3}\right)$$

$$= \frac{10}{15} + \frac{9}{15} = \frac{19}{15} = 1\frac{4}{15}$$

$$3 + 6 + 1\frac{4}{15} = 10\frac{4}{15}$$

$$6\frac{3}{4} \qquad \frac{3}{4} \times \frac{3}{3} = \frac{9}{12}$$

$$+ 5\frac{1}{3} \qquad \frac{1}{3} \times \frac{4}{4} = \frac{4}{12}$$

$$\frac{13}{12} = 1\frac{1}{12}$$

$$6 + 5 + 1\frac{1}{12} = \boxed{12\frac{1}{12}}$$

$$5\frac{3}{5} \qquad \frac{3}{5} \times \frac{4}{4} = \frac{12}{20}$$

$$+ 9\frac{3}{4} \qquad \frac{3}{4} \times \frac{5}{5} = \frac{15}{20}$$

$$\frac{27}{20} = 1\frac{7}{20}$$

$$5 + 9 + 1\frac{7}{20} = \boxed{15\frac{7}{20}}$$

Exercise

Add.

1. $7\frac{3}{5}$
   $+\ 8\frac{1}{4}$

2. $3\frac{1}{3}$
   $+\ 5\frac{1}{6}$

3. $7\frac{1}{9}$
   $+\ 6\frac{2}{3}$

4. $5\frac{1}{2}$
   $+\ 7\frac{1}{3}$

5. $11\frac{7}{10}$
   $+\ 13\frac{5}{6}$

6. $8\frac{1}{3}$
   $+\ 2\frac{2}{5}$

7. $10\frac{1}{4}$
   $+\ 12\frac{1}{5}$

8. $6\frac{3}{8}$
   $+\ 15\frac{1}{2}$

9. $4\frac{1}{3}$
   $+\ 9\frac{3}{10}$

10. $7\frac{2}{3} + 13\frac{3}{4} =$ _____

11. $6\frac{3}{7} + 18\frac{5}{6} =$ _____

12. $11\frac{1}{4} + 2\frac{1}{3} =$ _____

13. $15\frac{3}{8} + 10\frac{1}{4} =$ _____

14. $6\frac{3}{4} + 3\frac{1}{2} =$ _____

15. $2\frac{2}{7} + 5\frac{3}{5} =$ _____

16. $21\frac{1}{4}$
    $+ 35\frac{1}{5}$

17. $7\frac{3}{8}$
    $+ 25\frac{1}{2}$

18. $3\frac{1}{3}$
    $+ 2\frac{3}{10}$

19. $6\frac{2}{3} + 14\frac{3}{4} =$ _____

20. $9\frac{3}{7} + 11\frac{5}{6} =$ _____

21. $\frac{5}{6}$
    $+ \frac{3}{10}$

22. $\frac{1}{4}$
    $+ \frac{5}{6}$

23. $\frac{11}{12}$
    $+ \frac{7}{8}$

24. Joe's board was $11\frac{3}{4}$ inches long. Gilbert's board was $8\frac{7}{8}$ inches long. If the boys laid the two boards end to end and then measured them, what would their measure be?

_____

Multiply. Reduce to simplest terms.

25. $\frac{5}{2} \times \frac{2}{5} =$ _____

26. $\frac{9}{4} \times \frac{2}{6} =$ _____

Divide. Reduce to simplest terms.

27. $12 \div \frac{3}{4} =$ _____

28. $2\frac{1}{3} \div \frac{7}{3} =$ _____

1. Mother needed $1\frac{7}{12}$ yards of material for Katherine's dress, and she needed $\frac{5}{6}$ yard for a matching shawl. How much material did she need to buy?

   _____

2. Patrick painted $2\frac{2}{3}$ yards of the fence at St. Mary's but Father said he had to finish the job and paint $2\frac{5}{8}$ yards more. How many yards of fence did Patrick paint?

   _____

3. Father Hardon traveled $17\frac{3}{4}$ miles to the conference. He took a shortcut back that was only $15\frac{1}{2}$ miles. What was the round trip distance?

   _____

4. Doris had only $25 to buy Christmas presents, but the small presents totaled $36. How much more money did Doris need?

   _____

5. Last summer Daniel took 553 pictures when he visited Ireland. This fall, he took 224 pictures in Rome. How many pictures did he take altogether?

   _____

Practice Dividing Fractions

Divide.

1. $\dfrac{4}{7} \div \dfrac{1}{3} =$ _____

2. $\dfrac{5}{9} \div \dfrac{2}{3} =$ _____

3. $\dfrac{2}{3} \div \dfrac{2}{5} =$ _____

4. $\dfrac{2}{5} \div \dfrac{2}{3} =$ _____

5. $\dfrac{5}{8} \div \dfrac{1}{4} =$ _____

6. $\dfrac{3}{5} \div \dfrac{9}{10} =$ _____

7. $\dfrac{1}{6} \div \dfrac{2}{3} =$ _____

8. $\dfrac{2}{5} \div \dfrac{4}{7} =$ _____

9. $\dfrac{1}{2} \div \dfrac{2}{3} =$ _____

10. $\dfrac{3}{4} \div 8 =$ _____

11. $18 \div \dfrac{5}{6} =$ _____

12. $10\dfrac{6}{9} \div 3\dfrac{1}{3} =$ _____

13. $1\dfrac{5}{8} \div 13 =$ _____

14. $16 \div \dfrac{4}{5} =$ _____

To subtract fractions that have different denominators, we must first rename the fractions so that they have the same denominators.

We do this by finding a common multiple and using that as the new common denominator.

Then we multiply each of the fractions by a fraction that is equivalent to 1 to rename the fraction to one with the common denominator.

Subtract: $\dfrac{7}{8} - \dfrac{1}{4} =$

First rename the fractions so that they have the same denominator.

$\dfrac{7}{8} \qquad = \dfrac{7}{8}$ We find a common multiple and use that as the new denominator.

$\dfrac{1}{4} \times \left(\dfrac{2}{2}\right) = \dfrac{2}{8}$ Multiply by a fraction equivalent to 1 to rename to the common denominator.

Then subtract the numerators and write the like denominator.

$\dfrac{7}{8} - \dfrac{2}{8} = \dfrac{5}{8}$ Reduce the difference to simplest terms.
In this case the difference is already in lowest terms.

Study these examples.

Rename each pair of fractions so that they have the same denominator.

$\dfrac{5}{12}, \dfrac{5}{9} \qquad\qquad \dfrac{15}{36}, \dfrac{20}{36}$

12 $\quad$ 12, 24, 36
9 $\quad$ 18, 27, 36

$\dfrac{5}{12} \times \dfrac{3}{3} = \dfrac{15}{36}$

$\dfrac{5}{9} \times \dfrac{4}{4} = \dfrac{20}{36}$

$\dfrac{7}{10}, \dfrac{5}{9} \qquad\qquad \dfrac{63}{90}, \dfrac{50}{90}$

10 $\quad$ 10,20,30,40,50,60,70,80,90
9 $\quad$ 18,27,36,45,54,63,72,81,90

$\dfrac{7}{10} \times \dfrac{9}{9} = \dfrac{63}{90}$

$\dfrac{5}{9} \times \dfrac{10}{10} = \dfrac{50}{90}$

Rename each pair of fractions so that they have the same denominator.

1. $\dfrac{5}{6}, \dfrac{1}{2}$ _____

2. $\dfrac{2}{3}, \dfrac{1}{5}$ _____

3. $\dfrac{1}{3}, \dfrac{1}{2}$ _____

4. $\dfrac{3}{5}, \dfrac{3}{4}$ _____

5. $\dfrac{4}{5}, \dfrac{1}{7}$ _____

6. $\dfrac{3}{7}, \dfrac{7}{8}$ _____

After we have renamed the fractions so that they have a common denominator, then all we need to do is subtract the numerators and write the common denominator. Then simplify.

Study these examples.

Subtract.

$$\dfrac{5}{9} - \dfrac{5}{12} = \qquad \dfrac{20}{36} - \dfrac{15}{36} = \dfrac{5}{36}$$

$\begin{array}{l} 9 \quad \underline{18, 27, 36} \\ 12 \quad \underline{12, 24, 36} \end{array}$

$\dfrac{5}{9} \times \dfrac{4}{4} = \dfrac{20}{36}$

$\dfrac{5}{12} \times \dfrac{3}{3} = \dfrac{15}{36}$

$$\dfrac{4}{5} - \dfrac{1}{7} = \qquad \dfrac{28}{35} - \dfrac{5}{35} = \dfrac{23}{35}$$

$\begin{array}{l} 5 \quad \underline{10, 15, 20, 25, 30, 35} \\ 7 \quad \underline{14, 21, 28, 35} \end{array}$

$\dfrac{4}{5} \times \dfrac{7}{7} = \dfrac{28}{35}$

$\dfrac{1}{7} \times \dfrac{5}{5} = \dfrac{5}{35}$

$\dfrac{5}{6} \times \dfrac{5}{5} = \dfrac{25}{30} \qquad \dfrac{25}{30}$

$-\dfrac{3}{10} \times \dfrac{3}{3} = \dfrac{9}{30} \qquad -\dfrac{9}{30}$

$\qquad\qquad\qquad\qquad \dfrac{16}{30} = \dfrac{8}{15}$

$\begin{array}{l} 6 \times 5 = 30 \\ 10 \times 3 = 30 \end{array}$

$\dfrac{7}{8} \times \dfrac{7}{7} = \dfrac{49}{56} \qquad \dfrac{49}{56}$

$-\dfrac{3}{7} \times \dfrac{8}{8} = \dfrac{24}{56} \qquad -\dfrac{24}{56}$

$\qquad\qquad\qquad\qquad \dfrac{25}{56}$

$\begin{array}{l} 8 \times 7 = 56 \\ 7 \times 8 = 56 \end{array}$

Subtract.

1. $$\begin{array}{r} \frac{3}{5} \\ -\frac{1}{4} \\ \hline \end{array}$$

2. $$\begin{array}{r} \frac{1}{3} \\ -\frac{1}{6} \\ \hline \end{array}$$

3. $$\begin{array}{r} \frac{2}{3} \\ -\frac{1}{9} \\ \hline \end{array}$$

4. $$\begin{array}{r} \frac{1}{2} \\ -\frac{1}{3} \\ \hline \end{array}$$

5. $$\begin{array}{r} \frac{5}{6} \\ -\frac{7}{10} \\ \hline \end{array}$$

6. $$\begin{array}{r} \frac{2}{5} \\ -\frac{1}{3} \\ \hline \end{array}$$

7. $$\begin{array}{r} \frac{1}{4} \\ -\frac{1}{5} \\ \hline \end{array}$$

8. $$\begin{array}{r} \frac{1}{2} \\ -\frac{3}{8} \\ \hline \end{array}$$

9. $$\begin{array}{r} \frac{1}{3} \\ -\frac{3}{10} \\ \hline \end{array}$$

10. $\frac{3}{4} - \frac{2}{3} =$ _____

11. $\frac{5}{6} - \frac{3}{7} =$ _____

12. $\frac{1}{3} - \frac{1}{4} =$ _____

13. $\frac{3}{8} - \frac{1}{4} =$ _____

14. $\frac{3}{4} - \frac{1}{2} =$ _____

15. $\frac{3}{5} - \frac{2}{7} =$ _____

Add.

16. $5\frac{2}{3} + 2\frac{1}{6} =$ _____

17. $9\frac{7}{8} + 7\frac{11}{12} =$ _____

18. $\begin{array}{r} \frac{5}{6} \\ + \frac{2}{3} \\ \hline \end{array}$

19. $\begin{array}{r} \frac{1}{2} \\ + \frac{3}{4} \\ \hline \end{array}$

20. $\begin{array}{r} \frac{7}{12} \\ + \frac{2}{3} \\ \hline \end{array}$

21. Ruth's and Naomi's houses are $\frac{3}{5}$ of a mile apart.
Ruth is on her way to Naomi's house and has,
so far, walked $\frac{3}{10}$ of a mile. How much farther does
Ruth have to walk to get to Naomi's house?

_____

22. The recipe calls for $\frac{3}{4}$ of a cup, but I only have
$\frac{1}{3}$ of a cup. How much more do I need?

_____

Multiply. Reduce to simplest terms.

23. $4\frac{1}{2} \times \frac{5}{9} =$ _____

24. $\frac{3}{5} \times 6\frac{1}{3} =$ _____

Divide. Reduce to simplest terms.

25. $\frac{5}{9} \div 1\frac{1}{2} =$ _____

26. $2\frac{1}{3} \div \frac{3}{5} =$ _____

Triangles, Squares, Rectangles and Perimeter

A **triangle** is a 3-sided polygon. A polygon is a closed plane figure with straight line segments for sides. A closed figure is one with no openings and a plane figure has two dimensions. These are all triangles. Do they look familiar?

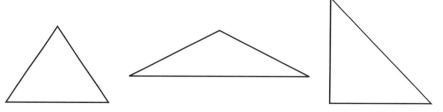

A **square** is a 4-sided polygon with 4 right angles and whose sides are all equal. A **rectangle** is the same except that it need only have its opposite sides equal. Look at the squares and rectangles.

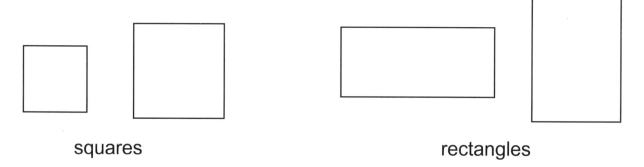

squares   rectangles

The distance around each of these figures is called the perimeter. We can find the perimeter of a figure by adding up its sides.

Find the distance around this figure: We simply add the sides.

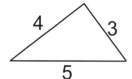

4 + 3 + 5 = 12

The perimeter is 12.

Study these examples.

Find the perimeter (P) of each figure.

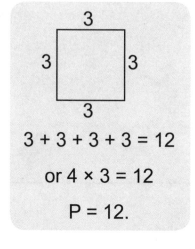

3 + 3 + 3 + 3 = 12

or 4 × 3 = 12

P = 12.

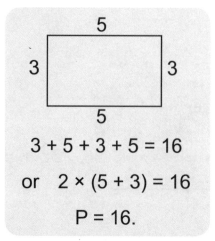

3 + 5 + 3 + 5 = 16

or   2 × (5 + 3) = 16

P = 16.

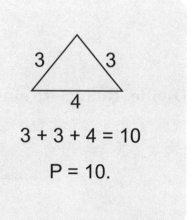

3 + 3 + 4 = 10

P = 10.

Exercise

Find the perimeter (P) of each figure.

1.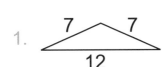

2.

3.

_____

4.

5.

6.

_____

7.

8.

9.

_____

Subtract.

10. $\dfrac{7}{12}$
$-\dfrac{1}{2}$

11. $\dfrac{17}{15}$
$-\dfrac{4}{5}$

12. $\dfrac{6}{3}$
$-\dfrac{7}{12}$

13. $\dfrac{9}{12} - \dfrac{2}{3} =$

14. $\dfrac{11}{12} - \dfrac{1}{4} =$

Add.

15. $5\frac{5}{9} + 2\frac{1}{6} =$ _____

16. $9\frac{1}{2} + 7\frac{2}{3} =$ _____

17. $\begin{aligned}&\ \ \frac{5}{6}\\+&\ \ \frac{1}{4}\end{aligned}$

18. $\begin{aligned}&\ \ \frac{5}{8}\\+&\ \ \frac{3}{4}\end{aligned}$

19. $\begin{aligned}&\ \ \frac{3}{2}\\+&\ \ \frac{2}{3}\end{aligned}$

20. The church is $\frac{2}{5}$ of a mile from our house.

    It is $\frac{1}{2}$ of a mile from our house to the library.

    How much closer to our house is the church than the library? _____

21. I worked for $5\frac{3}{4}$ hours this morning and then I worked an

    additional $7\frac{1}{2}$ hours this afternoon and evening.

    How much did I work altogether? _____

Multiply. Reduce to simplest terms.

22. $4\frac{5}{12} \times 4\frac{2}{5} =$ _____

23. $9\frac{1}{7} \times 2\frac{5}{8} =$ _____

Divide. Reduce to simplest terms.

24. $12 \div \frac{2}{3} =$ _____

25. $\frac{5}{10} \div \frac{2}{3} =$ _____

We have added fractions and mixed numbers with two addends; now we will add with 3 or more addends. The principles are all the same, but we will need to find a common multiple for 3 or more unlike denominators before we can add them. Let's find a common multiple for these three numbers: 3, 5, 7

When finding a common multiple for 3 or more different numbers, it is only necessary to find the multiples for the largest number and then check to see if the multiples of the largest number are also multiples of the lesser numbers.

If we are finding a common multiple for 3, 5, and 7, we will just write the multiples for 7 and then check the other numbers.

$$7 \qquad 7,14,21,28,35,42,49,56,63,70$$

In this case, we can check the multiples of 7 that are also multiples of 5, then check those multiples of 7 and 5 to see if they are also multiples of 3.

Do you remember the rules of divisibility for 3 and 5?

   Divisible by 5: Must end in 0 or 5

   Divisible by 3: Sum of the digits must be divisible by 3.

I chose an especially hard example to show you how difficult it can be to find a common multiple for 3 different numbers, especially if all three numbers are prime numbers.

We have listed the first 10 multiples of 7 and then picked out the multiples of 5 and then checked to see if they were multiples of 3. There were none. What do we do now?

There are two things we could do if we have trouble finding a common multiple. One way we could find the common multiple for all three numbers is to just multiply them together and that would obviously be a common multiple. Let's try that and see what happens. $3 \times 5 \times 7 = 15 \times 7 = 105$

We have a common multiple of 105!

Would it have been easier to do that from the very beginning? Perhaps. You can experiment to see what works best for you.

The other way we could find the common multiple for all three numbers is to continue to list the multiples of 7 and see if the multiples of 5 and 7 are also multiples of 3. Here we go, beginning where we left off with 11 × 7.

77,84,91,98,105,112,119,126,133,140,147,154,161,176,183,190,197

Finally! The multiple 105 is also a multiple of 5 and 3 at last.
That was hard work! Let's try some easier ones. We will show both ways.

2, 4, and 8   2 × 4 × 8 = 64   64 is a common multiple.

Multiples of 8: 8,16,24,32,40, . . .
All the multiples of 8 are also multiples of 2 and 4. Why?

Because 8 itself is a multiple of 2 and 4.

2, 5, and 6   2 × 5 × 6 = 60   60 is a common multiple.

Multiples of 6: 6,12,18,24,30,36,42,48,54,60 . . .
30 and 60 are common multiples of 2, 5, and 6

Try These

Find a common multiple for each set of numbers. Try both ways.

1. 3, 5, and 6 _____

2. 4, 6, and 9 _____

3. 3, 4, and 6 _____

4. 2, 3, 5, and 6 _____

5. 3, 4, 6, and 8 _____

6. 2, 4, 5, 8, and 10 _____

To add more than two addends containing fractions, the fractions must all have the same denominator. Using multiples, rename the fractional parts so that they have a common denominator. Then add as usual.

Study these examples.

$$\frac{5}{6} \times \frac{2}{2} = \frac{10}{12}$$
$$\frac{2}{3} \times \frac{4}{4} = \frac{8}{12}$$
$$+ \frac{1}{4} \times \frac{3}{3} = \frac{3}{12}$$

2, 4, and 8 $\frac{21}{12} = 1\frac{9}{12} = 1\frac{3}{4}$

Common multiple is 12

$$\frac{1}{2} \times \frac{15}{15} = \frac{15}{30}$$
$$\frac{2}{5} \times \frac{6}{6} = \frac{12}{30}$$
$$+ \frac{5}{6} \times \frac{5}{5} = \frac{25}{30}$$

2, 5, and 6 $\frac{52}{30} = 1\frac{22}{30} = 1\frac{11}{15}$

Common multiple is 30

Try These

Find a common denominator and add.

1. $\frac{1}{3}$
    $\frac{4}{5}$
$+ \frac{1}{6}$

2. $\frac{3}{4}$
    $\frac{5}{6}$
$+ \frac{2}{3}$

3. $\frac{8}{9}$
    $\frac{3}{8}$
$+ \frac{1}{4}$

4. $\frac{1}{8}$
    $\frac{3}{4}$
    $\frac{1}{6}$
$+ \frac{1}{3}$

Study these examples.

$$2\frac{1}{2} \qquad \frac{1}{2} \times \frac{4}{4} = \frac{4}{8} \qquad\qquad 2$$
$$\qquad\qquad\qquad\qquad\qquad\qquad +$$
$$3\frac{3}{8} \qquad \frac{3}{8} \quad\;\; = \frac{3}{8} \qquad\qquad 3$$
$$\qquad\qquad\qquad\qquad\qquad\qquad +$$
$$+\;7\frac{1}{4} \qquad \frac{1}{4} \times \frac{2}{2} = \frac{2}{8} \qquad\qquad 7$$

2, 4, and 8
Common multiple is 8 $\qquad\qquad \dfrac{9}{8} = 1\dfrac{1}{8} \quad + 12 = \boxed{13\dfrac{1}{8}}$

What is the perimeter of a triangle
whose sides measure $3\frac{5}{12}$, $4\frac{5}{6}$, and $5\frac{1}{3}$?

$$3\frac{5}{12} \qquad \frac{5}{12} \qquad\quad = \frac{5}{12} \qquad\qquad 3$$
$$\qquad\qquad\qquad\qquad\qquad\qquad +$$
$$4\frac{5}{6} \qquad \frac{5}{6} \times \frac{2}{2} = \frac{10}{12} \qquad\qquad 4$$
$$\qquad\qquad\qquad\qquad\qquad\qquad +$$
$$+\;5\frac{1}{3} \qquad \frac{1}{3} \times \frac{4}{4} = \frac{4}{12} \qquad\qquad 5$$

12, 6, and 3
Common multiple is 12. $\qquad \dfrac{19}{12} = 1\dfrac{7}{12} \quad + 12 = \boxed{13\dfrac{7}{12}}$

Exercise

Find a common multiple for each set of numbers.

1. 3, 6, and 9 _____

2. 2, 3, and 6 _____

3. 2, 4, and 5 _____

4. 2, 4, 5, and 8 _____

5. 2, 3, 5, and 6 _____

6. 2, 3, 4, and 5 _____

Find a common denominator and add.

7. $\dfrac{1}{3}$

      $\dfrac{5}{6}$

   $+\ \dfrac{8}{9}$

8. $\dfrac{1}{3}$

      $\dfrac{1}{2}$

   $+\ \dfrac{1}{6}$

9. $\dfrac{3}{4}$

      $\dfrac{4}{5}$

   $+\ \dfrac{1}{2}$

10. $\dfrac{1}{5}$

      $\dfrac{1}{2}$

      $\dfrac{7}{8}$

   $+\ \dfrac{1}{4}$

11. $\dfrac{1}{6}$

      $\dfrac{3}{5}$

      $\dfrac{1}{2}$

   $+\ \dfrac{2}{3}$

12. $\dfrac{1}{4}$

      $\dfrac{1}{6}$

   $+\ \dfrac{1}{8}$

13. $\dfrac{2}{5}$

      $\dfrac{3}{4}$

   $+\ \dfrac{3}{8}$

14. $\dfrac{1}{2}$

      $\dfrac{1}{3}$

   $+\ \dfrac{1}{5}$

Add.

15. $2\frac{7}{10}$
$3\frac{1}{2}$
$+ 4\frac{1}{4}$

16. $1\frac{1}{3}$
$6\frac{1}{4}$
$+ 2\frac{7}{8}$

17. $5\frac{1}{2}$
$2\frac{2}{3}$
$+ 5\frac{3}{4}$

18. $7\frac{3}{7}$
$3\frac{2}{5}$
$+ 5\frac{1}{7}$

19. $8\frac{3}{8}$
$1\frac{5}{9}$
$+ 9\frac{5}{6}$

20. $2\frac{3}{10}$
$7\frac{3}{4}$
$+ 3\frac{4}{5}$

Find the perimeter (P) of each figure.

21. $8\frac{3}{4}$ $8\frac{3}{4}$
15

22. $12\frac{1}{2}$
$8\frac{3}{4}$

23. $12\frac{1}{2}$
$12\frac{1}{2}$ $12\frac{1}{2}$
$12\frac{1}{2}$

272

Problem Solving
READ – THINK – PLAN – EXECUTE

1. Helen was mixing up a flour paste in the laboratory.
   She started with $\frac{1}{2}$ cup of flour and then added water.
   The paste was too soupy so she added an additional
   $\frac{1}{4}$ cup of flour. She realized that she was going to need
   more paste so she added another $\frac{1}{3}$ cup of flour. How
   much flour did she put in the mixture altogether?

   _____

2. Her grandpa took Mary on a little walk around the
   neighborhood. They walked $1\frac{2}{5}$ blocks before Mary
   stopped to look at some flowers. Then they walked another
   $\frac{3}{4}$ of a block before they stopped to visit with a neighbor.
   Then they walked $2\frac{1}{2}$ blocks before they decided to turn
   around and go back home. If they retraced their steps, how
   many blocks did they have to walk to get back home?

   _____

3. Mr. Jones, our building janitor, was emptying wastebaskets.
   There were 3 baskets in one area that needed to be emptied.
   They were $\frac{1}{2}$ full, $\frac{1}{5}$ full, and $\frac{3}{10}$ full. If he emptied them
   into a large receptacle, how many wastebaskets of trash
   would be in the receptacle?

   _____

Area - Squares and Rectangles

We learned that perimeter is the distance *around* a figure.

Area is the amount *covered* or *enclosed* by a figure.

The figure at the right is a square with 1-inch sides.

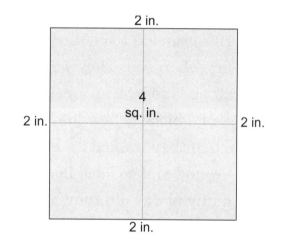

It covers an **area** of one square inch.

$$A = 1 \times 1 = 1 \text{ square inch}$$

Its perimeter is 4 inches. $P = 1 + 1 + 1 + 1 = 4$ inches

This figure is a square with 2 inch sides.

It covers an **area** of 4 square inches.

$$A = 2 \times 2 = 4 \text{ square inches}$$

Its perimeter is 8 inches.

$$P = 2 + 2 + 2 + 2 = 8 \text{ inches}$$

This is 1 inch.   ⊢————⊣ 1 in.

This is 1 centimeter.   ⊢—⊣   1 cm

There are about $2\frac{1}{2}$ centimeters in one inch

and a centimeter is about $\frac{2}{5}$ of an inch.

Look at this square and see if you
can figure out what its area is
and what its perimeter is.

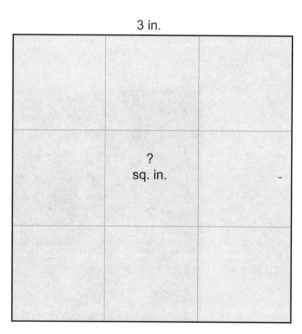

The sides measure 3 inches.

$$A = 3 \times 3 = 9 \text{ square inches}$$

$$P = 3 + 3 + 3 + 3 = 12 \text{ inches}$$

The area is 9 square inches
and the perimeter is 12 inches.

To find the area of a square:

Multiply the length of the side by itself.

A = side × side

Study these examples.

**Find the area (A) of each square.
Dimensions are in centimeters (cm).**

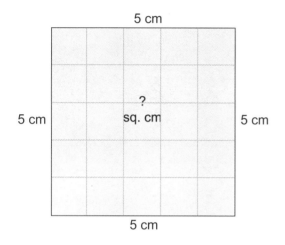

5 cm

5 cm   ? sq. cm   5 cm

5 cm

4 cm

? sq. cm

The sides are 5 cm.
The area is 5 × 5
   A = 25 sq. cm

The sides are 4 cm.
The area is 4 × 4
   A = 16 sq. cm

Try These

Find the area (A) of each square. Dimensions are in scaled units.

1.
9 units

? sq. units

2.
7 units

? sq. units

3.
10 units

? sq. units

_____ _____ _____

To find the area of a rectangle,
we multiply the length by the width.

Area of rectangle = length × width

$$A = l \times w$$

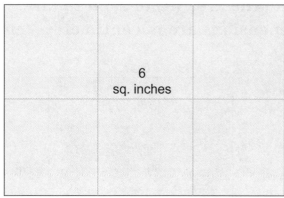

3 inches

2 in.

6
sq. inches

This rectangle covers an
area of 6 square inches.

The length is 3 inches.

The width is 2 inches.

The area is 3 inches times 2 inches.

A = 3 in. × 2 in. = 6 sq. in.

Study these examples.

Find the area (A) of each rectangle. Dimensions are in centimeters (cm).

7 cm

?
sq. cm

3 cm

The length is 7 cm.
The width is 3 cm.
The area is 7 × 3
A = 21 sq. cm

6 cm

?
sq. cm

2 cm

The length is 6 cm.
The width is 2 cm.
The area is 6 × 2
A = 12 sq. cm

The pages in this book are also rectangles.
The page dimensions are $8\frac{1}{2}$ inches by 11 inches.
Can you figure out how many square inches are on each page?

$$A \;=\; 8\tfrac{1}{2}\ \text{in.} \times 11\ \text{in.} \;=\; \frac{17}{2} \times \frac{11}{1} \;=\; \frac{187}{2} \;=\; 93\tfrac{1}{2}\ \text{sq. in.}$$

The next page is covered in square inches.
Count them to check the answer.

The page dimensions in centimeters are $21\frac{3}{5}$ cm by $27\frac{9}{20}$ cm.

Can you figure out how many square centimeters are on each page?

$$A = 21\frac{3}{5} \text{ cm.} \times 27\frac{9}{20} \text{ cm} = \frac{108}{5} \times \frac{549}{20} = \frac{59{,}292}{100} = 592\frac{92}{100} = 592\frac{23}{25} \text{ sq. cm}$$

The next page is covered in square centimeters.

Count them to check the answer if you wish.

Try These

Find the area (A) of each rectangle. Dimensions are in scaled units.

1.

5

?
sq. units

10

_____

2.

7

?
sq. units

6

_____

3.

18

?
sq. units

8

_____

4.

15

?
sq. units

12

_____

5.

17

?
sq. units

6

_____

Find the area (A) of each figure.
Dimensions are in centimeters. You may use the grid to help you.

1.

6 cm

? sq. cm

6 cm

_____

2.

8 cm

? sq. cm

8 cm

_____

3.

$4\frac{1}{2}$ cm

? sq. cm

$4\frac{1}{2}$ cm

_____

Find the area (A) of each figure. Dimensions are in scaled units.

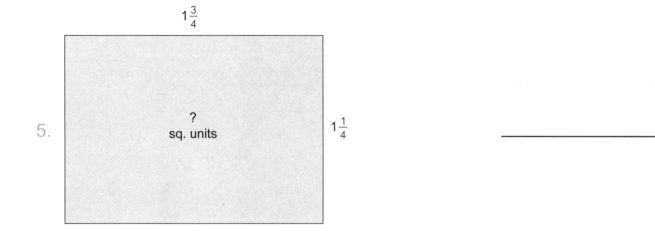

4.

$2\frac{1}{2}$

?
sq. units

$\frac{3}{4}$

_____

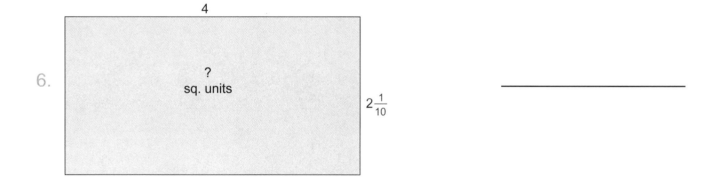

5.

$1\frac{3}{4}$

?
sq. units

$1\frac{1}{4}$

_____

6.

4

?
sq. units

$2\frac{1}{10}$

_____

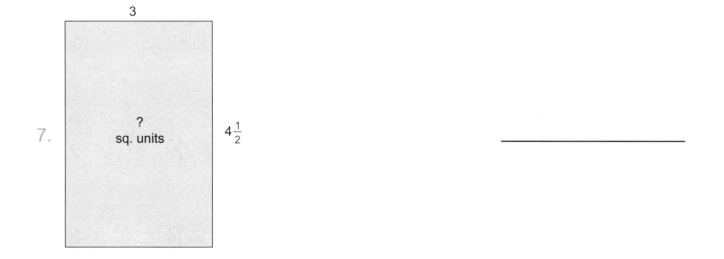

7.

3

?
sq. units

$4\frac{1}{2}$

_____

Facts Review

Add.

1. $\begin{array}{r} 4 \\ +\,3 \\ \hline \end{array}$	2. $\begin{array}{r} 9 \\ +\,2 \\ \hline \end{array}$	3. $\begin{array}{r} 3 \\ +\,3 \\ \hline \end{array}$	4. $\begin{array}{r} 5 \\ +\,7 \\ \hline \end{array}$	5. $\begin{array}{r} 2 \\ +\,4 \\ \hline \end{array}$	6. $\begin{array}{r} 9 \\ +\,9 \\ \hline \end{array}$
7. $\begin{array}{r} 0 \\ +\,8 \\ \hline \end{array}$	8. $\begin{array}{r} 2 \\ +\,1 \\ \hline \end{array}$	9. $\begin{array}{r} 7 \\ +\,1 \\ \hline \end{array}$	10. $\begin{array}{r} 8 \\ +\,4 \\ \hline \end{array}$	11. $\begin{array}{r} 6 \\ +\,7 \\ \hline \end{array}$	12. $\begin{array}{r} 0 \\ +\,3 \\ \hline \end{array}$

Subtract.

13. $\begin{array}{r} 17 \\ -\,9 \\ \hline \end{array}$	14. $\begin{array}{r} 15 \\ -\,6 \\ \hline \end{array}$	15. $\begin{array}{r} 16 \\ -\,7 \\ \hline \end{array}$	16. $\begin{array}{r} 10 \\ -\,8 \\ \hline \end{array}$	17. $\begin{array}{r} 14 \\ -\,6 \\ \hline \end{array}$	18. $\begin{array}{r} 11 \\ -\,4 \\ \hline \end{array}$
19. $\begin{array}{r} 7 \\ -\,3 \\ \hline \end{array}$	20. $\begin{array}{r} 5 \\ -\,5 \\ \hline \end{array}$	21. $\begin{array}{r} 6 \\ -\,2 \\ \hline \end{array}$	22. $\begin{array}{r} 9 \\ -\,4 \\ \hline \end{array}$	23. $\begin{array}{r} 8 \\ -\,6 \\ \hline \end{array}$	24. $\begin{array}{r} 17 \\ -\,8 \\ \hline \end{array}$

Multiply.

25. $\begin{array}{r} 1 \\ \times\,1 \\ \hline \end{array}$	26. $\begin{array}{r} 3 \\ \times\,3 \\ \hline \end{array}$	27. $\begin{array}{r} 6 \\ \times\,2 \\ \hline \end{array}$	28. $\begin{array}{r} 0 \\ \times\,7 \\ \hline \end{array}$	29. $\begin{array}{r} 8 \\ \times\,1 \\ \hline \end{array}$	30. $\begin{array}{r} 9 \\ \times\,3 \\ \hline \end{array}$
31. $\begin{array}{r} 7 \\ \times\,3 \\ \hline \end{array}$	32. $\begin{array}{r} 8 \\ \times\,2 \\ \hline \end{array}$	33. $\begin{array}{r} 4 \\ \times\,1 \\ \hline \end{array}$	34. $\begin{array}{r} 5 \\ \times\,9 \\ \hline \end{array}$	35. $\begin{array}{r} 3 \\ \times\,4 \\ \hline \end{array}$	36. $\begin{array}{r} 2 \\ \times\,8 \\ \hline \end{array}$

Divide.

37. $6\overline{)0}$	38. $4\overline{)32}$	39. $3\overline{)21}$	40. $9\overline{)45}$	41. $3\overline{)9}$	42. $2\overline{)10}$
43. $9\overline{)36}$	44. $7\overline{)0}$	45. $3\overline{)15}$	46. $5\overline{)40}$	47. $2\overline{)4}$	48. $8\overline{)24}$

READ – THINK – PLAN – EXECUTE

1. The Millers decided to add a room to their house for use as a classroom. Father said it should be square, with each side measuring twelve feet.
What would be the total perimeter?

_____

2. The Hibls wanted to add a rectangular room for use as a family recreation room. The length was to be 24 feet and the width was to be 12 feet.
What was to be the perimeter for their new room?

_____

3. Father needed a new driveway outside the rectory. He wanted it to be 8 feet wide and 24 feet long.
What would be the perimeter?

_____

4. Seton wanted a garden. Mr. Delaney said he would help, but needed to know what the perimeter would be.
It was decided that the garden would be square, with each side measuring 24 feet.
What would be the perimeter?

_____

5. In planting the garden, Mr. Delaney wanted to find the area. What is the area of the garden if it is square and one side measures 24 feet?

_____

Fractions Review (Part 1)

Find the GCF for each pair of numbers.

1. 8 and 12 _____

2. 6 and 21 _____

Reduce each fraction to its simplest form.

3. $\frac{5}{20}$ _____

4. $\frac{9}{15}$ _____

5. $\frac{3}{24}$ _____

Write the prime factorization for each.

6. 72 _____

7. 56 _____

8. 26 _____

Find the missing parts.

9. $\frac{3}{4} = \frac{?}{20}$ _____

10. $\frac{4}{7} = \frac{?}{35}$ _____

11. $\frac{1}{4} = \frac{?}{40}$ _____

Write each as a whole number.

12. $\frac{8}{1}$ = _____

13. $\frac{0}{8}$ = _____

14. $\frac{8}{8}$ = _____

Compare. Write <, =, or >.

15. $\frac{7}{8}$ ___ $\frac{3}{4}$

16. $\frac{3}{4}$ ___ $\frac{2}{5}$

17. $\frac{1}{3}$ ___ $\frac{1}{4}$

Find each part.

18. $\frac{1}{2}$ of 48

19. $\frac{1}{3}$ of 33

20. $\frac{1}{16}$ of 32

21. $\frac{2}{3}$ of 150

22. $\frac{3}{4}$ of 84

23. $\frac{5}{6}$ of 126

24. One fifth of the 25 students in the class
scored above ninety percent.
How many students scored above ninety percent? _____

25. How many students did not score above ninety percent? _____

26. The ushers counted 288 people at the noon Mass.
One third of them were adults. How many were children? _____

Convert the improper fractions to mixed numbers in simplest form.

27. $\frac{12}{5}$ = _____

28. $\frac{11}{3}$ = _____

29. $\frac{19}{4}$ = _____

Convert the mixed numbers to improper fractions.

30. $3\frac{1}{3}$ = _____

31. $5\frac{3}{4}$ = _____

32. $3\frac{7}{15}$ = _____

Add or subtract. Simplify your answer.

33. $\begin{array}{r} \frac{7}{8} \\ + \frac{3}{8} \\ \hline \end{array}$

34. $\begin{array}{r} \frac{11}{12} \\ - \frac{5}{12} \\ \hline \end{array}$

35. $\begin{array}{r} \frac{11}{12} \\ + \frac{5}{12} \\ \hline \end{array}$

36. $\begin{array}{r} \frac{8}{9} \\ - \frac{2}{9} \\ \hline \end{array}$

Add. Simplify your answer.

37. $3\frac{1}{6}$
    $4\frac{5}{6}$
    $+ 2\frac{5}{6}$

38. $7\frac{3}{10}$
    $3\frac{7}{10}$
    $+ 5\frac{9}{10}$

39. $6\frac{5}{7}$
    $3\frac{3}{7}$
    $+ 1\frac{4}{7}$

40. $9\frac{2}{5}$
    $8\frac{4}{5}$
    $+ 2\frac{3}{5}$

41. $3\frac{2}{7}$
    $+ 6\frac{5}{7}$

42. $1\frac{3}{4}$
    $+ 8\frac{1}{4}$

43. $11\frac{7}{8}$
    $+ 11\frac{3}{8}$

44. $3\frac{7}{12}$
    $+ 8\frac{5}{12}$

45. Mrs. Smith had 2¾ feet of blue ribbon for Mary's dress and 3¾ feet of red ribbon for Susan's dress. How many feet of ribbon did she have?

Subtract.

46. $7\frac{2}{9}$
    $- 4\frac{5}{9}$

47. 7
    $- 2\frac{3}{5}$

48. $22\frac{3}{8}$
    $- 13\frac{7}{8}$

49. $4\frac{4}{7}$
    $- 3\frac{6}{7}$

50. Father bought deli meat for the family. He bought 2¼ pounds of smoked turkey, 2¾ pounds of salami, and 3 pounds of ham. How much deli meat did he buy?

51. James walked $2\frac{3}{5}$ blocks to meet Matthew at the ball field. Matthew walked 4 blocks. How much further did Matthew walk than James?

1. Mary wanted to buy lace for several dresses. How much lace did she buy when she bought $2\frac{1}{2}$ yards of the white and $3\frac{1}{2}$ yards of the cream colored?

   _____

2. Lisa purchased $4\frac{1}{2}$ yards of some red print for her sister's dress, $1\frac{1}{2}$ yards of green, and $2\frac{1}{2}$ yards of pink material. How much did she buy altogether?

   _____

3. Our homeschooling cooking class used $2\frac{1}{2}$ pounds of sugar this week, $3\frac{1}{2}$ pounds last week, and 3 pounds today. How many pounds have we used in all?

   _____

4. Francis rode his bike for $8\frac{3}{4}$ miles to church, and then he rode to the grocery store, which was $5\frac{1}{4}$ miles from the church. When leaving the store, one of his tires burst and his Dad had to pick him up in his truck. How many miles did Francis ride on his bicycle?

   _____

5. On Monday, Peter practiced his organ music for $\frac{3}{4}$ hour in the morning and $\frac{3}{4}$ hour in the afternoon. For how long did he practice?

   _____

6. Mother bought cookies for the annual homeschoolers' picnic. She bought $4\frac{1}{2}$ dozen sugar cookies and $2\frac{1}{2}$ dozen chocolate cookies. How many dozen cookies did she buy in all?

   _____

Fractions Review (Part 2)

Multiply and simplify your answer.

1. $\dfrac{2}{3} \times \dfrac{3}{8} =$ _____

2. $\dfrac{3}{7} \times \dfrac{1}{3} =$ _____

3. $\dfrac{1}{12} \times 18 =$ _____

4. $30 \times \dfrac{5}{6} =$ _____

5. $2\dfrac{1}{8} \times 3\dfrac{1}{3} =$ _____

6. $5\dfrac{3}{10} \times 1\dfrac{1}{3} =$ _____

7. $8\dfrac{5}{6} \times 3 =$ _____

8. $16 \times 2\dfrac{3}{4} =$ _____

9. $4\dfrac{11}{12} \times \dfrac{6}{33} =$ _____

10. $\dfrac{6}{29} \times 4\dfrac{5}{6} =$ _____

Find the reciprocal of each. Multiply to check.

11. $\dfrac{7}{10}$ _____

12. $\dfrac{3}{4}$ _____

13. $\dfrac{7}{8}$ _____

14. $3\dfrac{3}{4}$ _____

15. $4\dfrac{1}{2}$ _____

16. 7 _____

Divide.

17. $\frac{3}{5} \div \frac{3}{10} =$ _____

18. $\frac{7}{8} \div \frac{1}{4} =$ _____

19. $2\frac{7}{8} \div 1\frac{3}{4} =$ _____

20. $1\frac{5}{9} \div 1\frac{1}{6} =$ _____

21. $3 \div \frac{3}{10} =$ _____

22. $7 \div 1\frac{3}{4} =$ _____

23. $8\frac{3}{4} \div 7 =$ _____

24. $\frac{2}{3} \div 7 =$ _____

Write each fraction as a percent with the percent sign (%).

25. $\frac{33}{100} =$ _____

26. $\frac{10}{100} =$ _____

27. $\frac{2}{100} =$ _____

Write each percent as a fraction with a denominator of 100.

28. 17% = _____

29. 53% = _____

30. 79% = _____

Rename each fraction as an equivalent fraction with a denominator of 100.

31. $\frac{3}{4} =$ _____

32. $\frac{9}{10} =$ _____

Reduce each fraction to its simplest form.

33. $\dfrac{40}{100} =$ _____

34. $\dfrac{18}{100} =$ _____

35. $\dfrac{75}{100} =$ _____

36. $\dfrac{50}{100} =$ _____

Add and simplify.

37. $\begin{array}{r} \frac{2}{5} \\ + \frac{5}{10} \\ \hline \end{array}$

38. $\begin{array}{r} \frac{5}{6} \\ + \frac{5}{12} \\ \hline \end{array}$

39. Jane needs $\frac{3}{5}$ of a basket to finish her work for the day. Felicity needs $\frac{3}{8}$ of a basket to finish hers. How much of a basket do they need in all to finish the day's work? _____

Add.

40. $\begin{array}{r} 3\frac{3}{5} \\ + 2\frac{1}{4} \\ \hline \end{array}$

41. $\begin{array}{r} 3\frac{1}{3} \\ + 3\frac{1}{6} \\ \hline \end{array}$

42. $\begin{array}{r} 2\frac{8}{9} \\ + 5\frac{2}{3} \\ \hline \end{array}$

43. $5\frac{2}{3} + 4\frac{3}{4} =$ _____

44. $6\frac{5}{7} + 4\frac{5}{6} =$ _____

Problem Solving
READ – THINK – PLAN – EXECUTE

1. Sister asked the lady for $5\frac{5}{8}$ yards of satin for
   the altar, but the lady gave her $6\frac{1}{2}$ yards.
   How much extra satin did Sister have?

   _____

2. Martha was told to pour $8\frac{1}{6}$ liters of milk
   but she poured only $4\frac{1}{9}$ liters.
   How many more liters does she still need to pour?

   _____

3. The trip from my home to Boston takes $3\frac{1}{2}$ hours.
   The trip from my home to Buffalo takes $5\frac{3}{4}$ hours.
   How much shorter is the trip to Boston?

   _____

4. Father Hardon traveled $17\frac{3}{4}$ miles to the conference.
   He took a shortcut back that was only $15\frac{1}{2}$ miles.
   How much shorter was the shortcut?

   _____

5. The turkey we bought for Thanksgiving weighed $15\frac{3}{4}$ pounds.
   The turkey we bought for Christmas weighed $17\frac{5}{8}$ pounds.
   How much more did the Christmas turkey
   weigh than the Thanksgiving turkey?

   _____

Rename each pair of fractions so that they have the same denominator.

1. $\dfrac{1}{6}, \dfrac{1}{2}$ _____

2. $\dfrac{2}{3}, \dfrac{1}{5}$ _____

3. $\dfrac{3}{7}, \dfrac{1}{2}$ _____

4. $\dfrac{3}{5}, \dfrac{1}{4}$ _____

Subtract.

5.
$$\begin{array}{r} \dfrac{3}{4} \\ -\dfrac{2}{5} \\ \hline \end{array}$$

6.
$$\begin{array}{r} \dfrac{5}{6} \\ -\dfrac{2}{3} \\ \hline \end{array}$$

7.
$$\begin{array}{r} \dfrac{11}{12} \\ -\dfrac{8}{9} \\ \hline \end{array}$$

8. $\dfrac{7}{10} - \dfrac{1}{3} =$ _____

9. $\dfrac{7}{8} - \dfrac{3}{4} =$ _____

Find the perimeter (P) of each figure.

10.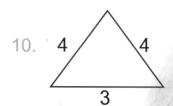

11.
```
        5
   ┌─────────┐
   │         │ 3
   └─────────┘
```

12.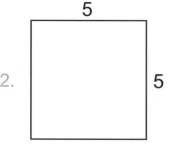

_____ _____ _____

Find a common multiple for each set of numbers.

13. 3, 6, and 12 _____

14. 2, 3, and 9 _____

Add.

15. $\frac{1}{8}$
    $\frac{2}{3}$
    $+ \frac{1}{2}$
    _____

16. $\frac{3}{4}$
    $\frac{3}{8}$
    $+ \frac{1}{2}$
    _____

17. $\frac{2}{3}$
    $\frac{3}{5}$
    $+ \frac{7}{10}$
    _____

18. $\frac{2}{5}$
    $\frac{1}{2}$
    $\frac{7}{8}$
    $+ \frac{1}{4}$
    _____

19. $6\frac{1}{2}$
    $2\frac{2}{3}$
    $+ 3\frac{3}{4}$
    _____

20. $4\frac{3}{7}$
    $3\frac{2}{5}$
    $+ 1\frac{3}{10}$
    _____

21. Mother and Father decided to retile the kitchen floor.
    The floor was $16\frac{1}{2}$ feet long and $12\frac{3}{4}$ feet wide.
    What was the perimeter of the kitchen floor?

    _____

22. The distance from St. Vincent's to St. Mary's is $8\frac{9}{10}$ miles,
    and the distance from St. Vincent's to St. Peter's is $6\frac{1}{4}$ miles.
    How much farther is the trip from St. Vincent's to St. Mary's
    than the trip from St. Vincent's to St. Peter's?

    _____

Find the area (A) of each figure. Dimensions are in scaled units.

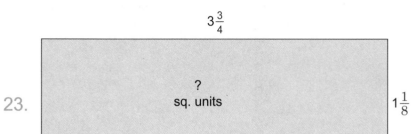

23.

$3\frac{3}{4}$

?
sq. units

$1\frac{1}{8}$

_____

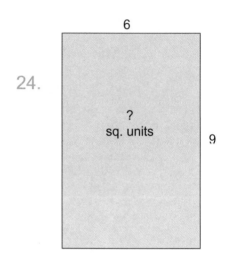

24.

6

?
sq. units

9

_____

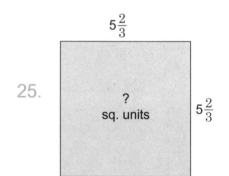

25.

$5\frac{2}{3}$

?
sq. units

$5\frac{2}{3}$

_____

26. How many square feet of flooring is needed to cover a chapel floor measuring 45 feet long and 18 feet wide?

_____

27. The measure of a rectangle is 16 cm wide and 35 cm long. What is the area?

_____

28. What is the perimeter?

_____

292

READ – THINK – PLAN – EXECUTE

1. The boys at Christendom wanted to set up a volleyball field. They thought it should be 14 feet wide and 20 feet long. What would be the perimeter?

   _____

2. David was given a ball of string his grandmother had been saving for him. He took the string out to the garden with 3 stakes and a wooden mallet. He drove the stakes into 3 different spots in the garden and then connected the stakes with the string, forming a triangle. He measured the string between stakes and the measurements were 6 feet, 8 feet, and 10 feet. What is the perimeter of the triangle?

   _____

3. The Clarks wanted to fence in their yard. They measured the length of the yard at 110 feet and the width at 75 feet. How much fencing would they need for their yard?

   _____

4. What is the area of a basketball court that measures 20 feet by 40 feet?

   _____

5. What is the area of a driveway measuring 15 feet by 7 feet?

   _____

Decimals

Decimal numbers are another way to express numbers that are less than one. When we studied place value at the beginning of the book, we looked at the 100 millions place, the 10 millions place, the millions place, the 100 thousands place, the 10 thousands place, the thousands place, the hundreds place, the tens place, and then the ones place. We can continue to move to the right, one place at a time to the **tenths** place, the **hundredths** place, and the **thousandths** place.

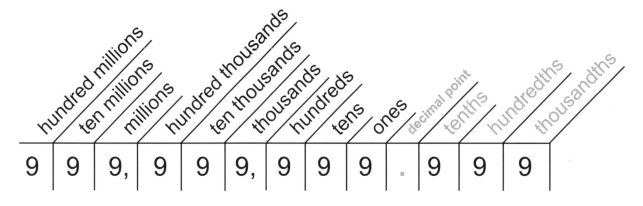

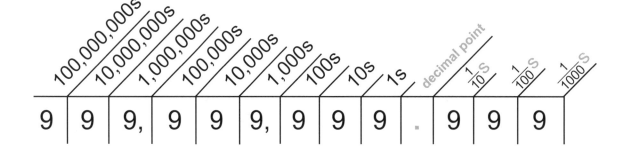

Like fractions, **decimals** can be used to show parts of a whole.

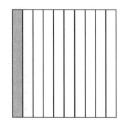

$\frac{1}{10} = 0.1$

one tenth

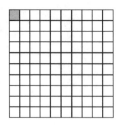

$\frac{1}{100} = 0.01$

one hundredth

If there are no numbers to the left of the decimal point, the number is less than 1. We fill the ones place with a zero to make the number easier to read.

$\frac{1}{1000} = 0.001$

one thousandth

 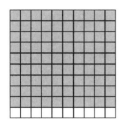 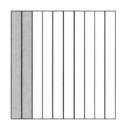 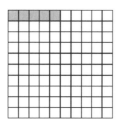

$\frac{8}{10} = 0.8$

eight tenths

$\frac{95}{100} = 0.95$

ninety-five hundredths

$\frac{2}{10} = 0.2$

two tenths

$\frac{5}{100} = 0.05$

five hundredths

$\frac{296}{1000} = 0.296$

two hundred ninety-six thousandths

$\frac{87}{100} = 0.87$

eighty-seven hundredths

$\frac{27}{1000} = 0.027$

twenty-seven thousandths

When the number is greater than one, as in a mixed number, the whole number part of the number will be written in the places to the left of the decimal point.

$432\frac{796}{1000} = 432.796$

$17\frac{35}{100} = 17.35$

Study these examples.

Shows how we write each fraction or mixed number as a decimal number.

$\frac{3}{10} =$ _0.3_

$\frac{6}{100} =$ _0.06_

$\frac{321}{1000} =$ _0.321_

$371\frac{49}{100} =$ _371.49_

$12\frac{6}{1000} =$ _12.006_

$9\frac{3}{10} =$ _9.3_

Try These

Write each fraction or mixed number as a decimal number.

1. $\frac{7}{10} =$ _____

2. $\frac{14}{100} =$ _____

3. $\frac{63}{1000} =$ _____

4. $76\frac{2}{100} =$ _____

5. $214\frac{2}{1000} =$ _____

Exercise

Write each fraction or mixed number as a decimal number.

1. $\dfrac{89}{100}$ = _____

2. $\dfrac{7}{100}$ = _____

3. $\dfrac{3}{1000}$ = _____

4. $12\dfrac{14}{1000}$ = _____

5. $2\dfrac{704}{1000}$ = _____

6. $\dfrac{3}{10}$ = _____

7. $\dfrac{4}{100}$ = _____

8. $\dfrac{11}{1000}$ = _____

9. $19\dfrac{7}{10}$ = _____

10. $11\dfrac{32}{100}$ = _____

11. $13\dfrac{912}{1000}$ = _____

12. $4\dfrac{9}{1000}$ = _____

13. $75\dfrac{5}{10}$ = _____

14. $81\dfrac{97}{100}$ = _____

15. $\dfrac{6}{10}$ = _____

16. $\dfrac{6}{100}$ = _____

17. $\dfrac{51}{1000}$ = _____

Write each decimal as a fraction or a mixed number.

18. 3.478 = _____

19. 2.109 = _____

20. 9.1 = _____

21. 6.72 = _____

22. 12.22 = _____

23. 7.09 = _____

24. 0.29 = _____

25. 0.346 = _____

296

Adding and Subtracting Decimals

When adding or subtracting decimal numbers, we must first make sure the decimal points are all lined up with one another. Then we look at the problems and add trailing zeros, if necessary, to even up the number of places after the decimal point. Adding the zeros makes it a little easier to keep everything straight, especially in subtraction when regrouping.

Then we proceed to add or subtract just the same as when using whole numbers. Then we make sure to put the decimal point in our answer so that it is lined up in the same way as in the other numbers.

For example, let's add 3.96 and 12.472.

First, we rewrite the problem vertically,
if it has not already been written that way,
and we line up the decimal points.
Then we add trailing zeros if necessary.

```
    3.96          3.960
+ 12.472       + 12.472
```

Then we add as we normally would with whole numbers.

```
    3.960         3.960         3.960         3.960         3.960
+ 12.472       + 12.472       + 12.472       + 12.472       + 12.472
       2            32           432          6 432        16 432
```

When we have finished,
we place the decimal point at the proper place, in our answer.

```
    3.960
+ 12.472
  16.432
```

Let's subtract 3.96 from 12.472.

First, we rewrite the problem vertically
and line up the decimal points.
Then we add trailing zeros if necessary.

```
  12.472         12.472
–  3.96        –  3.960
```

Then we subtract as we normally would with whole numbers.
When we finish, we place the decimal point at the proper place, in our answer.

```
  12.472         12.472       1  14           11 14
                             12.472          12.472         12.472
–  3.960       –  3.960      –  3.960        –  3.960       –  3.960
       2            12           512          8 512          8.512
```

Exercise

Add.

1. $\begin{array}{r} 1.101 \\ +\ 0.899 \\ \hline \end{array}$

2. $\begin{array}{r} 5.6 \\ +\ 7.15 \\ \hline \end{array}$

3. $\begin{array}{r} 13.01 \\ +\ 0.109 \\ \hline \end{array}$

4. $\begin{array}{r} 5.18 \\ +\ 1.66 \\ \hline \end{array}$

5. $\begin{array}{r} 5.9 \\ +\ 0.032 \\ \hline \end{array}$

6. $\begin{array}{r} 4.3 \\ 18.12 \\ +\ 6.9 \\ \hline \end{array}$

7. $\begin{array}{r} 6.23 \\ +\ 5.9 \\ \hline \end{array}$

8. $\begin{array}{r} 0.13 \\ 1.310 \\ +\ 7.1 \\ \hline \end{array}$

Subtract.

9. $\begin{array}{r} 38.26 \\ -\ 36.8 \\ \hline \end{array}$

10. $\begin{array}{r} 9.27 \\ -\ 3.1 \\ \hline \end{array}$

11. $\begin{array}{r} 2.163 \\ -\ 0.899 \\ \hline \end{array}$

12. $\begin{array}{r} 750.2 \\ -\ 9.04 \\ \hline \end{array}$

13. $\begin{array}{r} 9.28 \\ -\ 0.88 \\ \hline \end{array}$

14. $\begin{array}{r} 1.071 \\ -\ 0.719 \\ \hline \end{array}$

15. $\begin{array}{r} 8.5 \\ -\ 6.15 \\ \hline \end{array}$

16. $\begin{array}{r} 5.79 \\ -\ 1.23 \\ \hline \end{array}$

Add or subtract.

17. $\begin{array}{r} 7.24 \\ +\ 11.6 \\ \hline \end{array}$

18. $\begin{array}{r} 118.7 \\ +\ 137.3 \\ \hline \end{array}$

19. $\begin{array}{r} 62.40 \\ -\ 18.63 \\ \hline \end{array}$

20. $\begin{array}{r} 0.503 \\ -\ 0.303 \\ \hline \end{array}$

21. $\begin{array}{r} 76.467 \\ +\ 80.984 \\ \hline \end{array}$

22. $\begin{array}{r} 28.39 \\ 14.6 \\ +\ 9.8 \\ \hline \end{array}$

23. $\begin{array}{r} 0.907 \\ -\ 0.906 \\ \hline \end{array}$

24. $\begin{array}{r} 13.73 \\ -\ 11.87 \\ \hline \end{array}$

Problem Solving
_____

1. The boys weighed their fish and Peter found that his
   weighed 24.8 pounds, Timothy's weighed 25.70 pounds,
   and Daniel's fish weighed 27.6 pounds.
   How much did the fish weigh altogether?

   _____

2. How many more pounds did Daniel's fish weigh than Peter's?

   _____

3. The mail sacks Father Fox received were heavy. The one
   he received on Monday weighed 53.89 pounds, the one
   on Tuesday weighed 46.38 pounds, and the one on
   Wednesday weighed 24 pounds. How much did
   all three sacks weigh together?

   _____

4. How much heavier was Monday's than Wednesday's?

   _____

5. Daniel liked to run around the park. On Monday, he ran
   35.7 minutes. On Tuesday, he ran 41.75 minutes, and on
   Wednesday, he ran 45.68 minutes? How many minutes
   did Daniel run that week?

   _____

Multiplying Decimals

When we multiply decimal numbers, we multiply the same way we do when we multiply whole numbers. We start from the right and move left.

After we finish multiplying, we place the decimal point in the correct position. The correct position for the decimal point in the product is the same number of decimal places as there are in both the factors.

The product has the same number of decimal places as the sum of the decimal places in the factors.

For example: Multiply 7.91 × 2.5

We can see that the product will have a total of 3 decimal places in it.

$$
\begin{array}{r}
7.91 \\
\times\ \ 2.5 \\
\hline
\end{array}
\qquad
\begin{array}{r}
7.\underline{91} \\
\times\ \ 2.\underline{5} \\
\hline
\end{array}
\qquad
\begin{array}{r}
7.91 \\
\times\ \ \ 2.5 \\
\hline
3955 \\
1582\ \ \\
\hline
19.\underline{775}
\end{array}
$$

8.<u>12</u> × 0.<u>06</u>   The product will have 4 places in it.   0.<u>4872</u>

7.9 × 5.6   The product will have 2 places in it.   44.24

17 × 0.39   The product will have 2 places in it.   6.63

7.9 × 0.56   The product will have 3 places in it.   4.424

Try These

How many decimal places will be in each product?

1. 8.7 × 0.9 _____

2. 5.19 × 2.06 _____

3. 4.2 × 0.006 _____

4. 4.2 × 0.03 _____

5. 5.621 × 4 _____

6. 8.7 × 1.9 _____

Place the decimal point in each product.

7.
$$
\begin{array}{r}
9.43 \\
\times\ \ \ 7 \\
\hline
6601
\end{array}
$$

8.
$$
\begin{array}{r}
1.7 \\
\times\ \ 39 \\
\hline
663
\end{array}
$$

9.
$$
\begin{array}{r}
2.06 \\
\times\ 3.9 \\
\hline
8034
\end{array}
$$

10.
$$
\begin{array}{r}
0.79 \\
\times\ 0.25 \\
\hline
1975
\end{array}
$$

Exercise

1. 62.5
   × 7.6

2. 0.15
   × 16

3. 3.26
   × 8

4. 27
   × 4.9

5. 12.3
   × 1.4

6. 4.9
   × 5.7

7. 0.24
   × 3

8. 19.1
   × 2.40

9. 17.7
   × 1.06

10. 9.68
    × 0.36

11. 49
    × 7.3

12. 12.7
    × 6

13. 4.6
    × 2.7

14. 14.3
    × 2.5

15. 6.3
    × 4.8

16. 46.8
    × 0.43

17. 2.07
    × 0.13

18. 4.2
    × .006

19. 1.9
    × 0.7

20. 5.19
    × 2.06

21. 36.2
    × 1.4

22. 92.7
    × 0.03

23. 92.4
    × 8.00

24. 99
    × 0.7

Problem Solving

1. What is the area of a field measuring 3.5 cm by 6.8 cm?

   _____

2. If there are 2.54 centimeters in one inch,
   how many centimeters are in 8 inches?

   _____

3. Mary wanted to buy several copies of a book to
   give her friends for Christmas. How much
   would 9 copies be at $13.95 each?

   _____

4. The sides of a triangle measure 37.5 cm, 56.04 cm,
   and 86.435 cm. What is the perimeter of the triangle?

   _____

5. Eleanor had 28 music lessons last year. Each lesson
   cost $12.50. How much did Eleanor pay for music lessons?

   _____

6. Kevin loves to play tennis, but he needs to buy new tennis
   balls often. He admitted to Father Kim that, last summer,
   he had to buy 72 balls at $2.30 for each package of 3 balls.
   How much did Kevin spend on tennis balls last summer?

   _____

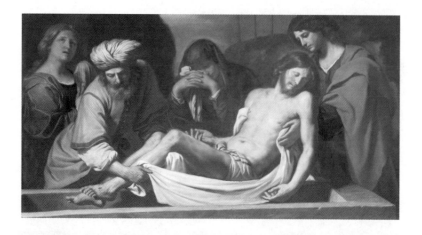

Art Index

Notes